D1242813

THE PERFECT INVESTMENT

THE PERFECT INVESTMENT

LOWELL MILLER

E. P. DUTTON, INC. New York

Published in the United States by E. P. Dutton, Inc.,
2 Park Avenue, New York, N.Y. 10016

Library of Congress Cataloging in Publication Data

Miller, Lowell.
The perfect investment.

1. Investments—Handbooks, manuals, etc. 2. Stocks—Handbooks, manuals, etc. I. Title.
HG4527.M52 1983 332.63'22 83-7824
ISBN: 0-525-93302-6

Published simultaneously in Canada by
Fitzhenry & Whiteside Limited, Toronto

COBE

10 9 8 7 6 5 4 3 2 1

First Edition

Contents

PART FOUR

MASTERING THE SYSTEM

Acknowledgments

Charts reprinted courtesy of Securities Research Company, a division of United Business Service Company, 208 Newbury Street, Boston, Massachusetts 02116.

PART ONE

THE ETERNAL SECRET

1

The Perfect Investment: A Special Kind of Stock

An entrepreneurial friend once gave me a valuable piece of advice. "You keep pushing up against the system," he said, "and pretty soon it gives way."

Nowhere is that idea truer than in the stock market. In the market you "push" through study and research, and if you push hard enough you find the market opening up to you, revealing its secrets. Behind all the obscuring jargon of brokers, behind the confusing wiggle and wobble of the daily fluctuations, behind the seemingly unmanageable mountain of information constantly processed by the market, there is a cogent and eternal truth. This book, I hope, will make that truth simple and useful.

I began a search for the Perfect Investment when I found that my market operations had become exhausting. I was making good money, but as an in-and-out trader the constant action had run me ragged. There was never any time or energy for the pleasures of living. Every morning I'd awaken and stick my nose in the newspaper stock tables. Then, even though I was far from the stock exchange trading floor, in my mind I could hear that starting bell go off at 10 A.M. sharp. And I danced all day to the jig of the quarter-point moves. What a life!

A change was needed. I set out to find stocks I could keep for a long time without sacrificing the kind of annual gains to which I'd become accustomed. But the very thought of holding on to a stock for a year or several years made my heart race. Long-term commitments frighten me.

What do you do if the stock goes down and you're hanging out there with a paper loss? I knew there were many investors (I imagined them, at least) who could stick with a stock through thick and thin out of the force of strong opinion. But I didn't think I was the type.

There was only one solution. In order to avoid the kind of situation I feared, I had to find a special kind of stock—one that didn't go down.

Ridiculous? Perhaps. Yet it surely couldn't hurt to look. If my years of studying stocks had taught me one thing, it's that the market is a huge mansion with many back rooms and dark corners where cobwebs can collect. Maybe, I thought, in one of those back rooms was a type of stock that never went lower once it reached a certain point.

If a stock could go no lower and there were good reasons why it might sell much higher, it would be simple, I felt, to hold a position with calm and confidence. I imagined myself one of the shrewd investors in the 1930s, buying up big chunks of General Motors and Procter & Gamble and General Electric because they knew beyond a doubt that the stocks could only go higher. Then they sat smiling as their visions bore fruit.

As a compulsive researcher, the prospect of this sort of golden fleece excited me. I stayed up into the wee hours of the morning poring over the histories of thousands of stocks—their ups and downs in all kinds of markets. Week after week, month after month I searched, trying first this formula, then that. The birds headed south for the winter, then came back the following spring.

Slowly I came to see that there was indeed a group of stocks that could meet my finicky standards. One had to choose them with care and apply strict rules to their selection. But once purchased they could be held with equanimity even if the general market became simply awful. When they were good, they were very, very good. And when they were mediocre they were . . . still pretty good.

Let's look at some examples of the sort of stock that fills the bill as a Perfect Investment. The three companies that follow may be in very different businesses, but their stocks displayed a communality of features. When found together, these features yield a potent formula for success.

In 1977 I came upon Diebold. This company is the major manufacturer of automated banking systems (as well as bank vaults and office equipment). That's a big and growing market, and it's the dominant company. Diebold also fit my newly developed model for a low-risk, high-return investment. I took the plunge at 8½ and held my breath, still unsure despite all the research I'd done. No brokers were recommending this stock. In fact, when I placed the order, my broker advised against it.

But what happened next appeared to validate my research most convincingly. From the moment the buy signal occurred, Diebold never looked back. By the time twelve months had passed the stock was at $14, despite a flat overall market for the year and the 1978 "October Massacre," when stocks suddenly collapsed for eight weeks. After another twelve months the stock was up to $22. Then, in 1980, Diebold reached $36 per share; I felt that a rise this strong simply had to end soon, so I took my profits. I'd quadrupled my money and was more than content. (Little did I guess that the stock would top $90 by the end of 1982—helping me to refine my selling rules so as to stay in for as long as a stock continued to rise, no matter how dizzying the heights.)

In 1978 I bought stock in Bergen Brunswig Corporation, the nation's second largest wholesaler of pharmaceuticals and surgical supplies. Selling then at about $3 a share, the stock had just barely qualified as a selection under my slowly narrowing rules. I didn't have particularly high hopes for it, but it did seem that if the stock got any lower some competitor would just have to come in and buy up the company. You can't even buy a candy store at a more favorable ratio of price to revenues, and this was a big organization with plenty of success in its history. Though the stock was hardly a favorite topic of conversation among Wall Street brokers—it wasn't high-tech, it wasn't glamorous, there weren't any great new products and there wasn't any special news—by the end of 1982 Bergen Brunswig traded at over $33, an elevenfold increase.

The same set of striking factors that had pointed out Diebold and Bergen Brunswig appeared in one of America's great corporate giants, Anheuser-Busch (maker of Budweiser and Michelob) in late 1979. Though the stock had sold at close to $70 per share earlier in the 1970s, it was out of fashion with investors and I noticed a buy signal at $24. Nothing was wrong with the company. Earnings and dividends were marching strongly upward. But buyers had lost their taste for it. Shortly, however, appearing just as inexplicably as it had previously vanished, a powerful thirst developed among investors for Anheuser-Busch. The stock tripled by the end of 1982.

What do these companies—each of which qualified as a Perfect Investment selection—have in common?

For starters, their stock had been hammered down mercilessly in the preceding five years. Prices had declined in a fashion analogous to the fall of the general stock market during the Great Crash from 1929 through 1933. There was not an ounce of optimism left in the share prices. Buyers were catatonic. Prior to the buy signal Anheuser-Busch had lost some 75 percent of its former value (the stock, that is, not the company).

Diebold and Bergen Brunswig had fared just as poorly. But at the time I purchased stock each company was earning *more* money than it had when the shares sold for four times the price. In other words, the stock prices were much worse even though the companies were much better. This had happened despite a generally upward stock market since 1975.

Why the discrepancy? There's a constant tension in the market between investors' rational, analytic capacities, and the subjective side of their minds. The rational looks at a company and determines its value through the use of yardsticks and standards that have evolved over the centuries. The subjective side takes the rational evaluation and inflates it with hope for a future far rosier than the present, or deflates the rational value in a swamp of pessimistic feelings. Booms and busts in the market and in individual stocks are a basic fact of life, a fact that any investment strategy must carefully heed.

When a stock is flying high, there's really only one central question for an objective investor: Can the company possibly live up to investors' optimistic hopes as reflected in the stock price? When a stock has collapsed, like Anheuser-Busch, Bergen Brunswig, or Diebold, the central question reverses: Can this company be as bad as the stock price would seem to indicate?

Our three sample companies had a visibly strong past, present, and future—as companies, as businesses. They had the sort of deep roots from which the prosperity tree can grow. They had factories, they had warehouses, they had distribution networks and a sales force, they had customers and a reputation. They had all the things you need to make money. And they'd already proved they can make money; they had a track record. They weren't the genetic-engineering dream of some young scientist turned entrepreneur; these were real businesses with real markets. They were making money at the time I invested, and they showed all the ingredients for making more money in the future.

During the years leading up to the stocks' qualification

as Perfect Investments, equity buyers didn't see it that way. Instead of feeling hopeful and expansive about the companies, they shrank back in a funk of worry. They worried that Anheuser-Busch would lose out to Miller in the nationwide beer wars, or that rising labor and materials costs would take huge bites out of Bud's profits. They worried about consumer acceptance of automated tellers, and this worry kept them from buying Diebold. Bergen Brunswig had a bad year in 1977. Shocked and surprised, investors wondered and worried that perhaps every year, from here on out, would be a bad year for the company. They fled like rats from a sinking ship, only this ship didn't even have a pinhole in its hull.

The buyers worried about these stocks, and, naturally, they didn't buy. When you don't have buyers for a stock, the stock won't go up. It only goes down. And as it goes down, the buyers who might've been interested find the scales of their judgment tipped against the stock. Investors who already own the shares become despondent over its prospects of rising anytime soon, so they join the selling. In an emotional environment—and let nothing dissuade you from the idea that the environment for any given stock does indeed become emotional at times—the true worth of the company disappears from view.

Each of the three stocks suffered from this subjective myopia about its real value for several years, so much so that the stock sold for a *fraction* of that value. Like any wave of emotion, however, over time the feelings of investors subsided. Looking at the companies with fresh eyes, new buyers saw a great deal of earning power for sale at a very low price. The pressures to sell eased off, for at a low enough price there are always interested buyers. When enough buyers began to act, the stock prices not only stopped sliding, they also slowly inched upward. There came a time—this time inevitably arrives for every such stock—when the upward price movement dispelled worries of investors, causing them to feel more optimistic about the future, and moved them to buy with greater passion than had been seen in years. At this point signals to buy that had been built into my system were triggered, and the rest, as they say, is history.

We often think that the stocks with the best gains are those wonderful growth companies bought when still at their beginnings—the IBMs and Polaroids and Xeroxes bought when they still sold for a dollar or two a share. But Perfect Investment stocks show gains that are just as great if not greater, without the uncertainties about whether their business plan will succeed, for it already has. These stocks rise so high not because they've suddenly taken the world by storm with their better mousetraps, but because they are *so unjustifiably low in the first place that a mere return to normal valuation implies huge price increases*. We know that once before buyers thought these stocks were worth four times what they were selling for when they became Perfect Investment candidates. The price of these stocks will quadruple if buyers merely pay what they've already demonstrated they might be willing to pay for them. In no other stock market situation do we have such strong evidence to support a vision of higher prices in the ultimately unknowable future. At the same time, as you'll see, any logic favoring still lower prices in the future has become almost nonexistent.

Fantastic Results through Systematization

Traditionally, investors have believed that in order to obtain low risk you have to settle for a modest potential reward. It is at this point that Perfect Investments depart from any other kind of stock. You *don't* give up the potentially rich reward that stock investing can bring, even though the risk is tolerable to even the faintest heart.

In this book you'll find a record of every stock selected as a Perfect Investment for the decade 1970–80.* If held

*From a sample group of eleven hundred major stocks tracked by Securities Research Company, Inc., Boston, Mass.

for twelve months, a full 96 percent of all investments proved profitable. If held for twenty-four months, the group was 97 percent profitable. In other words, for every twenty stocks you buy, only one will show a loss. And that loss will be small, because the rules are designed to keep any loss manageable.

The profits aren't small, though.

The average stock showed a gain of 53.5 percent after twelve months and average gain of 84.4 percent after twenty-four months. That's not the best price over those time periods, that's the actual price at the end of the period. If you used the best price reached, the figures would be considerably higher.

An astounding 91.8 percent of all stocks doubled at some point within five years of purchase.

In 1982—after the research record had been completed—the best-performing stock on the New York Stock Exchange, Chrysler, was a Perfect Investment stock. So was the best gainer among the stocks included in the Dow Jones Industrial Average—old Sears, Roebuck (now *new* Sears, Roebuck), which doubled. In fact, in a year when all the analysts were shouting "high-tech, high-tech!" fully six of the ten best gainers on the New York Stock Exchange were Perfect Investment stocks, and *none* of them were high-tech companies.

There are times that are better for finding Perfect Investment stocks and times that are less fruitful, but the system will find investments no matter what the market is doing. And the stocks are relatively immune from the movements of the market averages, so you don't have to be a Wall Street expert or seer to invest safely. When the market rises, Perfect Investment stocks rise faster. When it falls, this group of stocks just refuses to go down (the reasons for this are clear, and they will all be explained). Some Perfect Investment stocks were even picked in 1972 and 1973 and passed through the vicious crash of 1973–74 completely unscathed. In general, though, you'll find most Perfect Investments appearing when the market is ready to rise and fewest when it's ready to fall—automatically keeping you away from the dangers of "getting in at the wrong time."

The secret of this kind of consistency is systematization. In the end, every investment act is a prediction, and we predict by projecting what has happened in the past out into the future. We can never really know the future in all its specific variety, but we do know that what occurs today also occurred in some form yesterday and will again tomorrow. There's nothing new under the sun, and the market keeps repeating its old patterns just like everything else. Stocks go up, and stocks go down. Stocks get priced so high they lose any relation to the business of which they're supposed to be a share, or they get so low it's like being handed money on a silver platter. Fads for certain kinds of stocks come, and fads for stocks go. The market really hasn't changed since it began.

Once you realize that the past constantly repeats itself on Wall Street, you have to get specific. You need to know how long any given stock will be going up or down and when it will change direction. Getting specific means *pattern recognition,* discovering the narrowly defined factors that repeat themselves in the market, and learning to detect the signs that tell you a particular pattern is in its beginning, its middle, or its end. The best patterns are those that work virtually all the time; they become a kind of formula for describing the market's eternally repeating verities. Since they do repeat themselves, highly predictive patterns ensure that at the moment you invest, *the odds of probability are clearly and strongly in your favor.*

Getting the probabilities in your favor does wonderful things for an investor's pocketbook and emotional well-being. Stocks are always a gamble, but they're a unique kind of gamble, for you're not left to the vicissitudes of chance. You can control the outcome. If you possess a pattern of factors that show a predictable result time after time, you don't have to guess about the correctness of your decision. Indeed, you don't have to make a decision—the rules defining the pattern make the decision for you. You don't have to worry whether you're clever enough to spot the fly in the ointment of some broker's recommendation. You don't have to decide whether this is a good time to buy or sell. You needn't master the trickeries of annual reports or the fear that you've bought the right stock at the wrong time or the wrong stock at any time. Is the takeover rumor you've heard really true? Will the company really double its earnings next year and the year after?

None of these things matter to the investor who realizes that certain sets of factors contain a statistical truth that no "opinion" or speculation can hope to match.

This strategy gives you a way of investing without relying on judgment or opinion, so often clouded by emotions. Every move you make is dictated by rules. You'll need patience, but the system is designed to make it easy to be patient; patience isn't much of a problem when you have confidence in what you're doing and you know your investment is more than a stab into the dark void of the future.

Perfect Investments will help you avoid the most common mistakes of investors—faulty timing, inability to hold on, listening to the advice of others (which advice is usually self-serving), inability to take action when necessary, inability to recognize the low prices necessary if one is truly to "buy low and sell high."

You needn't devote much time to locating investments and following their progress—an hour a week should be sufficient. Close market watching is no help and can even be a disadvantage. The pitfalls experienced by most investors (noted above) are avoidable, but you can't go blindly into the fray. Armed with an understanding of the market, a proven investment policy based on that understanding, and a single-minded inner objectivity that refuses to be swayed, you can increase your capital enormously.

The next chapter is intended as a quick course in the eternal forces that make the market move. Even if you're experienced in the market, I think it will prove a useful refresher in remembering the sort of basics that investors all too often forget. More important, this material exposes a particular understanding of the market from which the Perfect Investment approach inevitably flows. Knowing *why* these stocks behave as they do is critical to perceiving the system not as just a set of rules but as a repeating pattern in which the relationship of investors to stocks expresses its essence.

2

Stock Market Realities

The most salient feature of the market is that it is a human arena. We often receive our impressions of stock activity as a swirl of numbers: the averages, the yields, the cash flows, the returns. What we know about a company's stock comes to us on computer screens, or on ticker tapes, or on vast tables of data. Shares of stock themselves are known as "intangibles." What we should not forget is that all the numbers are actually a kind of code or language that represents very real and tangible facts indeed. Above all, the key number—the price of a share—represents the judgment, clear or distorted, near or farsighted, of the human participants in their human arena.

What brings this arena to life is decision-making. Until a buyer and seller each make their individual decisions to buy or sell, nothing happens. If, one day, all the buyers and all the sellers just couldn't decide what to do, there'd be no market. Nothing would trade. All the ceaselessly changing bits of information with which investors are constantly bombarded have little value until they are *invested* with value through an act of decision.

In a perfect world, investment decisions could be made logically and rationally, based on calculations derived from reasonable projections into the future. If everyone were logical and rational and understood fully the companies they were evaluating, prices would be expected to change very little, for every investor would have the same opinion about the value of a stock. But everyone is not logical and rational, at least not all the time. And, at any given moment, different players in the arena have different reasons for buying and selling. (Some want long-term gains; some want quick, smaller profits; some need to pay taxes; some have tuition bills to pay, others have just received a windfall; some bought lower, some bought higher.) Decisions are made from a variety of perspectives—the "true" value of a company is not necessarily the paramount concern.

But one thing is certain. Every decision is made by a human mind. And the human mind is not nearly as rational or infallible as we'd like it to be, because it inhabits a human body. We don't just think, we *feel* at the same time. The mind, as all of us know, is influenced by innumerable emotional concerns. These emotional elements are just as present in the stock market as in any other realm of life. There are times when the feelings of investors completely overwhelm their rational faculties. Properly identified, these instances provide most of the outstanding investment opportunities. Prices change sharply when the blood of investors heats up, and prices change again when it cools. When there's not much doing emotionally, there's not much chance for profit.

What we always need to seek in the market is the evidence of *strongly felt* decisions. Put another way, stock prices can be seen as the result of a kind of electrical charge among investors. The charge always exists at some point along a continuum from extremely positive to extremely negative, with a neutral area midway between.

The positively charged state in the market (or in the micromarket surrounding an individual stock) is characterized by optimism, enthusiasm, avarice, hopes, dreams, faith, and, above all, by the impulse to buy. Prices and volume (the number of shares traded) head higher. The rational elements of decision-making about what the price of a share of stock ought to be (what the investor should pay) begin to erode in the face of the expansionist confidence that the positive charge of all *other* investors will be retained and will push prices still higher. Decision, in a sense, becomes an illusion as investors feel the infectious and magnetic pull of the positive charge. Analysis becomes a skewed exercise in justifying the wish to become a part of the swelling, throbbing, growing party. There is magic in the positive charge of the bull. There is salvation and grace. It is the money-maker's hallelujah chorus.

Negative charge is the dark side of the moon. When investors get negative, "reasons" to sell loom much larger than favorable prospects. Gripped by the fear of a loss, anxieties and worry color the decision-making process, causing share prices to drop as buyers take shelter.

There is always uncertainty in the future; if we know one thing about the future, we know it can never be predicted with 100 percent accuracy. When all the assets of a business have been counted, when all the earnings from existing and new products have been projected, when all the comparisons between *this* business and its competitors have been made, there still remains in the investment decision-making process an existential leap of faith in the fortuitous and supportive future. If the leap cannot be made, buyers are left with the feeling that calamity is just around the corner.

Inner Energy and the Market

This notion of psychic energy operating in the market is no metaphor. All of us—investors included—function in our lives based on the flow of inner energy. There's a single energy that animates us as organisms, flowing freely as pleasure or trickling laboriously as anxiety. We get high, we get low, we feel powerful, we feel weak, and *something is making it happen*.

Think about love and you'll see what I mean. We spot someone with a whole panoply of features (eyes, voice, personality, body, social class, talents) that attracts us, and we begin to feel desire. The energy within becomes excited, creating a current that gets stronger and stronger the more we want the person. We find that we suddenly exist at a higher energetic level, feeling the glow and warmth and increase in metabolism that accompany desire.

We try to find out more about the person. We try to spend more time with him or her. Tentatively, we seek touch, contact. The more we desire, the less objective we are in our perceptions. We overlook the faults and flaws and blemishes. The loved person takes on a kind of magical aura in our eyes. We don't think of the possible pain and hurt, we think of the pleasure oozing out of the future toward us.

We marry (we buy). We grow together (prices increase). We have children (dividends). We fight (prices retreat). We come back together (prices rally). We come to see each other more realistically, more objectively (prices become static). We realize the lover is not a miracle, but a mere mortal; we feel disappointment (prices gradually decline). Perhaps the fights become so hot and heavy that we must flee, we must divorce (prices crash). But the feelings of love, the pleasures that come from having one's inner energy excited and mobilized, are still yearning to be fulfilled within us. We begin looking for another lover, someone whom we can once again desire and possess.

It's no wonder that investments experts through the ages have advised people not to "fall in love" with a stock. That's exactly what we do, positively charged, optimistic, craving the high. In the stock market each individual, whether he or she be a small speculator or an institutional fund manager, is going through this same process of inner energy. All the individuals make up a group, and the group then becomes as one large individual, repeating as a mass mind the same characteristics that any of us can feel in our own minds if we make the effort. The human decision to buy comes from the mind's wish to have something it now does not have. The leap of faith required for buying is a kind of release of built-up energy, a climax of feeling, an expression of the self. The disbelief that leads to selling is its mirror image.

The year 1982 provided a powerful example of the way in which the positive or negative energy charge in the market can override the observable facts available to analysis and cause a highly profitable mass movement of prices.

During the first three months of that year, investors were depressed and negative, pessimistic about the future because of the recession, high interest rates, federal budget deficits of unprecedented porportions, a sense that the United States was dwindling as an economic power. There was much talk of major bankruptcies and possible bond defaults by local governments. Though short rallies occurred as some investors tried to fight the negative charge and some economists proclaimed an end to the recession, a parade of weak economic statistics continuously fed the negativity. Prices and volume of shares traded shrank, which is always the case when investors are *feeling* negative. Never mind the fact that numerous companies were prospering despite the general bad times, and never mind that they would prosper even more when things finally did get better. Many stock prices were so low that if you could buy all the shares in the company and then simply sell off its assets, you'd double your money.

The positive aspects of a company lose their visibility in a negative environment. It's as though a fog had been cast over all, preventing reason from compelling the decisions that analysis indicates. The value of a company is perceived, but it cannot be embraced. Fear intervenes.

By midsummer, prices had drifted below 800 on the Dow Jones Industrials Average. But it was a slow, mildly negative environment. There were no great slashing declines in individual stocks, no horrific drops into a vacuum of buyers. Emotionally, on a human level, the market presented a picture of depression and ennui rather than hair-raising terror. Gloomy economic numbers still flowed from Washington, but there was no collapse.

A change had occurred that was meaningful to professionals but largely unnoticed by the general public—preoccupied as they were with the sense that another Great Depression was at hand. Interest rates began to fall in July. There was still no letup in the figures that spelled recession, but professionals know that declining interest rates are the lifeblood of both the economy and the stock market. When companies can borrow more cheaply they can obviously turn interest costs into operating profits, and they can draw in capital for asset investment and subsequent growth. As for the stocks of those companies, they become much more attractive to investors as interest-paying instruments such as bonds and money market funds begin to show reduced rates of return on investment.

It's often said on Wall Street that stocks "climb a wall of worry." This seems less accurate than to say that stocks take a leap of faith. In August 1982 none of the basic problems in the economy had really changed. You could not *see* any evidence to contradict the notion of a helpless decline into depression. But experienced investors know that sooner or later things do get better. And the key to revival must be lower interest rates. Lower rates don't guarantee a recovery, but you cannot have one without them. So, despite evidence to the contrary, money managers at the big pension and mutual funds—cognizant of the importance of rates and their typical effect on both stocks and the economy—took the leap of faith that stocks and the economy would be much improved in the visible future. It was not so much that the prospects of many companies suddenly brightened, as the new willingness of these money managers to permit themselves to see those prospects, to become positively charged and make decisions with the force of that charge.

Obviously, many investors had been waiting for the opportunity to switch into a positive feeling. The market suddenly boomed upward on new record trading volume that was twice the level of the month before. The sharp rise in prices marked the commencement of a trend as more and more investors turned positive, sending the Dow Jones up over 50 percent within nine months—with many stocks more than doubling. And the economy *still* was not so hot, the figures still fragile and weak.

But a leap of faith feeds on itself. The market is a big, ungainly beast. No two investors see it exactly the same way. Some want to be first on the bandwagon, some want to wait until the wagon is rolling to jump on board, some run to it and catch up just as the ride is over.

The trend rolls and rolls, often defying the apparent facts. It always seems to go longer than it should, beyond the bounds of reasonable optimism or pessimism. And it is critical to recognize the point at which a trend has gone "beyond the bounds," the point at which it has become a kind of financial psychosis, a loss of sense in which mental objectivity is, for a time, completely overwhelmed by a subjective emotional charge. It can cause stocks to become so high-priced they have nowhere to go but down, or create such low-priced bargains that the reaping of large profits later on is virtually inevitable.

A Piece of a Business

The intangible quality of stocks is deceptive. Because most of us never even see a stock certificate, because they're so easy to buy and sell, because they so often seem like horses in a race over which we have no control, we forget what a share of stock really is.

In the end, a share of stock is still a piece of a business.

And the decision to buy or sell should bear some relation to the sort of thinking you would do if you were considering buying the *entire* business. If you truly approach investing as an investor, you want to have a strong sense of the actual, real-world value of the thing you're buying.

Any buyer of a business in the real world asks two essential questions: How safe is my money? When will I get it back? Only after those two questions will he then ask: How much can I really make? A business is an entity that makes money and thereby provides a return on capital for its owner. It makes money through mobilizing an idea, an organization, and property to create a salable product or service.

This may sound all too simple, but it is ignored with surprising frequency by stock investors. Often shares will float high in the stratosphere even when the underlying company is not making money, owns little productive property, and has a minimal organization. Only on the basis of a good idea, which may or may not produce real money in the future, stock buyers will pour in their hard-earned savings. It may not be earning money now, goes the rationale, but this new gizmo they've got will take the world by storm in two years. Forgotten is the fact that the world never has beaten a path to the door of the better mousetrap maker—the maker must go out and sell, and must manufacture and distribute, and must beat out the competition. The capability to do these things is of an order very different from merely putting together the mousetrap itself. Much can go wrong on the way to the bank.

Perfect Investments are stocks in real businesses that have already convincingly proved the ability to make real money. They embody the elements that a buyer of an entire business would want to see (these stocks often become takeover targets) as well as the fluid upward positive share price potential that a passive stock investor desires. When you buy a business, you want to be sure the capital you put in is safe. Your primary assurance is the existence of valuable property owned by the business (assets) that could be sold to recover your capital if necessary. A secondary assurance that your capital is safe is the fact that the company is indeed earning money and seems as if it will continue to do so—capital is not depleted when there are no operating losses. Earnings can disappear, of course, so this "protection" of your capital is less secure than salable assets. However, if the business has earned money for many years, the probabilities are certainly in your favor that it will continue to do so—the required elements for earnings are demonstrably present.

When you buy this asset-holding, income-producing business, you also want to feel confident that your capital will be worth more in years to come. Naturally, this is a key criterion in deciding which of several possible businesses you might want to buy. Ultimately, what makes a business worth more over the long term is increase in the value of its assets and increase in the level of its earnings. Preferably both will rise, but one—assets or earnings—*must* rise if the business is to be worth more.

Often stock market investors feel the way to this dual goal is through "idea" stocks of the sort discussed above, or small companies that are actually earning money and have favorable prospects for future expansion. The problem, as always, is uncertainty. What if they don't grow? Current prices for these stocks usually include a large premium, which assumes a certain level of future growth. If these assumptions are challenged by disappointing reality, losses quickly follow.

Investors err when they frantically search for the next new thing that will skyrocket in the financial sky. Old things are really much better for a long-term program of profits. You can count on them. They've been around. They know how to survive. They know how to prosper in good times and hold on in bad. They've proved it.

But, like other things in life, seasoned companies can become shunned, hated, or merely ignored. Sooner or later, though, investors with capital growth in mind see the assets and income of these companies as the bargains they truly are. The goal for us as investors is to *quantify* the essence of a bargain stock—a *true* bargain, not merely one that's a little lower than it might be. Perfect Investing provides a way to sift out the true bargains and buy them before they are recognized by the great bulk of the investing crowd.

How these bargains come to be is an instructive lesson in stock market dynamics. Emotionally, we always find something vaguely suspect about a bargain. "If this is such a great deal," we think, "how come nobody else knows about it?" The odd thing is that the creation of bargains is an intrinsic feature of the stock market process. A cheap price should whet your appetite, not scare you off.

The Creation of Bargains

Investment is wholly projective. When investors have sufficiently positive feelings to buy a business or a stock, all the factors they can see (or *choose* to see) foster the leap of faith that the future will be better than the past. Since the mind-set is projective, an investor's opinions are most strongly influenced by the relatively recent past. Most stock buyers are prone to say, "It did well last year, it's done well this year, so it'll probably do well next year." The investor's conditional grammar.

Projection, the commonest tool in the world of common stocks, is antithetical to the idea of reversal. The projecting mind most often repeats a single mantra, "more of same."

When the recent past has been negative, likewise, investors take on a negative emotional charge. It's quite an easy turn for the same mind that said things can only get better to now say things can only get worse. The content is less telling than the form of thought. When negatively charged investors shrink from buying and flee into selling, they've basically lost their faith and instead take a leap into disbelief.

I remember a meeting in 1974 when I was on the board of a nonprofit arts institution. We were trying to hash out new ways of raising money, for times were getting tough and donors had cut back drastically. Also on the board was a partner in the largest accounting firm in the world, a man who was appointed for his much-needed financial acumen. Though he hadn't contributed to the discussion yet, I noticed him getting increasingly nervous and fidgety, with a slight gleam appearing in his eyes. I'd no idea what could be upsetting him.

Finally he rose from his chair, raising his arms as if trying to hold up the sky. "You people are out of touch with reality," he said, his voice quivering and much too loud. "You're not going to raise any money with the ideas I've heard. You're not going to raise money with *any* ideas. There isn't going to *be* any money. We're sitting here gabbing about raising money for charity and the country is *already in a major depression*. You people ought to be thinking about cutting back and holding on. This is going to be worse than the thirties. America has *had* it!"

Well, I knew things weren't exactly rosy in the economy, but it was quite a shock to hear this highly trained and respected man of finance proclaim the presence of a depression. And he was wild about it. He was shaking. Out of control. Emotionally overwrought.

We all know that no major depression ever materialized and that even as he spoke, the groundwork was being laid in the stock market for a major advance that would propel many stocks to a tripling or quadrupling of their 1974 panic lows. The important point here is that even the conservative men who are responsible for the largest accumulations of capital in this country are subject to extreme emotionalism when they are economically terrified. It is caused by the tendency to project. When things get bad, the projecting mind sees the trend extending into the future and worsening. The possibility, not to mention the probability, of a *reversal* of the recent past is totally ignored. When emotions come to dominate reason and the lessons of history to such an extent—that is when you find bargains. No one is immune to making gross emotional mistakes, and that includes the money managers who control most of today's stock market as much as my colleague the C.P.A.

Three Routes to Bargains

1. Severe Market Declines

You can find emotionally produced bargain-priced stocks in virtually any market, but at no time is it easier than when the *whole list* has been crashing. During these periods nearly all investors become neurotically preoccupied with their fears and anxieties. The prior positive charge that had lifted stock prices higher becomes reversed with a vengeance. A state of negative shock sets in and there is mass flight. Blinded by the emotional charge of the moment, investors completely ignore the real earning power or asset value of the businesses whose shares they are selling.

In these periods, when the subjective component in pricing completely overrides the objective side, the negative charge within investors leads them to feel that the world is coming to an end. It really is not too strong to call these moments a kind of temporary mass insanity. Everything the investor knows to be true is simply abandoned in a primal reaction of flight from danger.

It should be noted that a steep fall is generally preceded by a sharp rise. One need only think of 1929 as a paradigm. During the rise, positive energy builds inside the bodies of investors, fostering hope, faith, and profit lust. Prices go up and up as the positive momentum grows. Certain stocks become shining stars.

But even as prices are still rising, a strange feeling forms in an investor's heart. Something is out of kilter. He feels it but doesn't know what it is. The breath doesn't seem to come as it did. The muscles aren't as strong anymore. What's going on?

What's going on is that the stock price has gone "beyond the bounds" of reasonable valuation, and analytic justifications for its high price are no longer available to support the emotional charge. Running now on subjectivity alone, with no support from the mind, investors find themselves out on a limb. *They can no longer stand the level of emotional charge.* They feel like balloons filled with too much air. Something's got to give. That air wants to escape.

And when it does, it does so explosively, carrying stocks back down the way they came, in a vicious, equally emotional reversal.

One need only think of the recent crash of 1974 as well as the 1929 catastrophe to realize that these events, on a greater or lesser scale, are a continuous feature of equity trading. Those two periods show us the extreme form, the boldly writ statement, of a principle that is constantly at work in the market. Indeed, on closer analysis we'll see that total market collapse yields a powerful model for investment in individual stocks even when the market itself is neutral or in an uptrend. Crashes of the 1929–33 or 1974 ilk are still the best times to buy stock as a long-term investment, but, sadly, whole-market bloodbaths appear too infrequently for an ongoing investment program. We need to find individual stocks that match the harsh emotional undervaluation produced by these spectacular bear markets.

2. *Growth Stock Trials and Tribulations*

The second route to bargains occurs when stocks are young and sexy and juicy, pounced on by every investor for miles, then dropped as if they had the plague—at the first sign of a gray hair. It happens every year, like clockwork.

The life cycle of most companies begins with skepticism by investors. This is especially true of any company whose business is based on a new idea. The new idea may be a technological innovation, like personal computers; a new method of marketing or sales, like Tupperware parties; a new way of packaging an old idea, like the way McDonald's repackaged the hamburger; or newly discovered resources, like oil on the North Slope of Alaska. The new idea puts a gleam in the eyes of investors. But the gleam is at first quite dim—things look good, but we want to be sure before we take the plunge.

And investors do well to approach the young company with caution. Many things can go wrong in the unproven, unseasoned business. As I mentioned earlier, you have to be able to *sell* the mousetrap, and make money on your sales, and somehow protect yourself from the bigger companies that will inevitably come sniffing around anything that seems as if it's making money. Seasoned investors, wounded over the years by too quick an infatuation with such small companies, stand back and wait for proof to appear. All the same, this caution produces inner conflict and stress, for if this company is going to be the best thing since sliced bread, the investor doesn't want to be too late. He doesn't want to buy in after the shares have seen most of their ultimate price increase. He watches, mounting positive energy held back in restraint.

Now the company starts to show earnings increases of 50 or 100 percent per year. Representatives of brokerage houses and investing institutions visit the company, see that it has more than a post office box—it has real employees, a parking lot, a tanned president. Hearing the reports of their messengers, investors begin to pick up some shares. They permit themselves to experience their feelings, if only tentatively.

The investors start to count on their fingers. "If earnings continue to double every year," they think quietly, "this company will be earning thirty-two times as much money five years from now as it is today." Investors can't seem to avoid thinking this way even though they *know* a company, in real life, can't continue to double its income year after year. The optimistic, positive side of an investor's personality—a side he must have to take any investment action at all—clouds his more rational faculties.

The company keeps turning out hot earnings reports. Investors, calculating their future gains, can no longer contain the inner buildup of positive, hopeful energy. They begin to buy in bigger lots, becoming less and less concerned about the price they're paying. Other investors, slower to act, see the price rising smartly; wanting to be in on a good thing, they begin buying, too. The original investors, now convinced by rising prices of their earlier perspicacity, become still more enamored of the company and invest again and again, rapidly swallowing shares.

All kinds of investors are going after the stock now, like fish on a feeding frenzy. Brokerage houses are touting it, and so are the writers of investment advisory newsletters. By this time it's really too late, but the stock still builds price momentum. There are hardly any sellers, though the ranks of buyers continue to swell. Demand far outstrips supply, the prices go up and up, further stimulating the expansive desire to buy. Anxieties about loss are forgotten; only the possible gains are visible.

The problem, of course, is that as the company succeeds, growing bigger and older, it begins to look more and more—as a financial entity—like other companies. The older it gets, the more conservative it becomes, with fewer new ideas. It becomes more bureaucratic, slower to act. The bigger a company gets, the harder it is to create huge *percentage* increases in earnings. If you add one hundred million dollars in sales to last year's hundred million, you've doubled your sales. If you add the hundred million to last year's billion, why, you've *only* shown a gain of 10 percent, and that's not hot!

From a psychological point of view, what happens next is fully to be expected. The expansion of positive inner energy among investors has driven the stock far higher than can possibly be warranted given the uncertain nature of the world, the economy, and the growth curves of businesses. The stock has become strangely out of control, detached from a sound basis in reality, and an undercurrent of anxiety—a note of negativity—enters the investors' emotional mix. Things cease making sense, but investors cannot abandon the stock, for the hope, faith, and greed engendered by positive feelings still exert a powerful pull.

Then some kind of event triggers the full force of the mounting but suppressed anxiety. In the typical case, the trigger is an announcement of disappointing earnings. "Disappointing earnings" are earnings that fall below the exuberant estimates of research analysts from brokerage houses who've been touting the stock to their clients. If a company is seen as really hot, an earnings gain of 50 percent—remarkable by any standards—can actually be seen as a failure by investors who were expecting gains of 100 percent, or even 75 percent.

The analysts and investors are suddenly terrified. "My God, maybe my analysis was wrong." (It's always the analysis, never the overemotionalism that's called into question.) They begin to count on their fingers again. Now they realize the stock has been selling for twice what it should be. They start moving out.

At first, the decline seems almost casual. Some investors see the first decline as a "buying opportunity," and their buying halts the decline. But it soon becomes apparent that there are no more avaricious buyers willing to push prices back up to where they were. The selling takes on a quality of deadly earnestness. The fear and anxiety underneath build to a raging momentum. Stocks of perfectly good companies can drop 20 percent *in a day* when the rush to sell is finally on. Negative charge completely overwhelms the former enthusiasts.

The stock that should have been selling for half its price (in a rational world) gets there in short order. And it keeps right on going, powered by the new negative

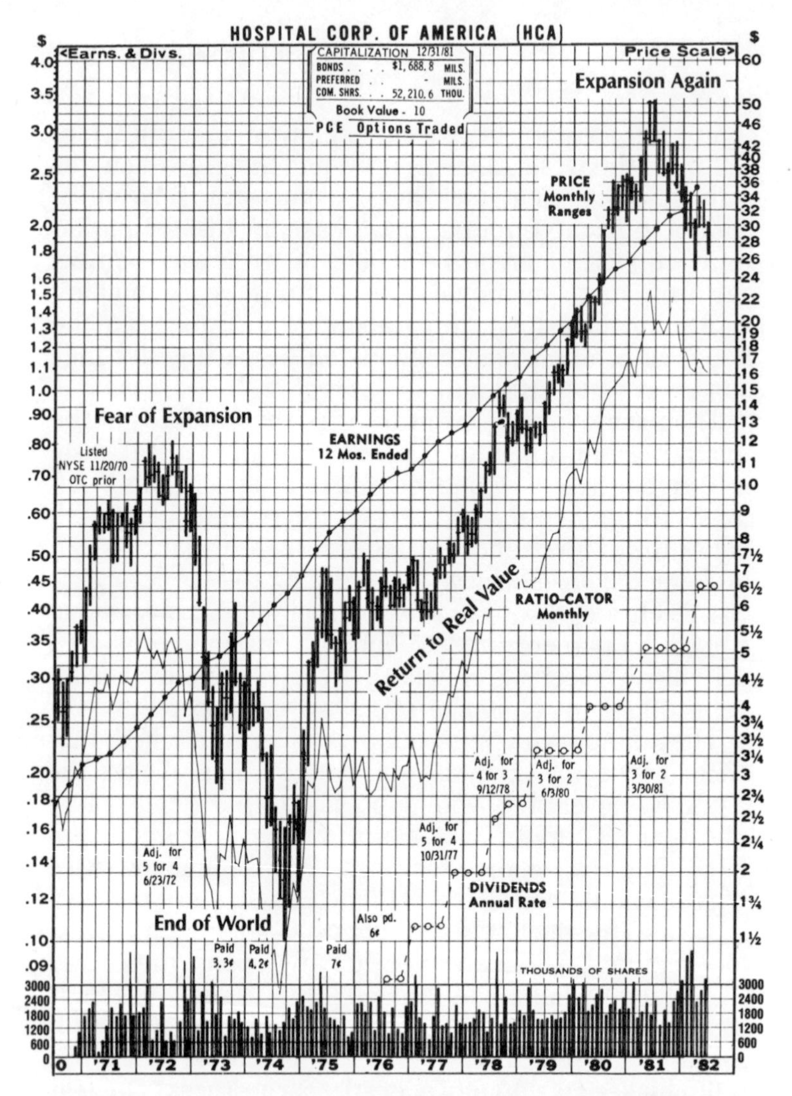

In 1972 investors began to become frightened of the high prices to which they'd bid up growth stocks. Even if a company did earn more year after year, it would take a theoretical lifetime before you got a payback on your investment were you a buyer of the entire company. At $12 per share in May 1972, Hospital Corp. of America was selling for some forty times its annual earnings. Previously expansive investors reached their limits and began to shrink from the stock. As they sold, fear gripped shareholders and they rushed to take profits built up in the previous years. But why was the stock going so low? There must be some horrible secret about the company. Meanwhile, what with the oil embargo, inflation, and New York's problems, it looked as if the end was nigh and people would never need health care again . . .

The stock dropped to 1½, then rose to *50* with never a down earnings report.

charge. The baby goes flying out the window with the bath water. The fact that the company might be a good one to own and might satisfy reasonable investment criteria at the right price is completely forgotten in the anger and repugnance over this beauty who, it turns out to the investors' dismay, actually has to sleep at night.

Soon enough, with no real change in the company's long-term prospects, the stock is selling at 40 percent of its former price, then a quarter; sometimes it even drops straight down, with no respite, to *10 percent of its former price*. The pendulum swings all the way to the other end of the spectrum, and we see a price that ridiculously *undervalues* the company's demonstrated ability to make more money tomorrow than it does today.

But investors cannot find it in themselves to buy now. Cheap as it is, the decline is frightening. The negativity is potent and repellent.

This process is inevitable for nearly every growth stock. Few can escape the emotional oscillation. Few can live up to investor expectation over a period of many years. *None* can do it when a recession comes along, and a recession is never taken into account by investors when they're counting up future profits on their fingers. Sometimes the stocks just drop. Sometimes they *really* drop, the drop is crazy, and if we know the right parameters of craziness, we can see without any doubt that a bargain has been created.

The list of stocks that have suffered this fate and gone on to become the biggest gainers and best companies in later years reads like a Who's Who of great investments: Boeing, Kodak, Fairchild, Levi Strauss, Loew's, Wang Labs, Humana, Loral, Hilton, Electronic Data, Syntex, Tektronix—the names go on forever.

3. When a Solid Company Stubs Its Toe

It often happens that a well-established, deep-rooted company runs into temporary troubles. A bank, for example, may have lent excessively to an industry that turned weak. A utility may have had troubles with a plant. A large manufacturer may come out with a product that just doesn't make it in the marketplace. A new acquisition may drain more of the acquiring company's resources than was anticipated.

Whatever the real or ostensible cause, the investment community—the pension and mutual fund managers—simply decide that owning shares in the company is for dummies. They ignore the long history of profitability, the depth of management, the enormous worth of the company's assets, its customer base, its distribution network—all the things that show a business has true intrinsic value and the ability to make money. Instead, only the troubles are in focus.

It's perfectly understandable, really, more a function of the way big players operate than mere stupidity. If a pension fund has decided, as a matter of policy, to hold 2 percent of its assets in automotive shares, why take the risk with Chrysler when they can buy GM? If Honeywell comes out with a mediocre computer, it's much simpler to switch your money into IBM.

Fund managers' heads are perpetually on the block. They need to justify their investments to employers, and they want to immunize themselves from criticism as much as they want to show good performance. ("Tell us why you own *that* one, you fool.") The net effect is to withdraw all "support" from certain companies, allowing their stock to fall to outrageously cheap levels. It then remains for the far fewer institutions whose guiding policy is the quest for bargains to begin buying these unwanteds just as the reason for their rejection is becoming past history and moot.

It's important to remember that even the biggest and best companies can make mistakes, and equally important to remember that they have the resources and resilience, the management ability and financial strength, *to remedy those mistakes*. No matter how great the company, whether it be General Electric or American Telephone or duPont or Exxon, they've all had their down times. And they've all rewarded investors who could look "beyond the valley."

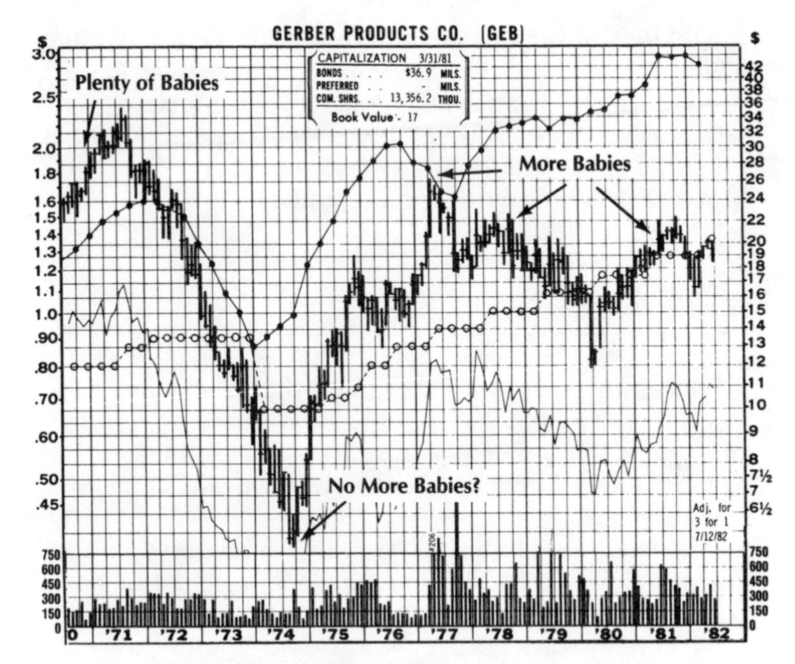

It is not uncommon for a company with a virtual monopoly to forget, temporarily, how to convert sales into profits. Or to forget that consumers must be encouraged to buy their products. Life gets too easy, discipline fades.

In 1971 Gerber Products reached a high of $35 per share. Shortly thereafter earnings began to deteriorate. Did it occur to investors that we haven't seen the last of babies and that they've all got to eat? Apparently not. Despite the clear and permanent market from which one could reasonably infer that Gerber would be able to extract profits as it had in the past, sellers fled GEB as if it were some fly-by-night operation. In the pits of the 1974 crash, sellers actually let the stock go for less than $6 per share. Had they lost their heads? This is *the* Gerber Products we're talking about—you know, puréed pears? Mashed peas?

Within three years normalcy had returned. No great new ideas, no hot stories or technological breakthroughs, merely normalcy. The stock reached 26, over *four times* its low price.

All kinds of major stocks have been beaten down, for all kinds of reasons. The capacity to analyze what's been beaten, why it's been beaten, what its current status is in terms of tangible value, and what its reasonable future might be is the hidden secret that makes the difference between wise investing and the typical win-a-little lose-a-little lot of most investors.

The Eternal Cycle

Bargains don't last forever.

Successful investors understand that stocks are subject to alternations of positive and negative charge among investors. The positive has its limits, as does the negative. And a reversal occurs when those limits are reached.

The fortunes of businesses, like everything in the universe, follow a cycle of growth, decline, and then new growth. All things change with a quality of cyclicality, and common-stock corporations are no different. Just as spring follows fall and sunshine follows rain, the economy swells and then deflates, interest rates peak and then trough, market rises are always followed by retreats, and retreats are always followed by new moves upward. The only thing that will change this pattern is the end of the world, in which case it won't matter whether you were right or wrong in your stock selections.

This idea of cyclicality is perhaps the most important single concept of investing. When Bernard Baruch announced "the market will fluctuate," he was talking about the ups and downs of cyclicality. Managements come and go, and so do fads and fashions on Wall Street. Earnings can look bright and then turn sour, or gloomy and then instantly sparkling. Cyclicality is the only fact you can count on. It will never let you down.

Imagine it is 1934, and you have money to invest. The stock market bubble has burst, leaving ruined lives and a nation depressed emotionally as well as economically. Someone tells you to buy stocks, because things can't possibly get worse. You blink in disbelief. Who can buy stocks when thousands are on bread lines? Who can buy stocks after what has just happened to your bankrupted uncle? "Oh, no," you think, "this is a terrible time to buy stocks." The air is filled with gloom and doom. Negatively charged, you simply cannot make a buy decision, no matter how cheap stocks may seem when you look at their assets and continuing ability to earn money.

And yet, as we all know in hindsight, this was one of the best times in history to invest in common stocks. The great stock market fortunes of this century were nearly all made by men who invested *after* the Crash of 1929, when companies were selling for a fraction of their true worth but few could bring themselves to see it.

Investors generally do not understand the cycling of the market so are afraid when stocks are cheap. Before plenty, there is famine. Stocks will continue to cycle as long as there are markets. The inner energy of subjectivity, the perpetual cycle of expansiveness and anxious contraction, desire and fear, will ensure it. In a way, investing is the simplest of all possible enterprises. All you have to do is buy stock when the downward side of a cycle is ending and hold on as your investment is revalued upward to a more rational level.

The primary secret of success, then, is knowing when you have arrived at a cyclical bottom.

3

Finding Your Own Private 1930s

The early 1930s represents the major cyclical bottom of the twentieth century. As such it provides a significant model in the quest for irrationally oversold stocks. How this low came to pass, and its ramifications and characteristics, are of crucial importance to understanding the low-risk, high-return quality of Perfect Investment stocks, for these stocks replicate, in their individual situations, the overall conditions of the market during the 1930s.

The Real Effects of the 1929 Crash

The specter of the stock market crash of 1929 continues to loom in the dark recesses of the minds of investors. Books continue to pour out about it, people still tell stories about some uncle or father or grandfather who lost it all. It was a major *psychic* as well as historic event—like World War II, or Vietnam—carrying with it emotional baggage that lasted far into the subsequent years. The Crash of 1929 is the investor's Frankenstein's monster, his Dracula, his Jack the Ripper. It is the dark powers of violence against which no plan can be formulated, which can strike at any innocent moment, which can destroy the self without reason, like lightning, like storms at sea, like cancer.

Since 1929, investors have known that 1929 can happen. To be sure, there were crashes before in American financial history, but never so severe and never with such broad-reaching effects on the entire structure and quality of society. Prior to the 1920s, investors mostly wore vests. They were the propertied, the advantaged, the aristocracy. In the 1920s, though, with greater communication spreading throughout society and greater affluence than ever before, even shoeshine boys were "investing." Every man with a small business was buying stocks; salesclerks were checking the latest prices during their lunch hour. Financial sages who predicted the indefinite rise of stock prices into the great beyond became pop culture heroes. The Crash of 1929 wasn't some isolated event that happened to "them," the rich people. The Crash happened to everyone. It became a matter of discussion for everyone. Its chronology and causes became a standard part of the curriculum in schools.

In 1929, and during the subsequent depression, the world seemed to come to the brink of extinction. Everyone—particularly investors—began to think that perhaps they'd been deluded all along. There was a flaw in the logic, a trick they'd missed, a lack of understanding about the way things worked. Indeed, in many parts of the world the free-market system was abandoned in favor of a parental and protecting state. Chastened by their own greed and failures, people headed in the opposite direction. Even in this country a serious socialist movement arose, insisting that an economy as old as man would no longer work. "I'll never buy stocks again," thought most investors.

But the market that had collapsed was never a market of true investors anyway. They were trading shares of stock, undeniably, yet the companies whose shares were being traded were quite tangential to the entire activity.

Investors buy a piece of a business that is expected to increase in value over time as the business earns more money and controls more assets. The so-called investors of the late 1920s were merely a positively charged crowd, blindly optimistic, frankly greedy, and quite ignorant of the rational boundaries governing the relationship of a company to its common stock.

Still, it's important to note that nearly everyone *thought* of themselves as investors. In truth, they were like children dressing up and playing financier. And the crowd of stock buyers today think of themselves as investors, even though they never examine a stock purchase in the same way they would for the outright purchase of an entire business. An insubstantial river of guesses, theories, and imaginings makes up most "strategies." Lacking a firm grounding in reality, most investors must have to cope with a potent repressed anxiety as they hold their positions. The expansive desire for profit must remain at an extraordinary level to compensate for the insecurity inherent when investors don't really know how to predict the future.

No one can be in the market today, over fifty years after the Crash, without experiencing anxiety over a Return of the Crash. The existence of the Crash made credible the concept of a crash, and now investors are compelled to coexist with the discomfort of that concept. It is as if every investor had an insistent little voice inside his brain saying, "Watch out, there could be another crash. Watch out, you could be wiped out, destroyed."

Those of us who recognize the reality of that little voice—who become aware of it rather than permitting it to undermine the unconscious—we have come into possession of one of the primary keys for investment success. We begin to understand the anxiety, the *uncontrollable contractions* that compel speculators and unaware investors to abandon an analytic approach and sell stocks down beyond all reason. Investors are assailed and assaulted by insecurity because they've seen securities vanish into thin air. It happened once and it could happen again, says the little voice.

Whenever things turn a little sour, whenever business goes a little soft (as we know it always does), the image of 1929 becomes brighter and brighter in the minds of shareholders. *They become unable to hold their shares.* The anxiety of a crash creates an unbearable negative charge that must be relieved. Four words shout inside sellers' heads: *I must get away.* Instead of looking twice to see if a declined stock might be a good long-term investment, investors can only remember the Great Crash and fall to imagining that the lowering prices point to dark and terrible secrets still to be revealed about the company. Selling frantically to avoid the final Great Crash in a stock, these weak hands actually create a reconstruction of the very process that has frightened them.

The bargain creation process outlined in the previous chapter is greatly exacerbated by the memory of the Crash of 1929, and the closer an individual situation is to the format of the Crash, the more likely it is to be an outstanding bargain with virtually no downside risk. As investors we want stocks as crazily thrown away as they were in 1929. We don't want stocks that have "dipped" a bit, or "declined." We want the ones that have been heaved out wholesale.

This is not so simple as it seems. It's very hard to look at a stock whose price has been beaten down, down, down. Most investors don't want anything to do with such a stock, for perfectly understandable reasons. *Stocks that have crashed remind the investor of the possibility of loss.* The positive charge and optimism needed to make an investment decision means the mind is focused on reward, not loss. The idea of loss is antithetical. That's why most of us are happier to invest in a stock that's been going up and why brokers and advisers almost exclusively recommend stocks that are well along in their rise. We like to imagine that what has been will continue to be. The fallen stock has the stigma of a loser. We want to get away fast from losers and anything that reminds us of losers.

Losers make us forget the immutable law of cyclicality in the market. As long as a company is in business, its stock can go only so far down. Unless the underlying company is truly worth nothing, a stock cannot go down to zero. The selling can't go on forever. Every stock in a going business is worth something more than zero. How *much* more than zero, over what time period, are the two issues that provide our challenge as investors. The answer always varies situationally, but one thing is certain: If the stock has reached bottom *now,* and we know with an extremely high degree of probability that this is truly the bottom, things can only get better.

Wait, you say, some stocks *do* go bankrupt! That may be, but Perfect Investment stocks don't. The system has built-in safeguards against buying a stock merely because it "seems" or "feels" low. You'll only buy stocks that are objectively undervalued—not those whose future has become improbable. And if a stock doesn't perform as expected, you'll sell it before significant losses develop.

A Sneak Preview

We're about to get into the nuts and bolts of the system. To provide you with a sense of context as the steps unfold, the following is a rough outline, in general terms, of the procedure for locating Perfect Investment stocks:

1. First, a crash. You'll become alert for an investment opportunity when a stock's price decline conforms to a model based on the overall market of 1929–32. When the model has been replicated you don't have to wonder whether the risk has been squeezed out of the stock.

2. Next, you'll remain a patient observer as the negative emotional energy of selling is discharged. There are objective criteria to determine when the selling is finally over.

3. While waiting, a very basic analysis of the company is undertaken, using a few simple but key factors to determine that it's still a viable company and that the shares are grossly undervalued relative to its worth as a moneymaking enterprise.

4. You will see objective signals of new accumulation of stock—indicating a buy point and confirming the notion of a much higher intrinsic value for the company.

5. Hold your stock as expansiveness and positive energy on the part of buyers reassert themselves, driving the price back toward its precrash levels.

The approach is simple and it works. Quantification of the critical factors has permitted the introduction of unambiguous rules governing your actions, so a great deal of expertise isn't required. All that's needed, really, is a will to win, to think independently, and to understand the truth and consequences of emotional behavior in yourself as well as in the marketplace.

First, a Crash

After the crash that began in 1929, the discrepancy between price and value for major companies was at its peak for the century. Further risk was almost an arithmetic impossibility. In developing the *Perfect Investment* guidelines I decided to use the post-Crash status of stocks as *a historic measure of true panic selling*. Once that measure is met, it is only necessary to determine, case-by-case, that the selling has in fact been emotional, and not *justified*.

It doesn't take long to assess the damage to stocks during the 1929 Crash. As you can see in the chart below, the first wave of selling, commencing on Black Monday, took stocks from an Industrial Average peak of 386 down to 195 in the space of little more than two months. Stocks were reduced to roughly *half* their former value. The market "valued" a company at 100 in September, and 50 by December.

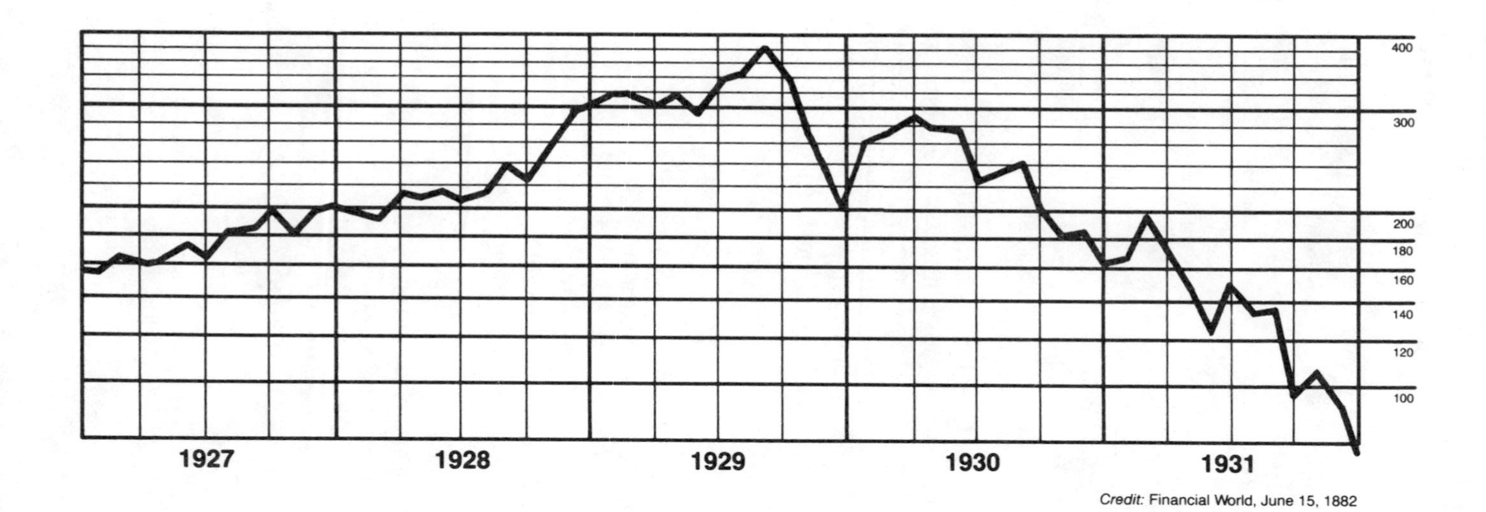

Credit: Financial World, June 15, 1882

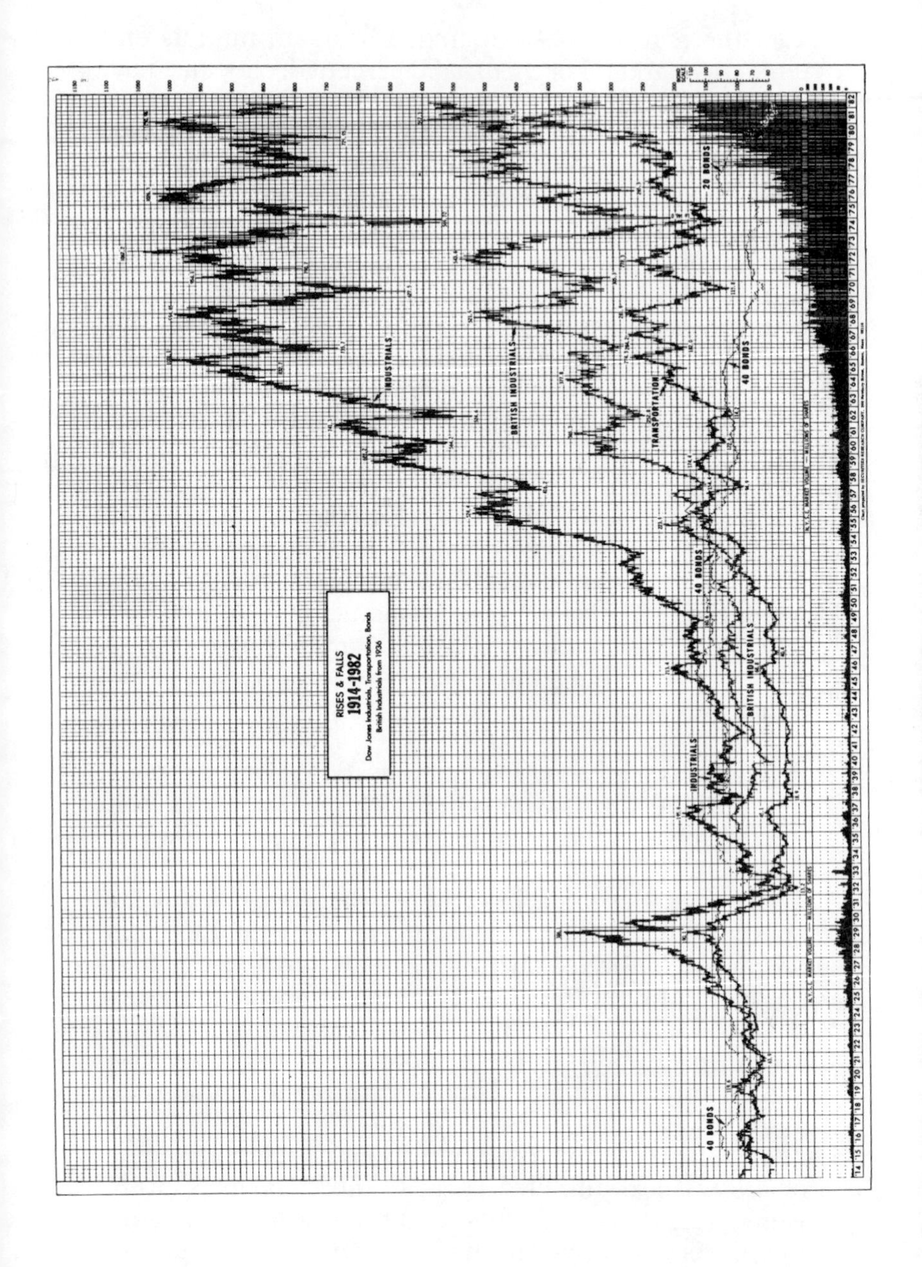
RISES & FALLS
1914-1982
Dow Jones Industrials, Transportation, Bonds
British Industrials from 1936
INDUSTRIALS
BRITISH INDUSTRIALS
TRANSPORTATION
40 BONDS
20 BONDS

At the end of 1929 overanxious bargain hunters entered the market. For them, a 50 percent decline just had to be as far down as things could go. Much to their chagrin, after a three-month rally stocks began to contract in price again, this time plunging steadily and inexorably down to find a bottom at an unthinkable 40.6 during the summer of 1932. Stocks had dropped to 10 percent of their former values. America's greatest companies—the ones that controlled over two-thirds of the country's total assets and earning power—were on the block for ten cents on the dollar.

Real stability entered the market in 1933 and 1934 at about the 100 level—roughly 25 percent of the former high. From this level the market was able to mount sustained rallies and, indeed, it has not gone lower during these past fifty years. (But the actual number touched by the market shouldn't be considered—inflation has so distorted the Dow numbers that in 1982, when the Dow broke 1,000, it had actually *declined* 50 percent, inflation-adjusted, from the 1972 high of just above 1,000. What's important here are *percentage* declines over relatively shorter time frames.)

I asked myself a very simple question: What happens to individual stocks when their own price histories look very much like the price history of the total market in 1929–34?

I studied the price histories of thousands of stocks, analyzing hundreds of thousands of weeks and months of price action. Narrowing the issue down to the past decade and omitting the 1974 crash (so many stocks crashed then that I thought it would skew the data for a system useful also in more "normal" times), I found a significant population of stocks who'd met a 1929-style Waterloo.

The answer to my question was equally simple. A few of these stocks tumbled because the companies really were going down the tubes, and the stocks disappeared into history. Virtually all the rest went up, and did they ever! As a group, they were some of the best performers I'd seen. And no wonder. Their prices could multiply tenfold merely by returning to the former price that investors had been willing to pay.

It was relatively easy to develop tests that would screen out the companies that were falling and would never get up. After all, companies don't go bankrupt *by surprise*. They provide plenty of pain first.

But at that severe level of ten cents on their former dollar, there were too few companies appearing as selections, I thought, and too many had to be screened out as "uninvestable." Unless a system can provide an investor with a fairly steady flow of opportunities it will lead to impatience, rule breaking, and subsequent losses.

When the market touched bottom in 1932, there were many factors that had led to its demise that are no longer present today. The regulation of orderly and honest trading in securities was virtually nonexistent then. The federal banking system was not nearly so strong as it is now. There was virtually nothing the federal government could do to help the situation—the private House of Morgan was far more influential.

Most important of all, during the boom years leading up to 1929, *investors could buy stocks for only 10 percent down* (that number keeps popping up). This excessively liberal margin requirement was perhaps the largest single factor in bringing about the severity of the bust, for investors then could lose far more than they put up. If you put up ten thousand dollars on a hundred thousand dollars' worth of stock, and the stock declines to fifty, you've lost fifty thousand, five times your original investment. If you haven't got the fifty, well . . .

Today the margin requirement is 50 percent of the value of the stock, and it's clear that the kind of wild selling pressure that results from highly leveraged trading is *much* less likely to develop in our times. Interestingly, in commodities, where you *can* still take a position with 10 percent margin, we recently saw silver rise to over forty dollars an ounce and then just as violently decline to near five dollars an ounce—12 percent of its former value. Quite close to the 1929 model, I would say.

Given today's higher margin requirements, I sought a slightly less horrific level of decline as the first qualification of Perfect Investment stocks. I ran through a computer screen a group of over one thousand stocks in mixed industries and of various size companies to determine a "crash" level in which further downside risk was all but eliminated. As a beginning, I left out all other variables except the extent of the crash. There had to be a sufficient number of stocks to create a workable system with investment possibilities occurring regularly, but the crash level had to be low enough to ensure against further decline.

Starting from the basic reasoning that stocks are often sold so unrelentingly that price and value become temporarily unrelated, my procedure became empirical—the crash level must be low enough to eliminate risk but not so low that investment opportunities became inefficiently restrictive. At the 50 percent level of decline, for example, you will find hoards of stocks. But the probability of a stock that has declined 50 percent declining still farther is far too great to be of any use—there is one chance in two of additional decline.

What I found, after much computer testing and cross checking, was that if an individual stock declined (in percentage terms) to a level comparable to the stabilization level of the Dow in 1933–35, it was highly unlikely to decline farther. And, at that level, there were ample investment opportunities. It could be argued that a stock might decline to this level and then go farther, to the very pits at 10 percent of its former value, so safeguards were built into the system. The primary decline, in any event, is only the *first* qualification in the method.

During the 1933–35 period stocks sold at roughly 20 to 25 percent of their 1929 highs. Interestingly, the Cowles Composite Index, an average no longer in use that measured a much broader group of stocks than the Dow, declined to 25 percent of its former value from the 1929 top to the 1932 *bottom*.

Empirically, over varying market conditions stocks seem to follow the broader Cowles model, while in a severe bear market, such as in 1974, they follow the Dow model. An interesting comparison of crashes between a group of 1929 and of 1974 stocks follows on pages 48 and 49. (Note that all of the 1974-crash stocks are still in business, and selling at much higher prices, and that only W. T. Grant, in the comparative table, is bankrupt.)

The system must be of use in all kinds of markets, so the Cowles model is more appropriate. Once a stock has crashed to the point where it is selling for twenty to twenty five cents on its former dollar, we know we've got a likely candidate. Indeed, with some exceptions, that's the first rule of *Perfect Investing*:

Basic Rule: A stock must decline to 20 percent of its former five-year-high price to be considered a potential investment.

But the basic rule must be adapted to the variety of situations one can encounter in the market. First there are certain kinds of stocks, such as utilities, which simply cannot be expected to decline so severely. Other stocks are clearly superior investments within the context of the *Perfect Investment* group because, for example, their earnings have *risen* even during the entire course of the decline; these are hardly companies in trouble. Since they're not in trouble, the evident risk is reduced and we need not apply such a stringent decline requirement.

My analysis of the various stock groups and company/stock characteristics has yielded the following set of rules for an initial screening. Obviously these rules are empirical adaptations of a primary reasoning or ration-

Bear Market Price Declines

1841

Stock	1837 High	Nov. 25, 1841 Price
United States Bank	122	4
Vicksburg Bank	89	5
Kentucky Bank	92	56
North American Trust	95	3
Farmers' Trust	113	30
American Trust	120	0
Illinois State Bank	80	35
Morris Canal Bank	75	0
Patterson Railroad	75	53
Long Island Railroad	60	52

Source: The Big Board

1962

	High	Low	Close
American Machine & Foundry	42 1/2	15 3/8	20 1/8
American Photocopy	32 1/8	8 1/4	11 3/4
Automatic Canteen	31 3/4	9 3/4	14 1/4
Brunswick Corporation	52 3/4	13 1/8	18 3/8
Cenco Instruments	68	28 1/4	32 1/8
Fairchild Camera	70 1/2	31	45 1/4
General Instrument	30	10 1/8	11 1/8
Hewlett-Packard	37	15 1/4	24 1/8
International Business Machines	578 1/2	300	390
Texas Instruments	125 1/2	49	63 1/2

Source: The Big Board

1929

Stock	1928–29 High	1932 Low	Percent Decline
Int'l Bus. Mach.	255	51	–80
Eastman Kodak	263	36	–86
Sears, Roebuck	197	9	–95
Coca-Cola	191	67	–65
RCA	114	1 1/2	–99
Packard	32 1/2	1 1/2	-95
New York Central	257	9	–96
Walgreens	108	8	–93
Burroughs	97	6	–94
Procter & Gamble	97 1/2	10	–90
Atch., Topeka & S. Fe	297	15	–95
Kresge	61	5	–92
Raytheon	85	1/2	–99
Loew's Theaters	96	8	–92
General Electric	101	9	–91
Babcock & Wilcox	141	19	–87

Source: Financial World

1974

Today's Counterpart	1967–72 High	1974 Low To Date	Percent Decline
Automatic Data Proc.	99 3/4	20 3/4	–79
Polaroid	149 1/2	14 1/8	–91
Best Products	66 3/4	3 1/4	–95
Royal Crown Cola	47 1/4	7 1/8	–85
TelePrompTer	44	1 7/8	–96
Winnebago	48 1/4	3 1/8	–94
Eastern Airlines	61	4	–93
Rite Aid	56 3/4	2 1/2	–96
Control Data	163 1/2	11 3/4	–93
Avon	140	18 5/8	–87
TWA	60	4 3/4	–92
Zayre	47 1/2	2 7/8	–94
Itek	171	5	–97
General Cinema	55	6	–89
Litton	101 3/4	4	–96
Combustion Eng.	107	21 5/8	–80

Source: Financial World

Comparative Price Declines, 1929 and 1974

Stock	The 1929 Crash					The "Second Crash"			
	High	(Year)	Low	(Year)	Percent Decline	High	(Year)	Low To Date	Percent Decline
Addressograph	38	(1930)	5 1/8	(1933)	–87%	92	(1968)	3 3/4	–96
Allis-Chalmers	82	(1929)	4	(1932)	–95	44	(1967)	6 3/8	–86
Chrysler	140	(1938)	5	(1932)	–96	72	(1968)	11 7/8	–84
Consol. Edison	182	(1928)	16	(1932)	–91	49 1/2	(1965)	6	–88
Detroit Edison	386	(1929)	49	(1933)	–87	38 1/2	(1965)	8 3/4	–77
W. T. Grant	72	(1929)	14	(1932)	–81	71	(1971)	3	–96
Honeywell	123	(1929)	12	(1932)	–90	171	(1972)	22 1/4	–87
Loew's Theaters*	94	(1930)	8 1/2	(1933)	–88	61	(1972)	10 7/8	–82
Pan Amer.	90	(1929)	11	(1931)	–88	40	(1966)	1 3/4	–95
Transamerica	66	(1929)	2	(1931)	–97	40 1/2	(1968)	5 1/2	–86
Westinghouse	292	(1929)	15	(1932)	–95	60	(1972)	8 1/4	–86
Western Union	272	(1929)	12	(1932)	–96	69	(1972)	8 1/2	–88
Woolworth	103	(1929)	22	(1932)	–79	56	(1971)	10 1/4	–82
Wrigley	84	(1928)	25	(1932)	–70	99	(1971)	38	–62

Source: Financial World
**Now Loews Corp.*

ale. It would no doubt be tempting to bend them if you've got a particular interest in a company, but you should strenuously avoid tampering with the rules by any more than a percentage point or two. For they've proven statistically valid over an enormous sampling of situations; if you adhere strictly to the rules, the probabilities of success are markedly in your favor. If you break the rules, well . . . the probabilities will change.

Complete Crash Rules

- The stock must decline to 20 *percent* of its former five-year high.

except

- A stock that has crashed to only 25 *percent* of its former five-year high may be accepted if the company's *earnings* have declined *less than* 25 *percent* from the stock's five-year high to the present low.
- A stock that has crashed to only 30 *percent* of its former five-year high may be accepted if:
  1. Earnings *or* dividends have increased from the five-year high to the crash-point low—or—
  2. Earnings have declined *less than* 25 *percent* from the five-year high to the crash-point low *and the company was previously valued in the market at over one billion dollars*. Market valuation is the number of shares outstanding times the share price. A company with fifty million shares selling at twenty dollars per share is valued at one billion dollars—or—
- A stock that has crashed to only 35 *percent* of its former five-year high may be accepted if:
  1. The stock is a component of the Dow Jones Industrials Average—or—
  2. The stock is a utility—or—
  3. The stock was formerly valued in the market at its five-year high at *over two billion dollars*.
  4. The company is a bank and ranks in the top two hundred in size nationally.

Option. When a stock has declined despite a strong upward trend in the overall market during its decline, you are permitted the option of *raising all figures by 5 percent*.

The exceptions in the complete crash rules are derived from exhaustive study of the price behavior of the different kinds of stocks, and each exception is based on a sound rationale of its own. The larger stocks are permitted less of a crash, for example, because these stocks are the most widely researched on Wall Street. Under closer scrutiny, it's to be expected that these issues are slightly less likely to reach extreme levels of undervaluation, and market action bears out this expectation.

Remember, the crash does not provide the buy point; it only gives you the first step in your Perfect Investment quest.

Once you've located a crashed stock it must then pass through the fivefold screen before you can actually invest. The screen should clarify the reasons behind the crash exceptions for you.

A sampler of crashed stocks follows.

30% of Former 5-year High

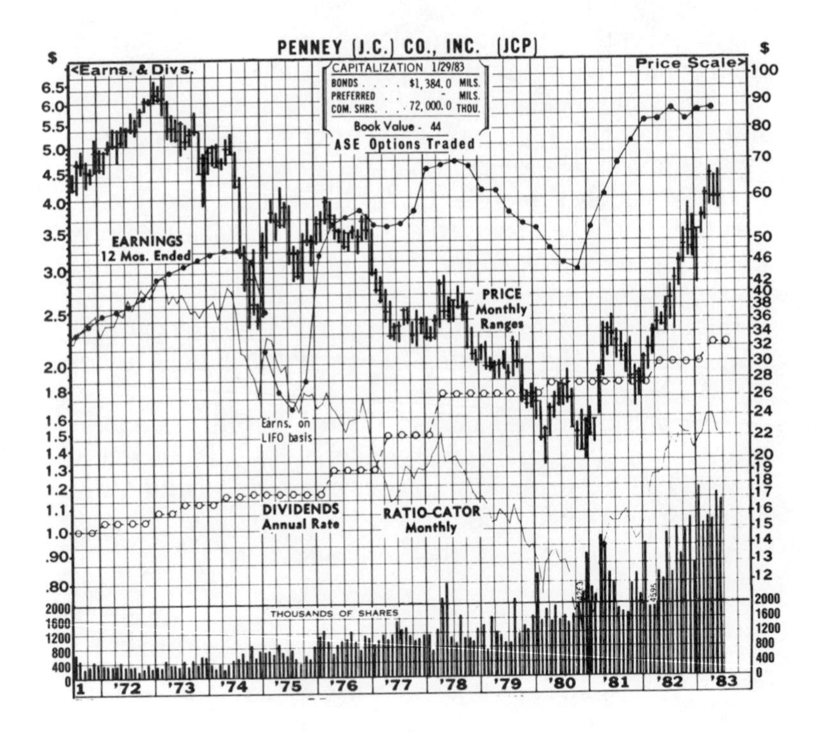

25% of Former 5-year High

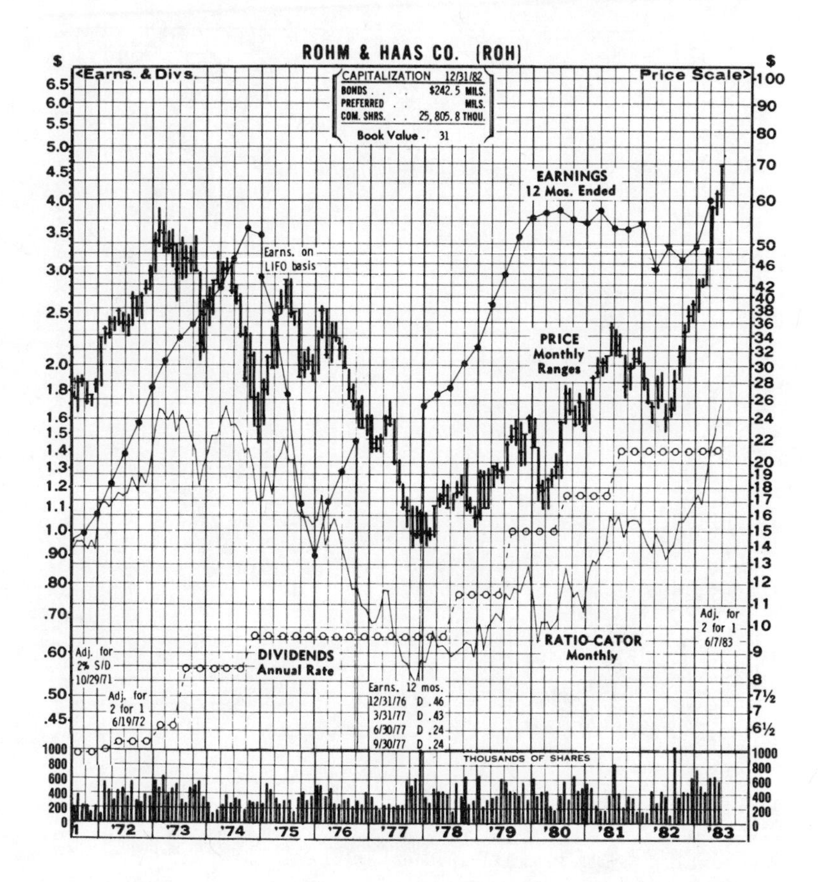

20% of Former 5-year High

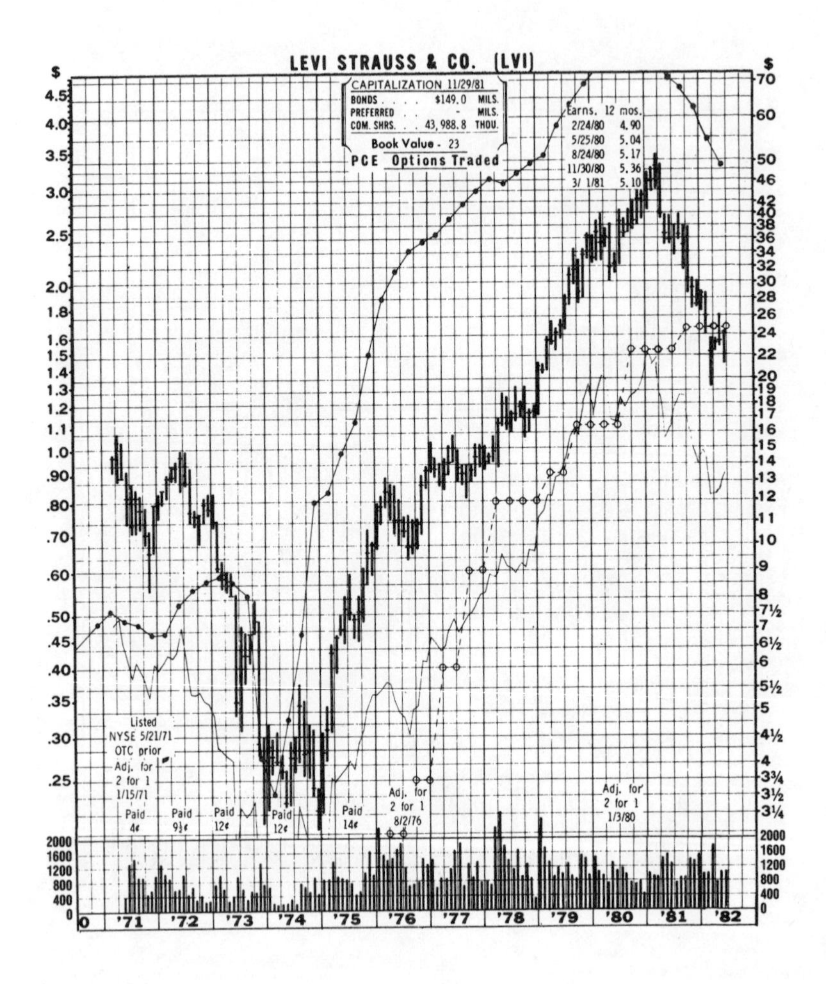

20% of Former 5-year High

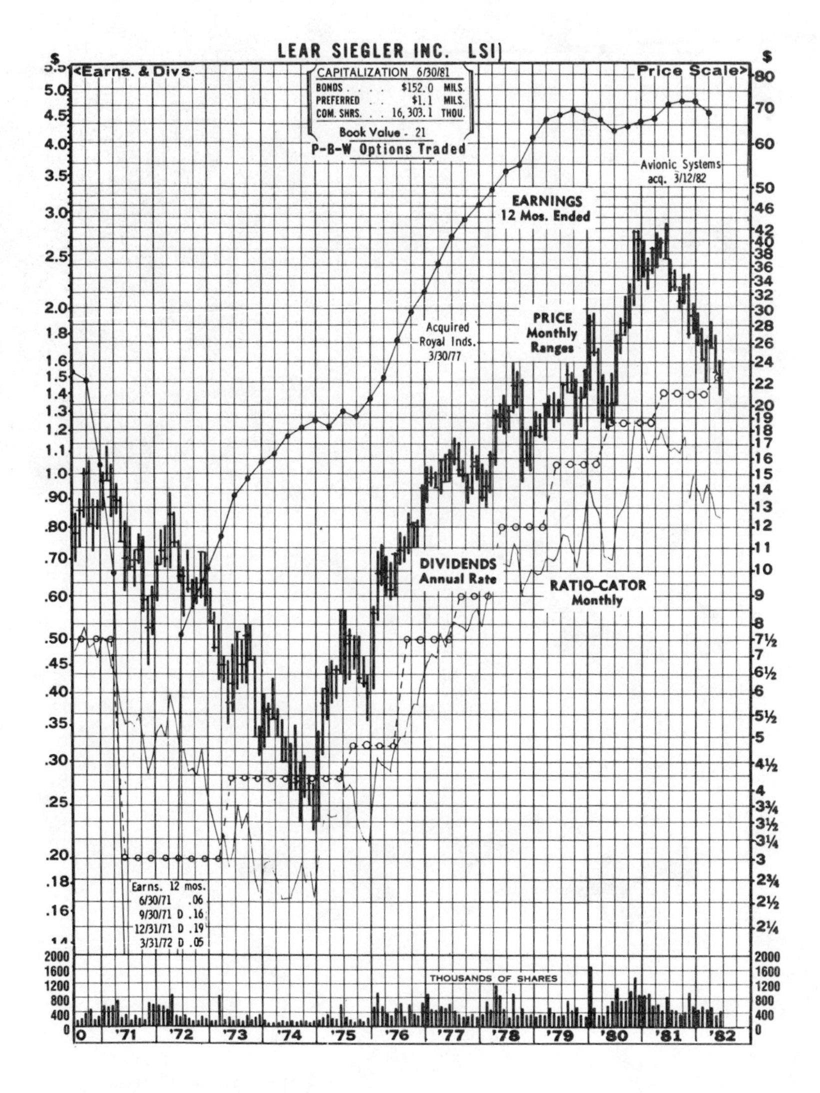

25% of Former 5-year High

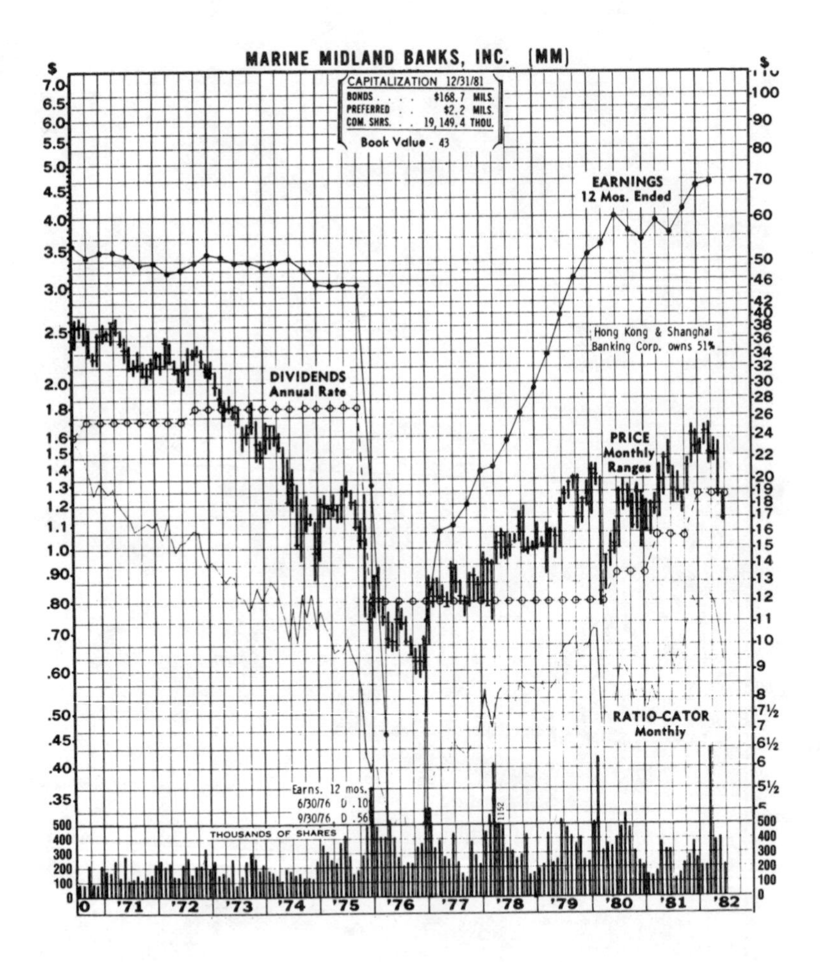

15% of Former 5-year High

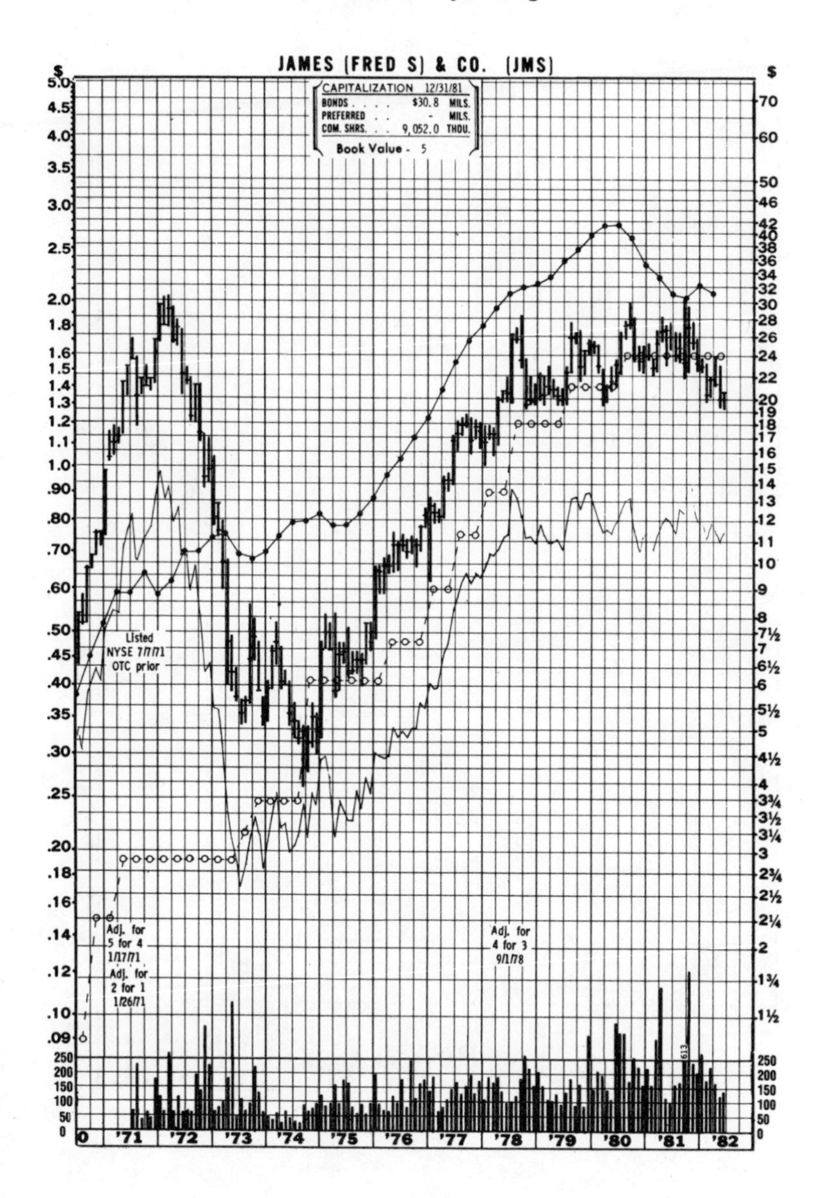

25% of Former 5-year High

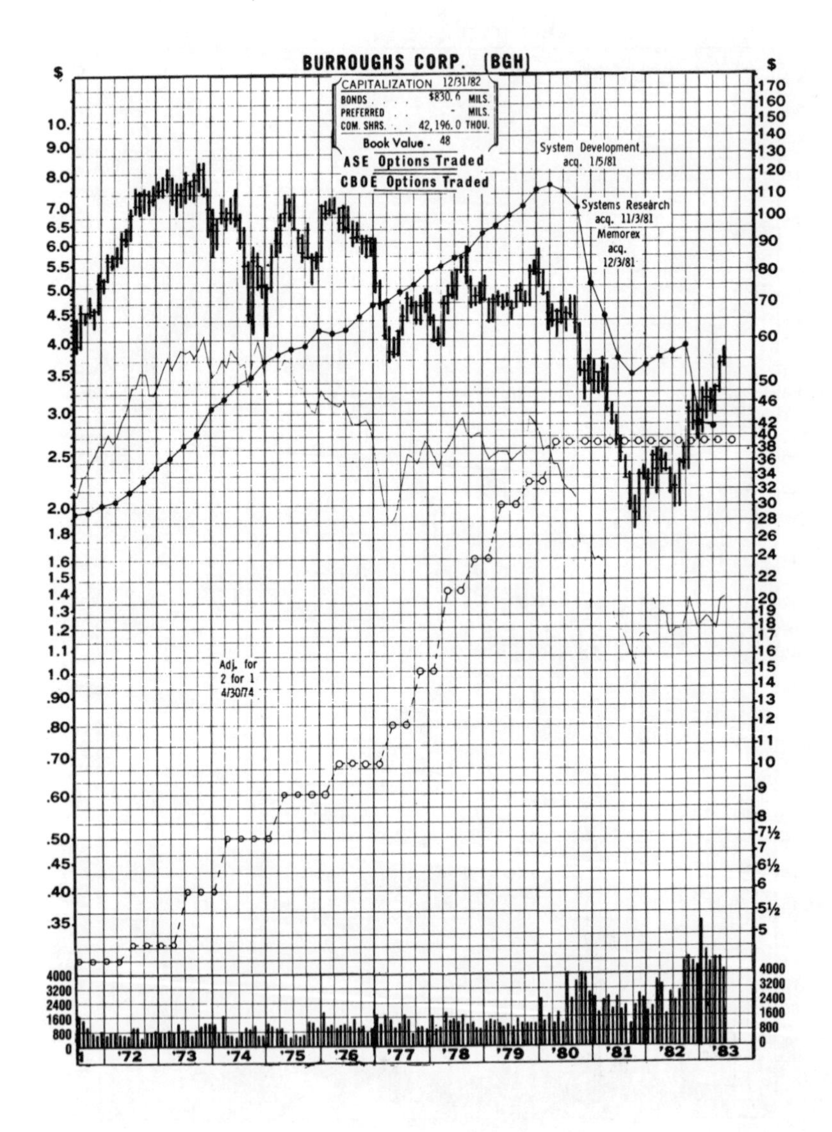

PART TWO

THE FIVEFOLD SCREEN

4

Screen One: There Must Be Assets

In every business, *the money made is produced by the assets the business owns*. In the case of a candy store, the business is able to make money because it has a location (long lease? short lease?), it has goodwill—loyal customers who've been coming in for years—and because it has an inventory of candy from which to make its sales. The worth of the inventory is reducible to a quick number based on inventory valuation formulas. The worth of the location and goodwill are more open to debate, but suffice it to say at this point that those two assets are worth *something*. If the business were sold, a buyer would pay some dollar figure over the inventory value *just because the store was a going business*—with all that that implies. A buyer would value the assets and consequent earning power (time earnings), deduct the debts, and come up with a figure he was willing to pay.

In the case of an apartment house, the asset is a building in a certain location with tenants who pay rent. The valuation of the building is arrived at by standard formulas, most prominently that of market value—what buyers have recently paid for similar buildings. Various factors that are not quite subject to formularization affect the asset—the improvement or decline of the neighborhood, subjection to rent-control or rent-stabilization laws, condition of mechanical systems, quality of tenancy—but these factors all resolve themselves in a "market price" dollar figure. This is the value of the asset. If a company's sole asset is a building worth ten million dollars, then that company is worth ten million dollars, less the debt on the building (or any other debt).

As businesses become more complex, the job of evaluating the worth of their assets obviously becomes more complex as well. Fortunately, there is a kind of standard of asset valuation known as *book value*. To arrive at book value—which is usually also considered the rough *liquidation* value—trained analysts assign salable value to a company's factories, inventory, land, patents and copyrights, leases, mineral rights, cash on hand, investments—anything of value that might be sold. From a total figure of salable assets the liablities of a company—loans that must be repaid, reserves for lawsuits that might be in progress, anything the company will or might have to pay—are subtracted to arrive at a book value. Book value is usually stated on a per-share basis, so that Perfect, Inc., might have a book value of twenty dollars per share. If the stock is selling at thirty dollars per share, you know that if the company went out of business tomorrow and all assets were converted into cash, you, a shareholder, would lose ten dollars per share. If the shares of Perfect, Inc., were selling at five dollars per share, on the other hand, and the company went out of business tomorrow, you would stand to gain, theoretically, fifteen dollars per share.

"Theoretically" is the key word here. While stated book value gives us a good starting point for gauging a company's cash liquidation value, it's hardly the whole story.

The actual worth of assets varies greatly as a function of changing market conditions, and the method for claiming value varies from industry to industry. Even within industries, companies list assets on their balance sheets in differing ways. One company might list, say, twenty thousand acres of land at its original cost forty years ago, thus giving it a book value considerably lower than its actual value if the asset were sold on the open market. Another company might list the same asset on its balance sheet with a replacement-cost valuation, thus giving the company an inflated book value if land prices turn down or if the land must be sold quickly under distress-sale conditions. While a General Motors factory might recently have cost five hundred million dollars to put up and be worth every penny, it's quite difficult to ascertain its true value as an asset on the open market. If it had to be sold, who would buy the plant? To be sure, the plant is an asset in the sense that it is an investment that provides earning power, but as an element of value in establishing book value, the plant has a definitely illusory quality. A small California company's factory for making computer chips, on the other hand, might be worth far more than its construction and equipment cost, for there might be many companies standing in line ready to buy the facility and increase their capacity to produce chips.

A manufacturing company I owned once held an auction to sell some top-quality equipment that we wanted to replace with newer and faster models. We thought we had conservatively "booked" the equipment at half our cost, but when the time came to sell, we could recoup only 15 percent of our cost. Our book value shrank accordingly. The point, of course, is that corporate assets are not sold that often, nor is the market for corporate assets so predictable that a reliable book value can always be established. A few years ago used planes sold for only slightly less than new ones. Recently, when Braniff announced bankruptcy, buyers for their fleet were nowhere to be found.

Still further weakening the concept of book value—or you might say lending to the concept a certain ephemeral quality—is the fact that cash and cash equivalents (investments in other companies, short-term money market accounts, T-bills, etc.) and working capital are considered part of a company's assets. Let's say a company has a loss this quarter. The cash to make up that loss is going to come from working capital or the company's cash chest. The book value of the company may be reduced by the amount of the loss. When a company runs into trouble, the losses can pile up quarter after quarter. And each quarter's loss, without a corresponding gain in the value of other assets (such as inventory), will reduce the book value.

Book value, then, while a handy and easily available concept (nearly all charts or brokerage information sheets will give you a book value figure), should not be seen as static. It is fluid, fluctuating, subject to rises and fallings based on earnings as well as the changing market for a company's assets, were they to be sold.

Still, book value remains a useful starting point for us. Barring special considerations, if a company's stock sells for, say, half its book value, we know that it will take some very special circumstances (or some very odd accounting) for the liquidation value of the company to drop below the price we are paying for the stock, at least in the foreseeable future. If Perfect, Inc., sells for ten dollars a share and its book value is twenty dollars a share, we can tell ourselves with more chance of being right than of being wrong that we have bought at half price a piece of the assets Perfect, Inc., owns. We're unlikely to lose money if the company shuts down tomorrow. Wall Street still may treat Perfect's stock badly—as it obviously already has—but that's a completely different issue, which we'll deal with later.

In a nutshell, it makes sense to start with book value in seeking a risk-free, crash-past stock. But then we must scrutinize the assets represented. What are their kind and quality? Are the assets expensive factories specially designed to produce products made by few other companies, so that there would be few potential buyers and a low market price? Not so good. Are they more "universal" assets, such as real estate, which could be useful to many buyers? Better. Are they the most universal kinds of assets, such as cash and securities, with a readily ascertainable market value? Best.

Are the assets listed on the company's books at cost, below cost, market value, or replacement value?* Obviously the former two are more attractive, for then the book value is likely to be even greater than stated. The problem here is simple: Though there are general rules for establishing book value, the rules are applied in different ways by different companies. What *we* want, as investors, is not merely the formalistic statement of book value, we want a more *realistic* figure.

The higher the book value relative to stock price (on a per-share basis), the safer we are as investors. Obviously, a stock selling at half its book value leaves quite a margin of safety between the stated book value and whatever the real-world book value turns out to be. If the stock is selling for one third of its book value, so much better.

Benjamin Graham (author of *The Intelligent Investor*), the most famous asset-oriented investor and theoretician of all time, had an almost fanatical attraction for book value and related techniques as investment criteria. Over the period 1925–75 his methods produced twice the rate of return of the Dow Jones Industrials Average. His underlying philosophy consisted in "buying groups of stocks at less than their current or intrinsic value as indicated by one or more simple criteria." Graham had a somewhat more sophisticated version of book value, which he called "net quick assets," but these two were close cousins. By the end of his life Graham was essentially saying that you should buy stocks at about 60 to 70 percent of book value and sell them when they rose to 100 percent of book value. That's a gross oversimplification, but what's more important than getting the formula right is the fact that Graham's concepts have *an enormous following on Wall Street*. When a stock gets way down below book value, you can bet there are people noticing: future buyers.

*See the Appendix for information sources that can help you discover an accurate book value.

One thing is certain: As investors in a company that has manifestly been rejected by other investors, we want to be sure we will at least get our money back if the company must be liquidated.

Given that need, no stock will qualify as a Perfect Investment unless it is selling for a per-share price equal to or lower than the stated per-share book value.

There are two exceptions to this rule. One is for the eager-beaver investor willing to do lots of homework. The other is for the sensible, objective investor willing to invest from a common-sense standpoint based on "unofficial" values.

In the first exception, the investor must seek out hidden values that the company is not claiming as part of book value but could claim if it so chose. Here we are basically talking about understated valuation of assets, as mentioned above. If you know that the company has, say, a hundred thousand acres of timberland, if you are able to find out the true value of those acres, and if you see that the company has valued the land at only one tenth of its real worth, then you have good reason to buy its stock even though its book value may be equal to or even greater than the share price. In this case, you have actually been able, through research, to generate the *true* book value of the business, as opposed to the stated value. (Often companies will understate values as a conservative accounting practice; sometimes they will do so to ward off potential takeovers.) Whatever the case, you can find out all the information you need from the annual report and the 10-K (more on these information sources later), but you'll have to solve the true-valuation problem through whatever means you can devise. One simple method would be to compare the asset valuation of your candidate with valuation of similar assets of another company.

To me, the more interesting and fertile area in which to find hidden values is in the group of off-balance-sheet assets. These are assets that, according to generally accepted accounting principles, cannot be included in the calculations arriving at book value. There are cases, though, where these off-balance-sheet assets can be as valuable as the entire sum of the tangible assets of the company. Such values can include goodwill, patents and technology whose value is rarely stated at full worth, a strong, loyal sales force, a difficult-to-create distribution network, or simply a "franchise"—when a business dominates its market through the absence of competition. (The only candy store in town is surely worth more than one of three in a similar-size town.)

Several years ago I visited with Roy Ash, one of the founders of the giant Litton Industries and former chairman of the Office of Management and Budget of the federal government. At the time he had just taken on the presidency of seriously ailing Addressograph-Multigraph Corporation. AM International (as it was renamed) had been left in the dust of the booming office automation/ computerization industry, and it seemed as though its clanking old machines would have no place in a new world of word processors. Belatedly, the company purchased small California firms with new computer products, graphic transmission products, and got hooked up in a new business satellite venture with the likes of IBM and Aetna.

These new additions were moves Ash had made in the year since he'd joined AM International, and it seemed as though he were breathing new life into an old firm that had previously been wheezing and gasping its last. But something intrigued me. Upon taking the presidency Ash had purchased a substantial percentage of the company, and had taken options to buy more later. He was no mere hired savior, he'd put his money—plenty of it—on the table, too.

I asked him what strange whim has possessed him to invest heavily in a company with problems potentially too serious for it to survive.

"I don't go by the book," he said, unintentionally making a pun. "I learned something very important at Litton," he went on. "We made a study in 1972, and at that time we found it cost us nearly thirty thousand dollars to train a salesman. And salesmen are the lifeblood of any business. If you've got a good sales force you've got a business. Now, I'd been in Washington for a while before I took over here, but I figured that today it had to cost at least fifty thousand dollars to train a new salesman. AM International had over four thousand highly trained, loyal salesmen who'd been with the company for years. These guys, because they are already selling our office equipment, could get their foot in the door of virtually every office in America. I knew they could get our products in front of the buyers, and hell, that's more than half the battle. We could bring new products on stream, one after the other, and we'd have this army to march them into customers across the land.

"But a sales force, according to the rules this group of accountants has set up, is valued at zero on the books. I don't live in the world of accountants, I live in the real world. And I know how much it costs to train a salesman, so I know how much a sales force already in place with proven guys is worth. To replace that sales force would cost some two hundred fifty million dollars! And that's how much I figured the book of this company was undervalued. I'm a businessman, I know I would pay to have a sales force in place, so I know some other businessman with intelligence would also pay for a living, breathing sales force. As far as I'm concerned, the force was an asset as real as any other, and I bought my stock because I figured it was an utter bargain."

For a time, anyway, Ash proved absolutely right. Within two years AMI was selling its new products, making money, and seeing its stock price soar. Ash's stake tripled in value, for he had seen the hidden value, *the hidden income-producing power* of owning the means of distribution. In today's business world you need to operate on a large scale, and you can do so only if you can sell on a large scale. Only if you have a distribution network can you sell on a large scale. Someone else always can make your products for you, but you have to get them into the hands of your customers. (In all fairness, I must add as a

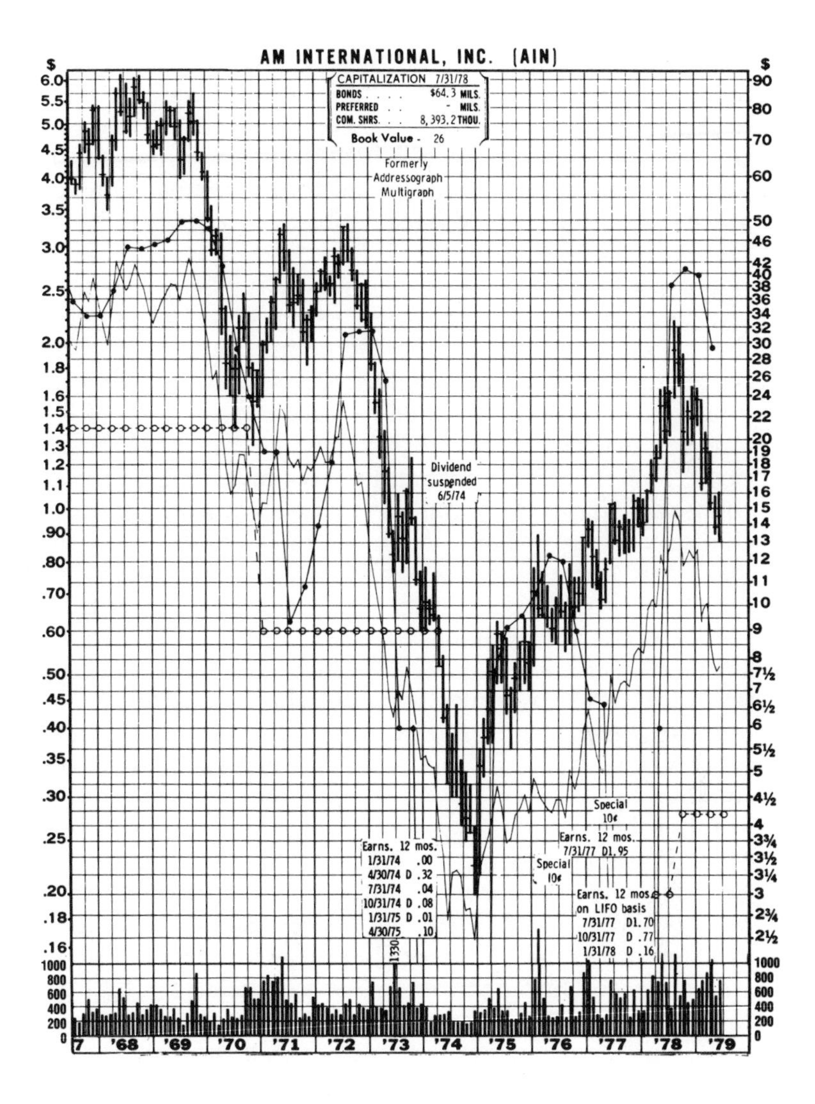

AM INTERNATIONAL, INC. (AIN)
CAPITALIZATION 7/31/78
BONDS . . . . $64.3 MILS.
PREFERRED . . - MILS.
COM. SHRS. . . 8,393.2 THOU.
Book Value - 26
Formerly Addressograph Multigraph
Dividend suspended 6/5/74
Earns. 12 mos.
1/31/74 .00
4/30/74 D .32
7/31/74 .04
10/31/74 D .08
1/31/75 D .01
4/30/75 .10
Special 10¢
Special 10¢
Earns. 12 mos. 7/31/77 D1.95
Earns. 12 mos. on LIFO basis
7/31/77 D1.70
10/31/77 D .77
1/31/78 D .16
1330
'68
'69
'70
'71
'72
'73
'74
'75
'76
'77
'78
'79

footnote that AMI ran into trouble another two years down the road—they simply didn't have enough money to finance their renewed growth, but we as Perfect Investment investors would have taken our long-term gains and been gone long before the problems became apparent. And we would have doubled our money in little more than a year.)

The lesson of Roy Ash's logic should not be lost. He is, after all, one of the gods of the postwar business pantheon, one of the leaders of the conglomerating 1960s whose special skill was finding other companies to buy at a bargain. His mind is tuned as a true investor—as I've stressed earlier—to the idea of buying the entire business. The thinking of an individual investor buying a thousand shares or a mutual fund buying a hundred thousand shares should be no different. You've got to look beyond the numbers. You've got to think about the company. You've got to ask yourself: What gives this company the power to make money? Certainly you want to know about the generally accepted tangible assets, but you also want to know more, for the real assets of a company go beyond its book value. The real assets are whatever characteristics it has that enable it to make money.

When I built up my stake in Marine Midland (MM) in 1977 I wasn't looking for the most sparkling bank in America with the best "numbers" and every pension fund on Wall Street buying its shares. Since this was a time of economic recovery, I was looking for a bank whose shares had been mercilessly sold down, thrown away by investors contracting from the anxiety of declining share prices and temporary business troubles. I knew that banks make up an important part of institutional portfolios, and I also knew that no portfolio manager wants to have to explain to his superiors why he's got the worst bank around on his list.

At the time, selling for $12 a share, MM had a book value of about $35 a share. In late 1975 MM's loan portfolio began to show problems, and by 1976 there were minor deficits. In 1976, during a bull market, MM's stock reached a low of $8.50 a share, having sold as high as $40 a share within the previous five years. As I saw it, MM as a company was not much changed from five years earlier, except that its assets, whatever those proved to be, were surely not showing as much earning power as they once had.

As the stock's decline to the area of ten dollars a share seemed to stabilize, I had to ask myself this single, all-important question: Will the assets of the company enable it to earn money once again as it had in the past?

In other words, is this horse dead or just sick?

Every company gets its time of trouble, I knew. Problems are to be expected. It is precisely the successful resolution of problems that makes a company strong. When a company has seen hard times and gotten through them, it is much more likely to get through hard times in the future. We all make mistakes—nobody's perfect. Yet investors seem to insist that a company *be* perfect. One mistake and they'll drop the stock like a hot potato, taking their money elsewhere. They'll pay forty dollars for a stock yesterday, but let some clouds pass on the company's future and they'll pay no more than ten dollars tomorrow. Same company, different stock price.

To forgive a company when it has been bad, like forgiving a child, can be not only divine, mature, and compassionate, it can also be very profitable. I looked at Marine Midland and asked myself: Is this just sickness, or is it death? If just sickness, I already knew that the stock price was cheap, for it had already met the crash criteria. I also knew that the stock was selling way below book value, so in a liquidation I was likely at least to get my money back.

I also knew that Marine Midland had important off-balance-sheet assets. There was plenty of value beyond the books. In terms of numbers of branch offices, Marine Midland was the largest bank in New York State.(That, of course, made it one of the largest banks in the United States.) That meant it had thousands of locations all over the state, many, no doubt, in small towns where it was the only bank in town, or the largest and most secure bank in town in the eyes of customers. That gave it, in addition, thousands of pieces of prime property and/or leases, most of which would be carried on the books at an acquisition cost years old. In those thousands of offices were more thousands of trained employees, and officers who know the local populace and are trusted by their customers. Having spent considerable time living in a small town, I knew that the attraction of the local people for the officers, and the knowledge of the officers of whose word is good and whose isn't, is a business asset of incalculable value; for a bank in a small town is the linchpin of an entire society—it really does hold the "franchise," for no one wants to drive twenty miles to cash a check. So, on top of those thousands of offices and the significant assets located therein, add now *millions* of loyal customers who already have their accounts and loans at Marine Midland and would just as soon stay right where they were.

If that horse is dead, I thought, there certainly is going to be quite a flock of vultures picking over the carcass.

And another tidbit caught my eye. Despite the bank's showing a small deficit, the directors of Marine Midland—presumably a group with substantial combined experience and savvy—had elected to maintain payment of a dividend. To be sure, the dividend was cut in half, but it was still being paid. This is an issue we'll get into later, but at this point it's worth noting that the directors of the company did not feel that business was so bad that they couldn't pay the stockholders a dividend. Looking into the future, as they are far better able to do than any outside investor, they collectively said, "We have enough money to pay a dividend, and we'll have enough in the future to pay the dividend then, too." If things were *really bad,* they would have cut the dividend altogether, preserving that cash for the company's fight for survival.

So I saw that not only was MM selling way below book value, it also had hidden "common sense" assets that were not valued at all in the stock price but were worth much to any businessman. The stock wasn't just cheap, it was supercheap. And it wasn't supercheap because the company was going under—not only did a dividend remain, but also, by the beginning of 1977, earnings had begun to return. That wasn't too late to invest, though—once Wall Street turns, like a lover abandoning an old mistress, investors will literally cross the street to *avoid* hearing the news that they were wrong, that the end of the world has not come, that the horse is coming back to life.

I was sorry I didn't have more money so I could buy up *all* of Marine Midland's stock. Imagine, being able to buy the largest New York State banking network for, I figured, around twenty cents on the dollar! With a business like that, you could surely figure out a way to make those assets earn income!

I didn't have that much money, but the Hong Kong and Shanghai Bank did, and two years later they bought 51 percent of MM at $24 a share. They added working capital, making it a still stronger company, and by December 1981 Marine Midland showed earnings of $4.55 per share and had a book value of $43 per share. The stock hasn't gone much higher than $24 a share yet, but 100 percent profit plus dividends is okay in my book—I've long since sold to seek new bargains.

When you're dealing with a big, big business that has been around for many years, through up and down cycles in the economy, through Republicans and Democrats, wars, acts of God, and through errors of judgment and correction of those errors—*the odds are much greater for survival than for dissolution*. Investors never view a troubled situation or an out-of-favor stock (the two can be quite different) this way and always sell the stock down for a fraction of its intrinsic, asset-based value. If you can see both the visible and invisible assets and how they might be put to use to *regain past earning power*, you are exactly one fifth of the way to locating a *Perfect Investment*.

5

Screen Two: There Must Be "Signs of Life"

The fact that Marine Midland was still paying a dividend—even in the face of two quarters of losses—presents us with a "message" about the company. We may not have access to any of the facts that the corporate directors have seen and on which they base their decision to continue paying a dividend, but we *do* know that they—who have far more information than we—don't feel the corporation is on the edge of oblivion. Crash in the stock or no, the company still has the money to pay its bills *and* share some of the wealth with the stockholders.

The maintenance of a dividend is an example of what I call a "sign of life." It's a clue that the crash in the stock price is creating a bargain rather than pointing out the end of the world for the company. While directors have certainly been known to pay dividends when they shouldn't, in general we can rely on them as major-league businessmen who would keep the dividend cash inside the corporate treasury if it's really that badly needed. When a dividend is maintained, the "message" is that those closest to the company do not believe the problem is permanent or life-threatening.

A cut or omission in the dividend is poison for stock prices. If this occurs during a company's crash it is no reason to reject the stock—you're just going to have to look for your signs of life elsewhere. Maintenance is a point in the company's favor, cut or omission's not a point against it. (Increases, reinstatements, and first institutions of dividends are discussed in the chapter on Plus Factors.

One of the best signs of life is when the assets are doing what they're supposed to do—bring in dollars.

If a company still is able (or once again is able) to earn money, then its assets (its earning power) are still worth something. Just how much they're worth is open to question, but our presumption is that a company has the ability to earn at least as much money as it did before its crash.

We don't have to look for great new products or technological breakthroughs, we don't need to find the next IBM or 30 percent growth in earnings compounded over the next ten years. All we want to see is that the company has the potential to earn as much money as it did when its stock sold four times higher.

There's no point in asking too much of a company or its stock. All that's needed to show huge investment profits is a return to normalcy.

The simple fact is that any company that *survives* earns more money over the years, if only because of inflation. A bad quarter or two, even a bad year or two does not necessarily indicate the beginning of a downtrend in earnings. It's almost impossible to find a substantial company that has shown consistent earnings declines over the past, say, five or ten years. If the company is to survive—and our asset test begins to give an answer to that question—we can expect that over a period of years its earnings will be much higher than in the past. If the stock was not insanely valued previously (tests to come), it is only reasonable to expect that when the company finally does get back on the earnings track it will not only earn as much or more than it did before its problems, but also that its stock will be valued in constant dollars at the same price or higher than it was before. In that sense, every investment that passes the Perfect Investment tests has at least the *potential* to increase in price fourfold over the three-to-five-year period usually required for a company to rid itself completely of earnings-depletion problems. In the case of the stock that has experienced a price crash *without* attendant corporate problems, we're of course in a better position, having only to wait for sanity to return to investors.

To establish confidence that the company's earning power is intact, *we must see earnings*. This is a minimum requirement.

To qualify for investment, the stock must not be showing losses *at the buy point*.*

The reasoning here should be obvious. Current losses deplete current assets, which deplete book value, which means the liquidation value of the company declines and our shares are less "protected" by the underlying breakup value of the company. Furthermore, we already know that this company's assets were once useful tools in earning money and that other investors recognized that fact and paid relatively higher prices for the shares. As investors, we cannot profit until some degree of that past profile reasserts itself, until other investors once again see that this company can be a money-maker, a wealth builder. If the company is not now earning money, it is abundantly clear that the management has not yet learned, or relearned, how to harness the company's earning power right now. Promises and plans mean nothing. Other investors will be looking only at the bottom line (profits or no profits), and that's all we can afford to look at as well. Precisely how the company is able to make its earning power a reality is of no concern to us—all we want to see are the results. Again, *no losses*. Losses diminish the value of the assets and show us that the assets are not being properly used.

*Based on the most recent quarterly report.

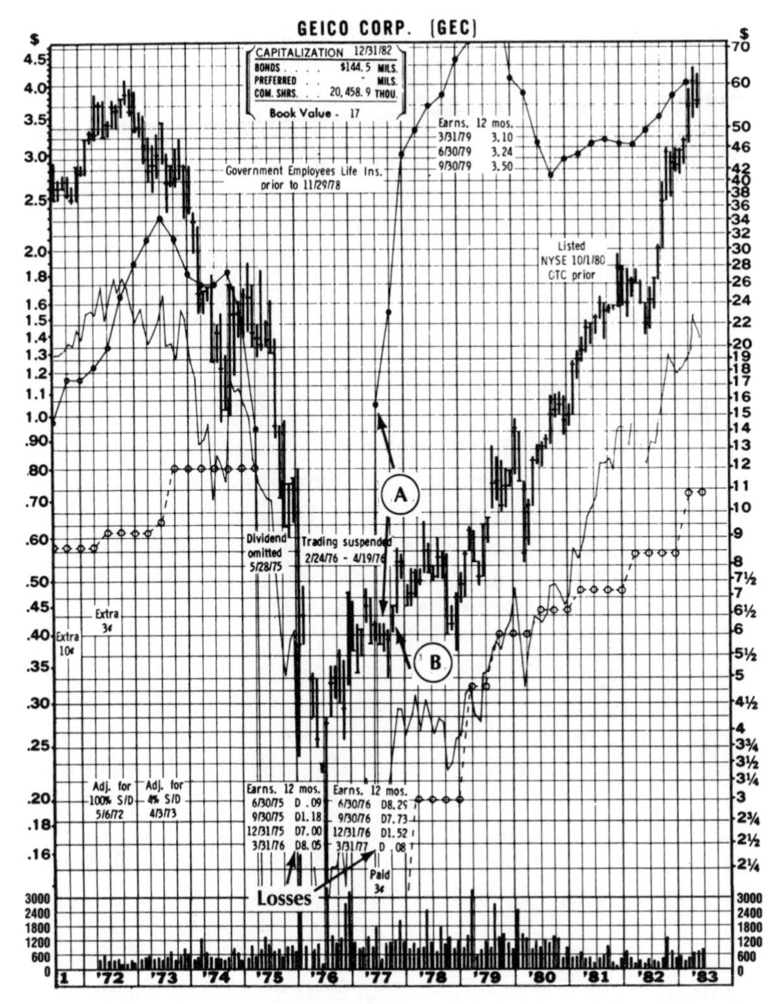

Geico is a perfect example of a stock that renews its upward cycle once it verifies that it is, indeed, still capable of earning money. The stock had losses for two and a half years, and, perversely, when earnings were finally announced (at A) the shares dipped a bit. *Perfect Investors* would have been laying in wait to buy, as you'll see, at point B.

Companies whose earnings don't founder are the easy ones. What about companies who present severe earnings problems—losses or sharp declines?

As noted in the beginning of this section, we proceed on the assumption that a company can, if not set the world on fire, return at least to its former level of earnings. We have already seen evidence of the earning power of the company's assets—in its former earnings. So we don't really have to guess, as we do with a "growth stock," how well it can do in a few years. We already know. We know it can make as much money as it did before, in the typical case.

There is a pattern in the decline of this kind of stock—that is, the trend of earnings and the trend of stock prices usually proceed in tandem. Each fresh earnings decline seems to bring a new decline in stock price, and each decline in stock price seems to be followed shortly by a new negative earnings announcement. At some point, however, the trend of both slowly flattens out and ends. If the company is to survive, you will one day see the earnings on the rise once again. The trick, of course, is to have the patience to wait for this sign of life, this sign of return to strength. If there have been losses, suddenly the company posts a profit. If the earnings have been way down, a quarterly report comes in with earnings jumping nicely upward. From that point, earnings can often rise sharply and quickly, for the company is well on its way to returning to its former glory.

There's another important sign of life we can use in conjunction with renewed earnings, rising earnings from a low level, or stable earnings at a high level. This is really a *confirmation* of earnings and an indication of future growth. Earnings, of course, are a measure of profitability. And profits are, on the simplest level, the difference between gross sales and the cost of sales (just as your stock profits are the difference between your selling price and your original cost, plus the broker's ounce of flesh!) There are only two ways to increase profits; then: You must cut your costs, or you must increase your sales.

Cost-cutting is almost always the preliminary route for bringing a sick company back to health. Why so many companies don't cut costs when they're doing well is beyond me, but that's really beside the point. Though it's of utmost importance to cut costs, costs can be cut only so much. Corporations reach a point at which cost-cutting becomes a game of diminishing returns: There is, for every company, a minimum cost level for effective operations below which the organization cannot go. You do, after all, have to pay your workers and your rent, even after you've gotten both down to the minimum.

That leaves the other half of the profit equation—increasing sales. Once the necessary cost cutting is in place, increasing sales is the *only* way to increase profits. But increased sales don't always increase profits immediately—each new sale has its cost, each new customer requires a certain amount of effort and expense to bring "into the fold." Sooner or later, though, any company with competent management should be able to turn increasing sales into increasing earnings, demonstrating the underlying value of the assets. Once you see increasing sales, you have a very good "sign of life" from an investment standpoint.

If you're unsure, for example, of whether an earnings increase for a given company is meaningful, look to see if it's accompanied by rising sales. Profits on rising sales can always be augmented by cost-cutting, but increasing profits on static sales don't bode well for future profit increases. Only if there are rising sales can you have confidence that the probabilities favor a continuing trend of rising earnings.

In addition to rising earnings and rising sales, there are several other signs of life that are significant clues to a turnaround in the company's fortunes and its stock price. All of these signs might be grouped under the heading of "movement." You want to see, as an investor, that the company is doing something, that it is trying, that it recognizes the fact that there is a problem and is seeking the solution. As in any aspect of life, unless a problem is recognized as a problem and taken seriously, you cannot expect change.

Among the signs that the directors have decided to do something are:

1. Selling of unprofitable divisions or assets.
2. Replacement of top management.
3. Issuance of new bonds (interest expense is increased, but the creditworthiness of the company is demonstrated).
4. Formation of joint ventures with other companies.
5. Purchase of large blocks of stock in the company by outsiders—who study value and future potential in great detail before committing their millions.
6. Purchase of substantial share positions by insiders (as when Roy Ash bought into AM International).

None of these actions are conclusive, but each shows us directly or indirectly that something is being done to correct a troubled situation or take advantage of a stock price that is unrealistically and irrationally low.

6

Screen Three: Avoid Obsolescence

You will recall that the screens we're discussing here constitute a technique for assuring ourselves that a stock whose price has crashed dramatically has experienced an *unjustified* disaffection by shareholders. There are, of course, rare occasions when panic selling by investors is justified, and one important reason would be a company whose entire business has been made superfluous by changes in the economic or political climate, or by radical changes in popular taste and overall demographics. For some, stocks of buggy and harness makers may have looked like great bargains in the 1920s and 1930s. But they weren't.

In today's world, the analysis of obsolescence is both more pressing and more subtle and complex than ever before.

Most obvious are the technological advances that make products or processes worthless. AM International's famous Addressograph machine, a fixture in nearly every office in the country, simply had no chance in the face of computer word processing and mailing list maintenance. The old clanking machines were to the new devices as a scrubbing tub was to a washing machine, and obsolescence brought the sleeping company to its knees. Black-and-white television becomes color, prop airplanes become jets, tubes turn into transistors, eyeglasses lose out to contact lenses. These are the kinds of things most of us are aware of in life—unfortunately, knowledge of many similar kinds of supercessions in business and industrial processes is not so available to the layman. Auto manufacturers, in their quest for fuel economy, turn away from steel and toward aluminum and plastics, for weight savings. Makers of silicon chips seek ever more efficient processes to speed up production—a whole generation of machines can become obsolete overnight.

As outsiders we can't always be on top of the latest developments that might tune us in to an impending decrease in value of a company's basic business. There are, still, some ways to seek for hints. A careful reading of the company's annual report might reveal mention of new competing products or processes (no doubt viewing them with skepticism), or you might find that the company is suddenly devoting much more research and development money to a new evolution or new "generation" of its lines. That's not necessarily an indictment, but it must be considered a possible tip-off. Brokerage reports sometimes can be helpful here, for the research analysts at brokerage houses usually cover an entire industry and will have an idea about what the competition is up to. Of course, declining sales in a company with a narrow range of products or services is one of the best clues to obsolescence you can find. Often a company that has built its business on a single concept for many years simply doesn't *believe* that a new idea will steal its market. By the time it wakes up and joins the march of progress, it may be too late.

There are two kinds of companies for whom the obsolescence factor is particularly ominous. The first is a company whose fortunes are entirely hinged to the products or services of another company. The symbiotic company may be a supplier—such as a supplier of tools to Sears—and have great difficulty maintaining its margins because its bargaining position is so poor. Symbiotic companies are literally at the mercy of their one or two large customers (suppliers to a single area of the federal government are another example), and the risk of being dropped as a source is ever present. So it is no feather in the cap of a company that they have such an intimate relationship with a lord and protector company of great renown and size—it is a danger sign.

Even if a company is not a supplier, dangerous relationships can develop. Itel was a major lessor of large IBM computers to companies that couldn't or didn't want to pay in full for the equipment. Sadly for Itel, when IBM radically changed its model lines, the customers had the right to cancel their leases, leaving Itel stuck with all these machines, for which it had to pay but that were no longer creating income. The calamity drove Itel, as you might expect, almost immediately into bankruptcy. Similar fates have awaited other small companies involved with "second sourcing" or supplying parts and accessories to other companies' machines at a cheaper price. When the machines change, no one wants the second-source accessories. On the other hand, second-source companies serving, for example, automobiles, have always done well, for there is a constant need for replacement parts on a basic product that has not radically changed since its invention.

The second category of company for whom obsolescence is a major threat is the one-product company or its cousin, the fad company. These are so often the stocks that get hot, look as if they're heading for the sky, then suddenly fall out of bed as the market becomes saturated or some bad news about the product emerges. Too, the success of any one product company is sure to attract competition from others. Will the market be big enough?

During the 1970s there were many examples. Zenith flew high as the demand for color television really came of age. But the Japanese entered the market with high quality at low cost, gobbling up Zenith's market like an industrial Pac-Man. But after Zenith's stock hit bottom, tumbling from near 60 to less than 10, it still wasn't attractive. With an eroded market and no new products to replace its mainstay, color televisions, the stock did little to bring pleasure to investors. Only in the past year, after entering the computer monitor market, has Zenith stock shown significant upward movement.

One recent fad was the rush to buy wood stoves during the energy crunch caused by soaring oil prices. Stove shops blossomed from coast to coast, as did the manufacturers of cast-iron heating units for them to sell. All went fabulously for a couple of years. Millionaires were made overnight. Then, almost as suddenly as the boom began, it seemed that most people who wanted stoves had already bought them. Inventory piled up in manufacturers' warehouses. These single-product fad businesses had no other source of income to see them through the shake-out and hard times to follow. One could hardly think of them as bargain purchases in their time of distress—their past was short and exceptional, their future uncertain.

The wood-stove companies served a kind of life-style fad, albeit a fad with serious underpinnings and implications. There are changes in the needs of the marketplace that are far more important, though, than the sudden urge for a particular product. These are the larger demographic changes in society—the age of the population, where people are living and working, income levels, etc. And there are often major shifts in basic social attitudes or long-term styles that can have tremendous investment impact. Where would Levi Strauss be without the jeans phenomenon? And for every Levi Strauss there is a crowd of defunct tailored trousers manufacturers who were left behind in the wake of change. When a stock has crashed you need ever to be alert to the possibility that a mismatch between the company's products and its market has developed.

Times change, tastes change, needs change. There's no point in fighting these changes or guessing that they'll return. If you like a company in a business that seems to be suffering from demographic obsolescence, *wait* until the demographics turn more favorable. Some smart investor might have bought a brassiere manufacturer in the late 1960s or early 1970s when women were rejecting the underwear as a torture device—the smart investor thinking the bra would "come back" quickly, its large market reestablishing itself. Indeed the fashion has returned, but it has taken ten years—perhaps ten years of manufacturers' losses and ten years of the investor's money lying fallow when he could have bought great companies by the bushelful in mid-decade.

A friend of mine made a terrible investment (though he really thought this would finally be his ship coming in) that was destroyed by *political obsolescence*—an increasing hazard for investors. He'd read in an investment advisory newsletter about a small Guatemalan oil company that had oil leases on property contiguous to the giant Mexican oil fields. My friend waited as test well results came in, seeming to prove the possibility of an enormous bonanza. It looked as though every time they scratched the earth, oil came pouring out. The stock had all the earmarks, for him, of an issue that could increase tenfold, and even fiftyfold, if crude oil went to a hundred dollars a barrel, as many seers were predicting and as he so fervently hoped.

The story about this company wasn't some rumor planted to hike the price of the stock. The oil was there. The problem was that the military junta in Guatemala also was there. Every six months they renegotiated the share of the oil revenues the government was to receive. And soon enough, the violence and instability we've all heard so much about broke out in the country. Investors fled the stock—uncertainty is anathema to the investment community, overruling even greed. Now my friend sits with stock he purchased at twelve dollars a share currently quoted at about a dollar.

Do not invest in companies whose business is dependent on the vagaries of politics in unstable countries. Too many unpredictable misfortunes can befall you. Take the safe route. Invest in the United States, in companies who do most of their business here. Even in the United States you've got to watch out for political obsolescence. Tax laws can change, products can be banned, pollution control installations can be mandated. Ordinarily, in this country most measures won't destroy a company beyond repair. Still, you need to be careful. Obsolescence lurks everywhere.

I don't mean to scare you with all these warnings. Remember, we're in the process of screening for a Perfect Investment. We're looking at stocks whose price has crashed. There are many, many stocks whose price has crashed for whom obsolescence is not an issue. But if a stock has gone down greatly and the reason for the decline is any of the possible forms of obsolescence, you certainly don't want to hide your eyes from the problem. Coming to terms with the real reasons why stocks go down, or why they've gone down but shouldn't have, is essential in the screening process. You want to eliminate candidates whose stock might not rise again, stocks whose fair and rational price is right where it should be.

7

Screen Four: There Must Be a Technical Bottom

In our consideration of the past three screens there were many questions to which we could propose a reasonable answer, but we lacked certainty—for an individual investor never has enough information. And even if all the information available to a specialist or corporate insider were known, experts would disagree about its interpretation. What are the hidden assets really worth? More than we think? Less? Are the company's real-estate holdings worth ten million dollars in a liquidation? A hundred million dollars? Are the rising earnings an accountant's trick? Are the rising sales due to special promotions that are impossible to sustain? Can increasing revenues really be translated soon into rising profits? Was the writedown of a division that caused last quarter's loss large enough? Too large? Is the new management going to be effective? Are key executives leaving? Are they really key? Are the company's products no longer relevant to its markets? Is there a chance that new laws will put it out of business? Is its exposure in a foreign country dangerously large?

All these questions can be answered in theory, and with reasonable assurance of accuracy, but we lack sufficient information to arrive at conclusions with absolute certainty. There are, however, other investors who *do* have the information we need. "Oh, goody," you say, "let's phone them." Well, there's not much chance of reaching them, and not much chance of them telling you anything if you do, but that's okay. We don't need to talk to these other investors. We can let them talk to us; and they *are,* they are talking constantly to us.

Informed investors talk to us through their actions.

They tell us when to buy and when to sell stocks.

All we need to do is know when and how to listen. This when and how is called technical analysis.

A Brief Introduction to Technical Analysis (So Simple Even a Child Could Do It)

There is a whole armamentarium of factors about a stock that technical analysts use in attempting to decide whether it is a good investment. There are technicians who say you can buy or sell stocks based on a variety of cycles (a 3.6-year cycle, an 8-month cycle, a 20-day cycle, etc.). Others use moving averages of prices to determine buy and sell points. Still other technicians look at oscillating averages that indicate when a stock is "overbought" or "oversold" (too much, too fast), momentum indicators, stochastics, arcane formulas of all kinds. The world of technical analysis is strange and fascinating. No matter what the particular formula or strategy, though, all technical methods have the same basic goal: *to uncover a systematic way of buying and selling stock that is based entirely on what happens in the market and pays little or no attention to the company whose stock is being traded.* That is, there is much more than intrinsic value affecting the price of a stock. There is an entire world of the dynamics and interrelationships in the market that bears greatly—some would say decisively—on the price of any stock.

Put most simply, technical analysis seeks to discover whether the forces of acquisition and expansion are dominant among those who consider the stock, or whether they feel contractile and want only to sell. After all, stocks will move up only if there are plenty of buyers, or buyers with vast resources buying. And stocks will inevitably move down if the supply-and-demand balance favors the sellers. No matter how great the company, the stock won't move up unless someone buys it. And no matter how silly the company, if the stock gets hot it will stay hot until the sellers are more powerful and/or more numerous than the bulls.

A stock can be seen less as a security and more as an emotional barometer of the investors who have examined the company. It's no wonder we call quickly rising stocks "hot"—they charge up the covetous emotions of investors. A stock price, we can begin to see, is not really a stock price—it's more a measure, a gauge.

As I write this book the stock market is experiencing the historic rally that began in August 1982. Two months ago the Dow stocks were selling for about 780. Today they are over 1,000. Nothing has really changed in the economy. *Are the Dow stocks really worth 25 percent more today than they were worth two months ago?*

Absolutely.

Why? What has changed in two months?

Investors had a change of heart.

So, one reason the technical view of the market pays no attention to the companies whose stocks are being sold is that technicians know investors are fickle and emotional. One day a company with a certain level of assets and income will have nothing but sellers. The next day the same company, with the same assets, will find itself the object of covetous investors from all over the world. Knowing that's often so, technicians reason that it isn't important to pay attention to the company. What you want is clues to whether investors are buying or selling and how strongly, so you'll know whether the buying or selling will continue.

Technicians feel this way because they have a god. The god is called trend. Whoever has studied the history of stocks or any other market knows that prices tend to follow a trend over time. Trend rules. Stocks don't go up a month, then down a month, then up a month, then down a month indefinitely. Sooner or later they start going in one direction and keep going in that direction for months, years, even decades. The trick, of course, is to find a formula that will spot a trend near its commencement.

There's a second important reason why many investors are drawn to technical analysis, and this has little to do with the fickleness of the investing crowd. As we discuss this, don't forget that the trick is to find a formula that will spot a trend near its commencement.

The second reason, and I think perhaps the more important and substantial justification for technical analysis, has to do with what you might call *information conversion.*

The essential problem of stock market investing, whether you are an individual with twenty thousand dollars or the investment manager for Prudential Insurance Company of America, is information: quantity of information, quality of information, and speed of information. There are facts about a company, about the thousands of companies whose shares are traded daily. There are facts about the stock of the company. These facts are the content of the river of information important to investors, and it is a tricky river indeed: The information is not always accurate; not everyone has access to it, and even among those who do, the access occurs at different times; and, most hopelessly, the meaning or importance of the information is subject to debate. In other words, though the investing world exists on the flow of information, no one really knows if they have received the right information at the right time and in the right place.

Large investors who have the most at stake tend to spend the most time and effort on the accumulation of information. Brokerage firms, banks, insurance companies, and companies interested in takeovers all have armies of M.B.A.'s busily researching stocks to buy and sell. These research analysts study industry as well as corporate prospects—they know the real value of assets, whether the competition is a serious threat, whether orders are coming in at the rate they should, whether earnings are real or an accounting chimera.

Be you individual investor or giant pension fund, the information you have obtained and the interpretation you've put on that information are all you have to go on when making an investment decision. But technical analysis provides a potent new source of information that, in effect, instantly tells you whether your information is correct and/or if you have interpreted it correctly. Through technical analysis you can discover the single most important fact about a stock (as distinguished from the underlying company). You can tell whether the stock is being bought or is being sold.

Recall that the whole trick is to spot a trend near its commencement. For us, as Perfect Investors, because we are looking for stocks that have been emotionally sold down to the superbargain level, that trick becomes a kind of inversion. Information, when it is timely and correctly obtained and correctly interpreted, becomes converted into price changes by substantial investors. Small investors usually don't have access to the right kinds of information, nor can their small investments affect the price of a stock. But large investors do have the kind of information that, when coupled with their enormous buying or selling power, converts into stock price.

The way to see when the force of negative information has become exhausted in the market is to examine the patterns of stock price. In this way we will see that large investors are finished cleaning out their portfolios of this stock that scares them so. When the selling pressure is over, the tide, as it were, begins to change. The inversion

I referred to is this: Since stocks nearly always trend in one direction or the other, when we see a pattern of prices that indicates the selling has ended, we can then begin to look for evidence in the price pattern that the new buying that will inevitably follow is ready to begin. For this kind of stock we first look for signs of a bottom, for signs *in the price pattern* that the stock has been sold below its real value and that some major investors, at least, are beginning to think in terms of buying rather than selling.

There is absolutely no point in buying a stock before the large investors have finished selling. Our whole goal is the elimination of risk, so we will never buy when the stock is still declining, or when technical analysis tells us that the stock may well go lower.

We will use technical analysis as a kind of weather vane to tell us when the winds of decline have become gentle breezes and to tell us when they are about to change direction.

Further, *technical analysis will keep us away from the relatively few stocks whose crashes are justified by corporate problems that may be too serious to correct.* We get to make use of the armies of M.B.A.'s free. In the service of their rich employers they have been busy analyzing the situation with the troubled or out-of-favor company. They know whether bankruptcy is imminent, if there is a chance that the stock will become worthless. If the analysts discover too much that is negative about a company they will never recommend purchases to their employers. *If the large investors don't start buying, we won't see price action that indicates an end to the selling.* The stock will just keep on going down and finally out. Fortunately, we'll be on the sidelines, watching with interest but with no losses.

Technical analysis puts the probabilities in our favor. The previous "fundamental" screens have put reason in our favor, but reason is not always triumphant in the practical world. What *is* triumphant in the practical world is probability. If we can find a pattern of prices that has shown itself to be predictive of the future price action, say, nineteen times out of twenty, we really don't have to be concerned with the one time it misses the mark. That one time we may show some loss—only partial loss, as you'll see—but the other nineteen correct predictions will show gains that completely cancel out the loss. Combined with the fundamental reason of our other screens, the net result is high profit.

We can determine that the probabilities are in our favor because we have tens of thousands of weeks, months, and years of price histories on the whole spectrum of publicly traded stocks. Prices fall into patterns—just as an emotional price crash is itself a pattern of prices—because of the essential mechanics of the marketplace.

Every stock has its own pattern, reflecting the relative interest of buyers and sellers in the company and its stock. But the price patterns are not unique. Indeed, there are about twenty major price patterns into which virtually all stocks fall. Each of these price patterns gives us a varying degree of predictive power about the future of the stock's price. Further, for each of these patterns there is also a point at which we know if the pattern's predictive ability has broken down, so that we can take a loss before it gets too great.

As Perfect Investors, we develop a rationale for purchasing a particular stock. Basically, the rationale is always that the stock has been terribly oversold, that the stock is selling so low that it is amply "covered" by the value of the company's assets (on the books or off), and that we have seen evidence that the earning power of the company's assets is reasserting itself.

Technical analysis gives us a way to discover whether this rationale is correct or incorrect. *Reason will tell us what to buy and why, technical analysis will show us when to do it.*

The Technical Bottom

Before we can see evidence of a new, upward trend, we need to see a price pattern that indicates a lasting cessation of selling pressures. Technical analysts call these patterns "bottoming out," and, while there are quite a few patterns that have been identified as showing bottoms, we are going to look only to the handful that have proven most reliable. If you see one of these patterns you will have as much assurance as is humanly possible that the crash is over and the company will survive. The bottom is the first sign that the stock will return to its more glorious price levels.

Technical patterns are easiest to see when looking at bar graph charts, so we'll be using them in this section and for the remainder of this book. If you don't know how to read a chart, please consult the Appendix before reading farther. Charts are available from numerous publishers, also listed in the Appendix, and usually you can consult charts at any good library. Your broker will be happy to let you look at his charts, and often your local bank will subscribe to them. All of the patterns we'll be looking at can be stated numerically without the need for charts; I'll show you how to do this at the end of the next section.

To find bottoms we use *monthly basis* charts, showing the high, low, and close for each month. Monthly basis charts are used to get a longer-term perspective—since we're looking for long-term investments—and because shorter-term charts ordinarily will not show us the high price for the past five years.

Following are the patterns that indicate the crash is over, and an interpretation of their meaning. *If you don't see one of these bottom patterns, don't invest.*

The Double Bottom

The double bottom is perhaps the easiest to identify as well as the most reliable of all the bottom patterns. It has

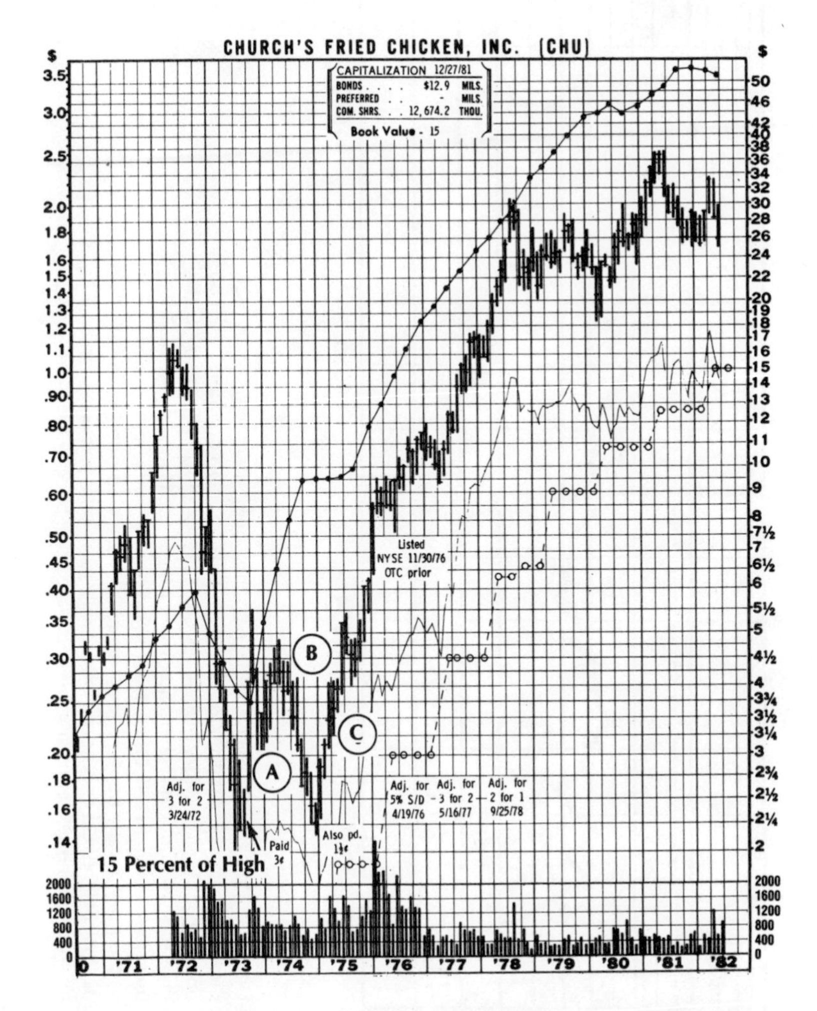

Double Bottom: You won't see a cleaner or more classic double bottom than in this chart of Church's Fried Chicken. First, prices swoon in 1973, falling well below the required crash level. Then the bargain hunters can no longer resist, and a rally ensues as they buy cheap assets. But as prices rise, these buyers begin to take quick profits and trapped sellers see their chance to get out (B). Selling pressures drive the stock back down—in this and the classic case—to a point just above the previous low (C). The next rally, which commences from a level clearly "pointed out" as the low, is the good one. Virtually all the other bottom patterns are variant on the double bottom—compressed in time or scale or price movement.

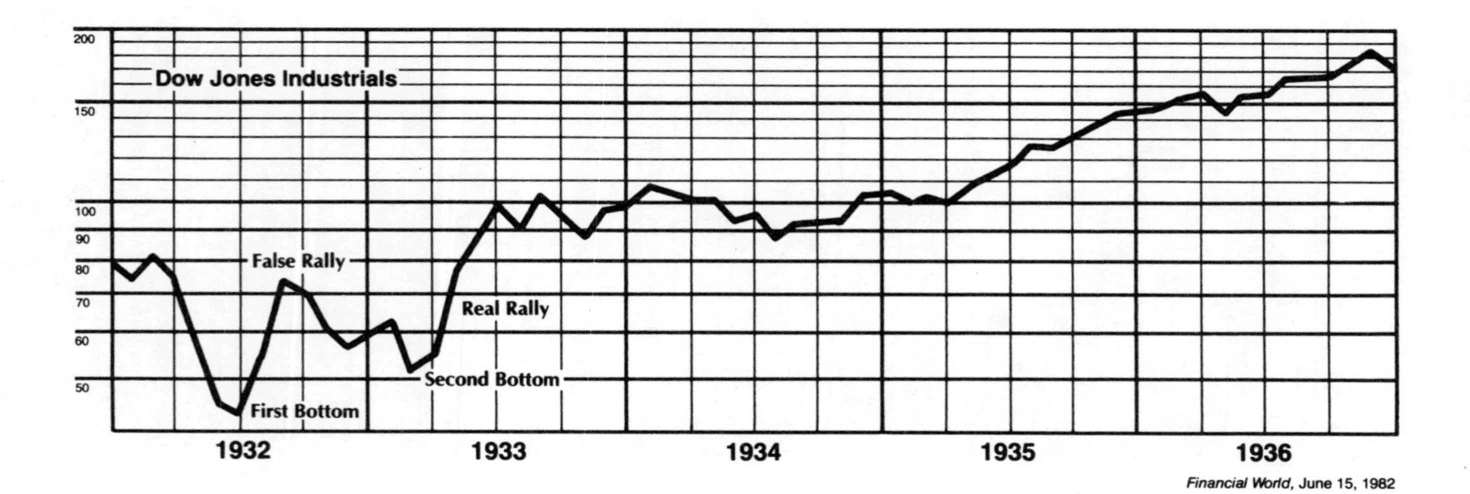

Financial World, June 15, 1982

Double Bottoms aren't exactly modern phenomena. After the Crash of 1929, the market displayed this textbook action, alerting smart investors to get on board in 1933. The story's such an old one—a short rally, and all the investors who bought higher and can no longer stand the anxiety of sitting on losses rush in to sell. Once these "weak hands" have washed themselves of their psychically burdensome holdings, there's no one left to sell. The next rally is the real one, as the longs freely mark their prices up and up and up—now that the "depressing" sellers have gone back to the farm.

several variations, but most look pretty much the same, and the underlying reasons why double bottoms occur remain constant in all the variations.

First you will observe the crash. The crash may have lasted for several years, or it may have occurred in a chilling six months. Most commonly, at the end of the crash there is a sort of final minicrash, a blowout, an exhaustion, in which prices drop suddenly, as if the long slide were about to begin all over again from a lower level. But this final spurt downward, if it occurs (and it need not occur for a double bottom validly to appear), usually is short-lived—a kind of final shock that shakes out the last diehard holders of the stock. At this point there are very few sellers left. Then, often suddenly, the stock begins to rise again. *Do not mistake this for a new uptrend.* The quick first rise results from a handful of bargain hunters trying to buy stock when there are few sellers anxious to sell to them. Specialists on the exchange who have an inventory of stocks also like to try to give the stock a goose at this point to unload some of their holdings and draw in buyers who have been looking at the stock and marveling at what a bargain it is. There are rare cases when a stock will crash, turn on a dime, then begin to rise nonstop, but these cases are indeed rare and the probabilities do not favor investment in such stocks.

When the stock does rise from its low point it soon encounters what's known in the market as "resistance." Resistance means two things. First, buyers do not want to pay any more at the present time. Second, the rise in price has flushed out some more sellers. Perhaps they bought too early on the way down and now see a chance to get out. Perhaps they were lucky enough to buy at the very bottom and now want to sell for a nice, quick profit. Whatever the case, the stock quickly reaches a point—usually around a 30 percent gain from the nadir—when the rally abruptly halts and the price begins to decline again.

This new decline often is not as sharp as the final-spurt decline on the crash leg, and it usually lasts no longer than the time required for the first rally. The price declines again to the area of the original low.

So far we've got a bottom, a rally, and a decline toward the bottom again. The movement that completes this pattern is a second rally as the price nears the original bottom level. Here are some lovely examples:

Vee Bottom Plus Correction

This is a variation of the double bottom that is far enough away from the basic pattern to deserve a category of its own. If you'll recall, I mentioned a few paragraphs ago that stocks sometimes will crash and then turn on a dime to march upward. Much of the time we will have to pass these by because the pattern is too unpredictable (it usually turns into a double bottom), but there's one kind of vee bottom that has a lot in common with the double bottom. In this case you'll see the stock take off immediately from a crash bottom and then show a brief, sharp pause or pullback in its rally, only to resume the rally in short order. It looks almost as though the rally line becomes shaggy for a month or two, then gets sharp again. This too becomes a valid bottom pattern, though if the velocity of it scares you, don't hesitate to wait for another stock with a bottom whose pattern makes you more comfortable. There are plenty of fish in the sea, a cliché that eludes most investors, to their disadvantage.

Vee Bottom with a Flag

There are times when a double bottom refuses to double. You'll see the terminal decline, the rally moving up from the extreme low, the rally fading, and then, just when you expect the stock to decline down near the first bottom, nothing happens. The stock just moves sideways in a flat congestion pattern, often for months. The rally this time has not flushed out enough sellers to drive the stock down, and at least some buyers are still interested.

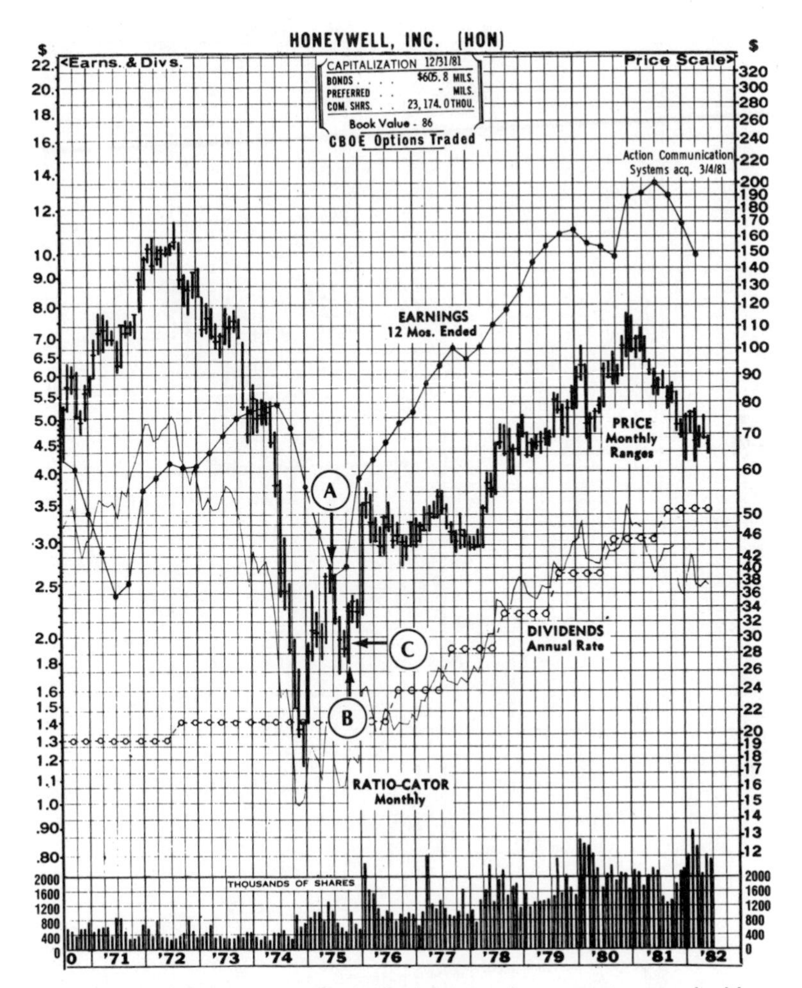

Vee Plus Correction: You might think of the vee plus correction as a double bottom with a very quick right-hand side. The second decline lasts only a few months and will rarely return to the level of the first bottom. Indeed, in the case of Honeywell, Inc., the second decline (correction) lasted only two months (A), followed by one inconclusive month (B), and then a sharp renewal of the rally in October 1975 (C). The stock hasn't been lower since.

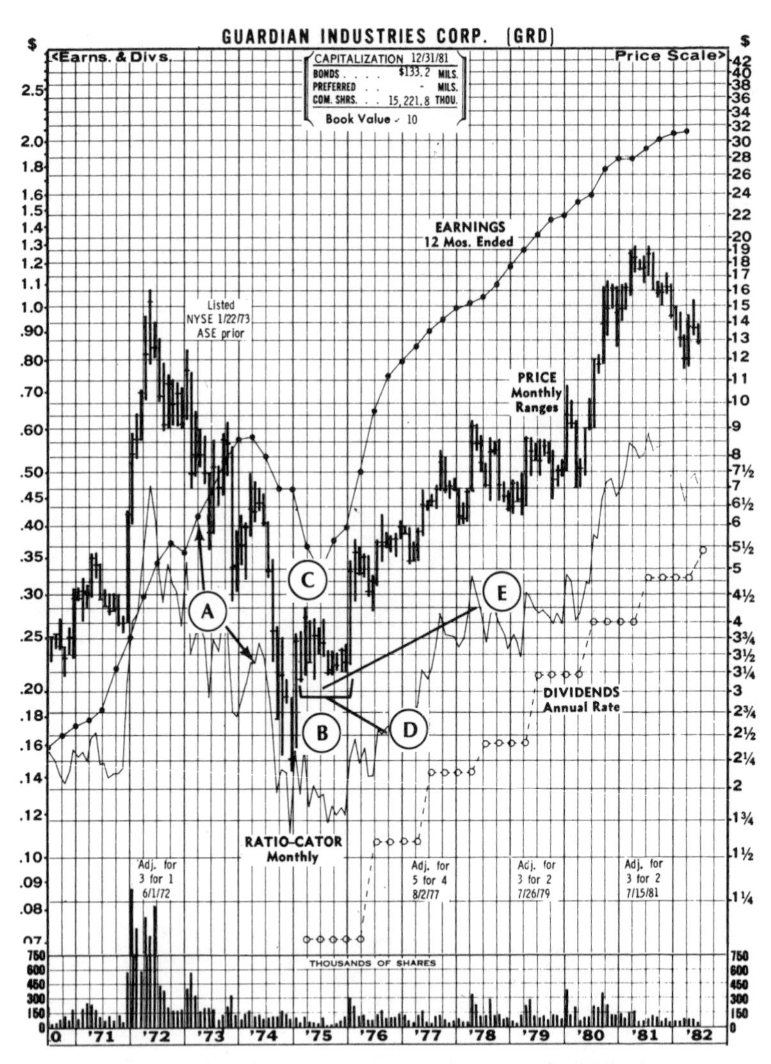

Vee Plus Flag: A vee with a flag is like double bottom that refuses to happen. You see the first decline (A), the rally (B), and the slowing down of the rally (C). But instead of the second decline ensuing, prices remain stable, with an upward bias for about the same length of time that would ordinarily be required for the second decline (D). If the monthly lows do not decline (E), the pattern is more positive.

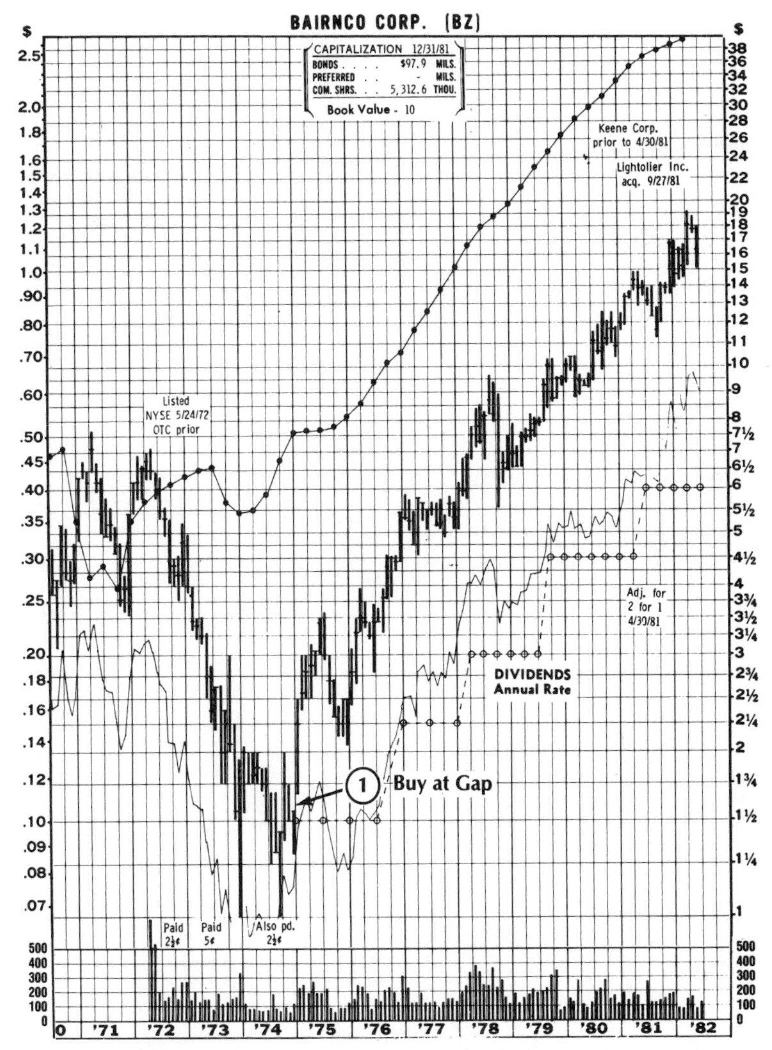

Vee Plus Gap: In the usual case, it's a far better policy to wait for a second bottom or correction in a stock, since it almost always comes. The problem with a vee bottom, even when it's reached the level of a Perfect Investment crash low, is that you never know if the prices are going to keep heading south. One exception, however, is the appearance of an upward gap in prices. When you see it, there's no need to wait for a more substantial rally. It's a signal that says, "Here is the ground floor. Get on." As you can see for Bairnco, the appearance of the gap (1) was certainly the appropriate time to buy. Of course, you could have waited for the correction, but with a gap, it may never come.

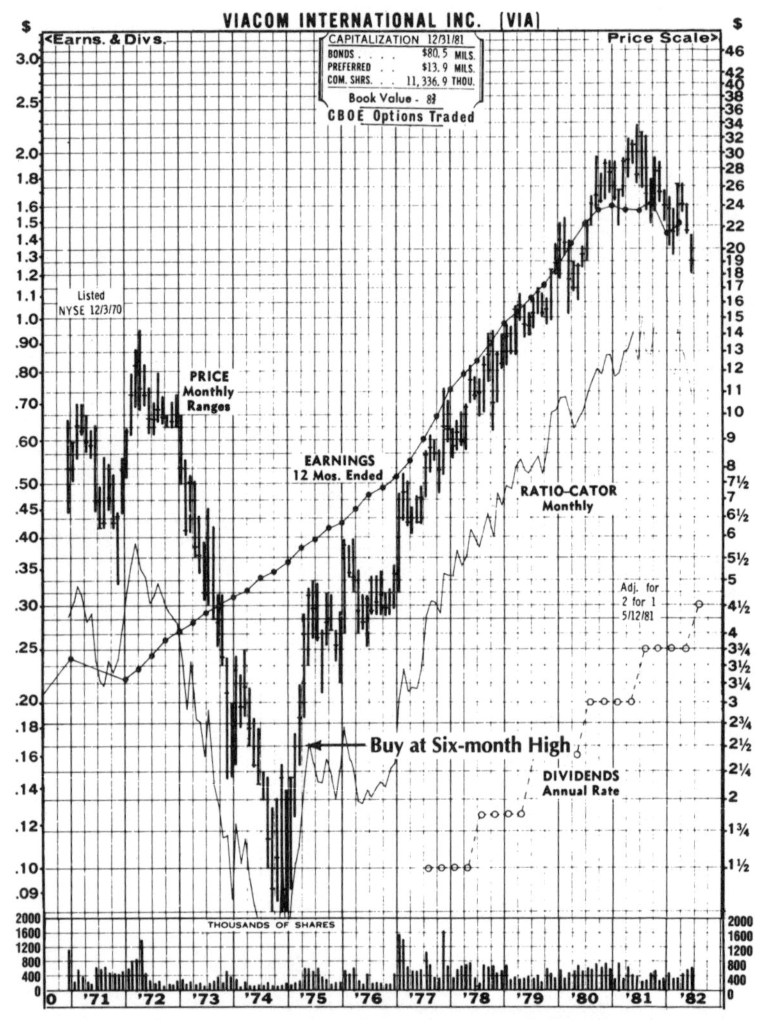

Vee Plus Six-Month High after 90 Percent Decline: This is the hairiest and scariest bottom pattern, one to use very rarely. But often it is the most profitable. To use this bottom, you must first locate a stock that has lost 90 percent of its former value (former five-year high) *and* did not suffer an earnings decline of more than 25 percent during its decline *and* did not suffer a dividend cut. When you see a stock like that, you're looking at a ridiculous situation. Somebody—the bulls at the top or the bears at the bottom—must be *very* wrong. Usually it's both of them. In any event, when such a stock has been blasted in such a way, buy it when it rises to a six-month high on the monthly close. Losses will be limited under the selling rules, and you might really get the ride of your life, as in this exhilarating chart of Viacom, International.

The stock is caught in a balance of buying and selling, a no-man's-land of indecisive market pressures. This is a wonderful bottom pattern. It has all the virtues of the double bottom in demonstrating that investors no longer will permit the stock to fall, and it has the added plus of showing more buyers and fewer sellers than the primary double bottom pattern.

Reverse Head and Shoulders

If you have a friend who knows something about technical analysis you may hear him or her spout some impressive certainties about an inverted head and shoulders. This pattern is an icon of technicians, but it's really no more than a form of double bottom, as you can see from the chart on page 104. The second shoulder is the second bottom, or the break from a vee bottom. I show it here because it does appear with some regularity, and you might as well know what you're looking at.

The Swing Bottom or Saucer

This second major type of bottom provides more of what you'd expect after a long period of extensive price decline. This is a bottom in which the previous downtrend ends not with a bang but with a whimper. Prices stop declining, but they show no real impetus to begin going in the opposite direction. Here sellers have finished contracting but buyers have not yet begun to enter an expansive phase. Looking at the charts on pages 105–107, you get a sense of stasis, a kind of humming, of spinning wheels going nowhere. The swing bottom can look something like a pendulum at the base of its arc, with the long crash on its left side and a rounded arc below, preparatory to what is ordinarily a slow and orderly rise on the right. I like the swing bottom because the price action following it is usually nonviolent and predictable, a succession of small gains over time, which makes it easy and anxiety-free to hold the position. In my

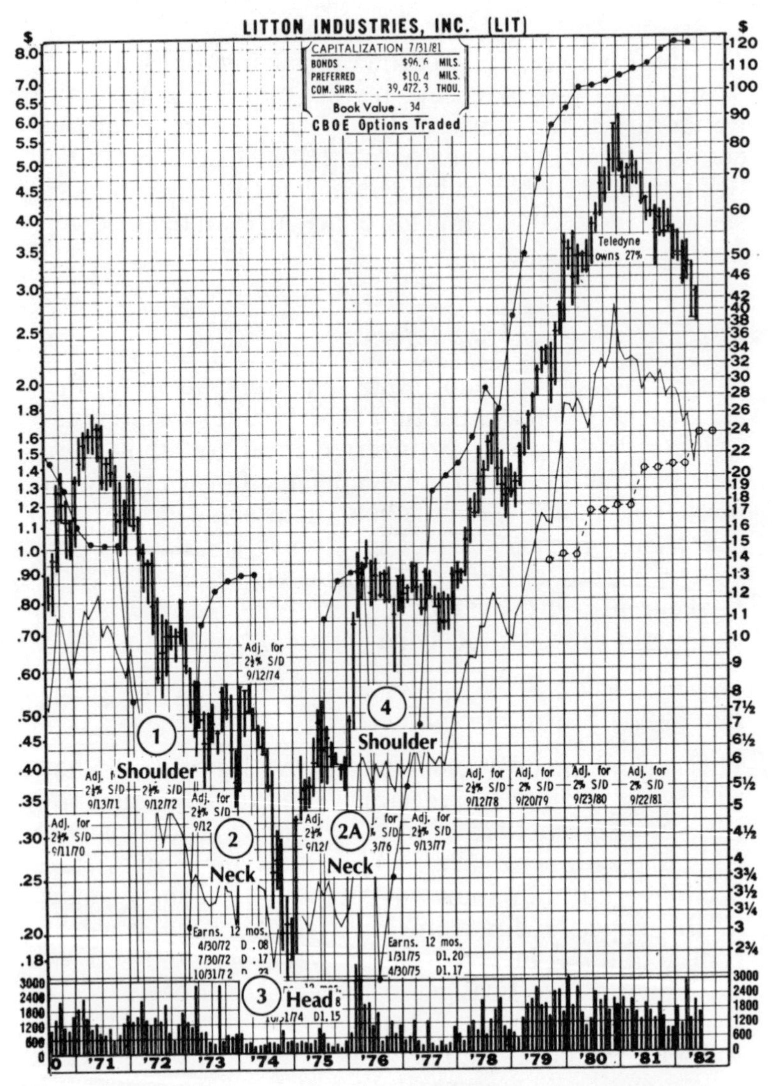

Reverse Head-and-Shoulders Bottom: Litton Industries shows us a rather extreme form of the head-and-shoulders pattern. At the left shoulder (1) we see a preliminary area of congestion following an extended period of decline. This congestion doesn't turn into a rally but rather a further sharp decline (2) known as the neck. When prices begin to rise again, the second side of the neck is established (2A), and the head (3) demarcated. Congestion then renews in an area roughly similar to that of the first shoulder, forming the second shoulder (4). The two shoulders reveal a price level at which buying and selling are nearly in balance—the neck and head are the price levels at which the last frightened sellers jump ship.

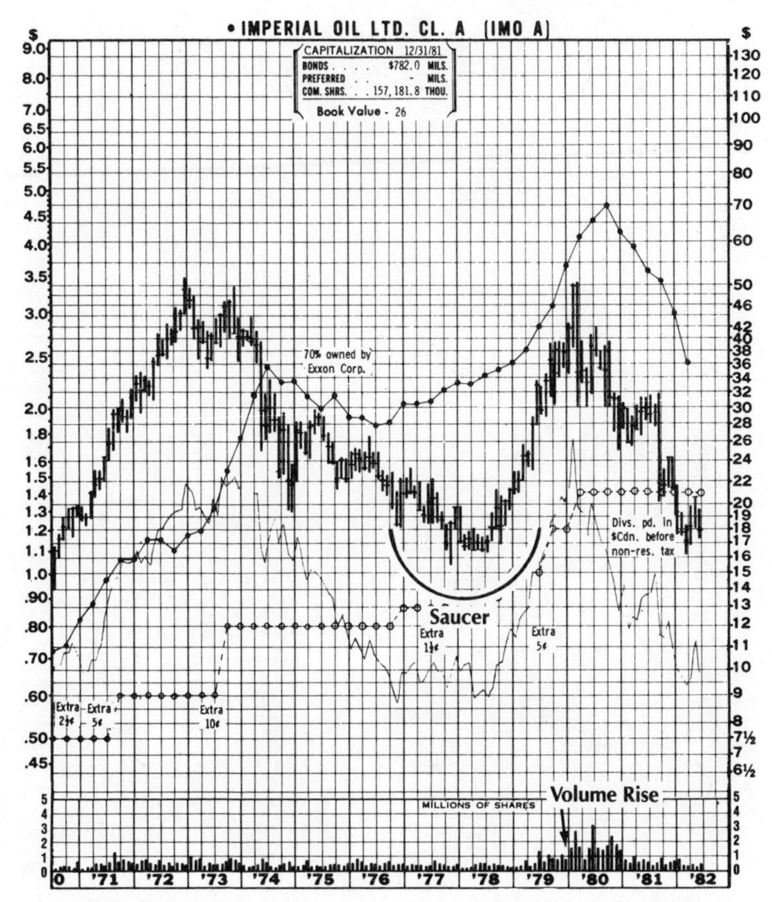

Saucer or Congested: These are two names for the same phenomenon—when prices get hung up at the end of a decline. You don't see the sharp rally that so often begins the double bottom process (or one of the variants). Instead, prices just seem to go out with a whimper. They can make a saucer shape, with a rounded bottom and increasing volume on the right-hand side of the saucer as prices rise, as we see for Imperial Oil.

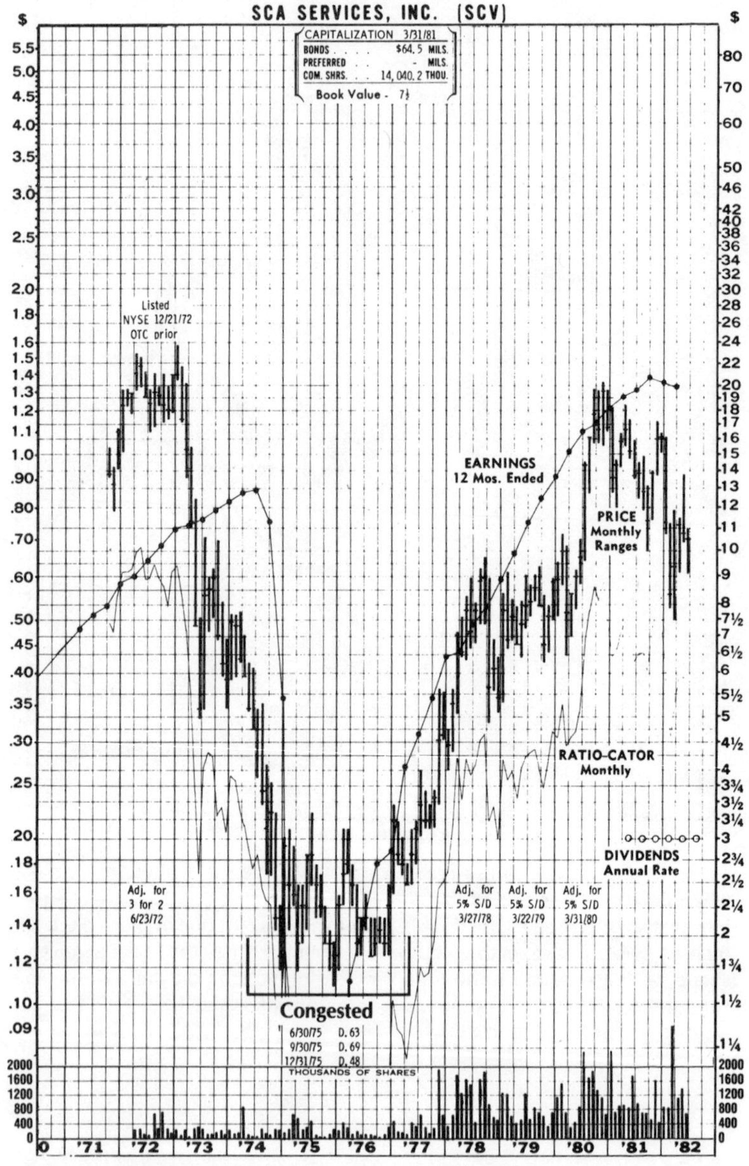

Or, as for SCA services, prices can get stuck in a tight trading range for two years or more (though that is a particularly long time—six months is enough to warrant being called congestion), terminating their stasis with an upside burst out of the locked range.

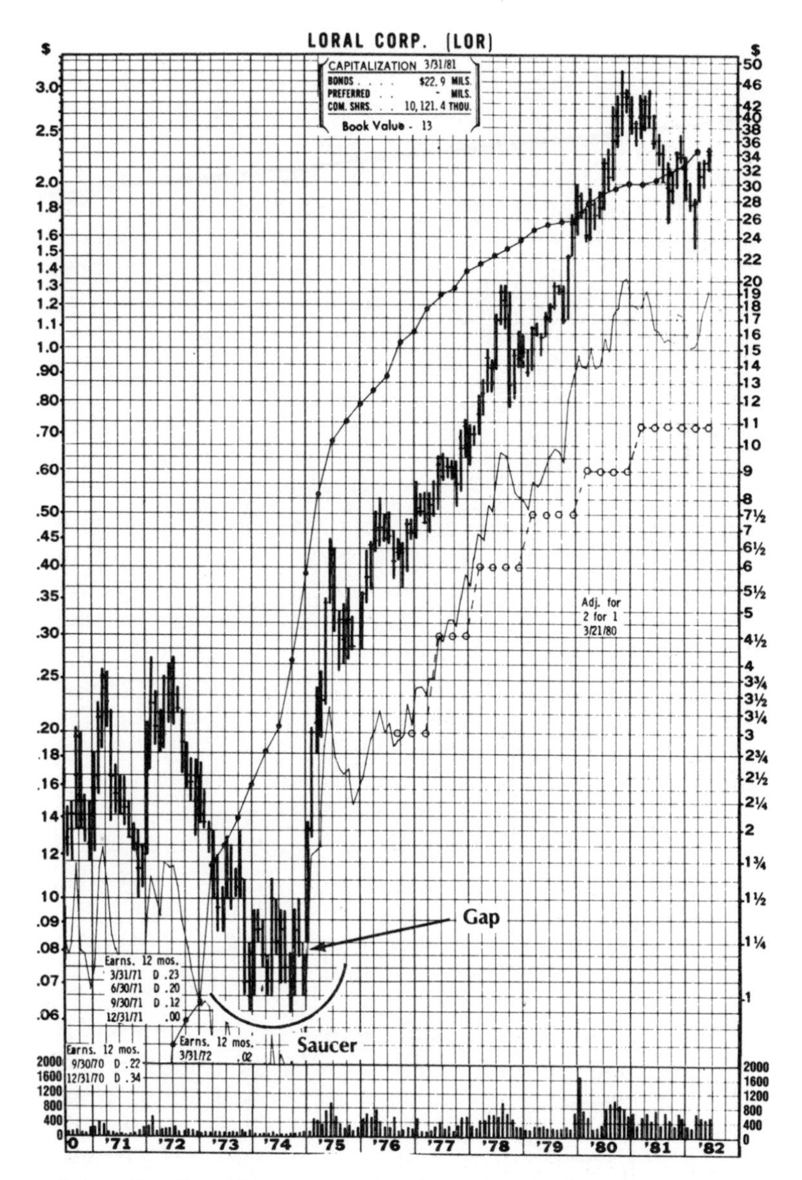

Saucer Plus Gap: This is my personal favorite. It's the safest and most predictable bottom for any kind of stock. First you see congestion at the lows, as here, when Loral lost 75 percent of its value during 1973. Prices were locked between 1½ and 1 for a year. Then, as the market came to life in 1975, there was a price range gap and a clear surpassing of the former highs. The stock increased fifteenfold over the next five years.

opinion, the longer and flatter the congestion of prices at the bottom, the better. During this long, flat period, the stock builds up a large base of buyers willing to buy at that price level, which serves as downside protection in the future. Indeed, a long, flat saucer (saucers come quite rounded and quite flat, depending on the manufacturer) followed by one of the technical turn signals discussed in the next section is perhaps the very best investment posture you can take in the stock market.

The Climax Bottom

Most investors will be well advised to stick to the double bottom or swing/saucer bottoms or one of their close relatives. For those who want their action fast and furious, one other type of bottom has a fairly consistent record of future prediction. This bottom is quite useful in predicting bottoms for the *overall market averages* after a prolonged decline, and I mention it here more for that purpose than for its use with individual stocks.

In the climax bottom we see the typical crash pattern with its final extra crash. When this final crash is accompanied by extraordinarily high volume of trading and equally extraordinary extension of the ranges of high and low prices (the distance between high and low in a given month or week becomes two or three times greater than in the previous months or weeks), technicians begin to speak of selling climaxes. It is something like a dull toothache suddenly becoming a screaming pain, or slowly building anger suddenly venting itself in a rage.

And it seems that when one of these selling climaxes is reached there are trolls waiting under the bridge for the stock price to get so low they just can't resist jumping out and gobbling it all up. The price suddenly spurts upward at an even faster rate than it had been careening downward. On the chart you'll see big spikes of downside price, then an even bigger spike sending the stock skyward. Good technicians can spot this climax turning point based on the price action of even a single day.

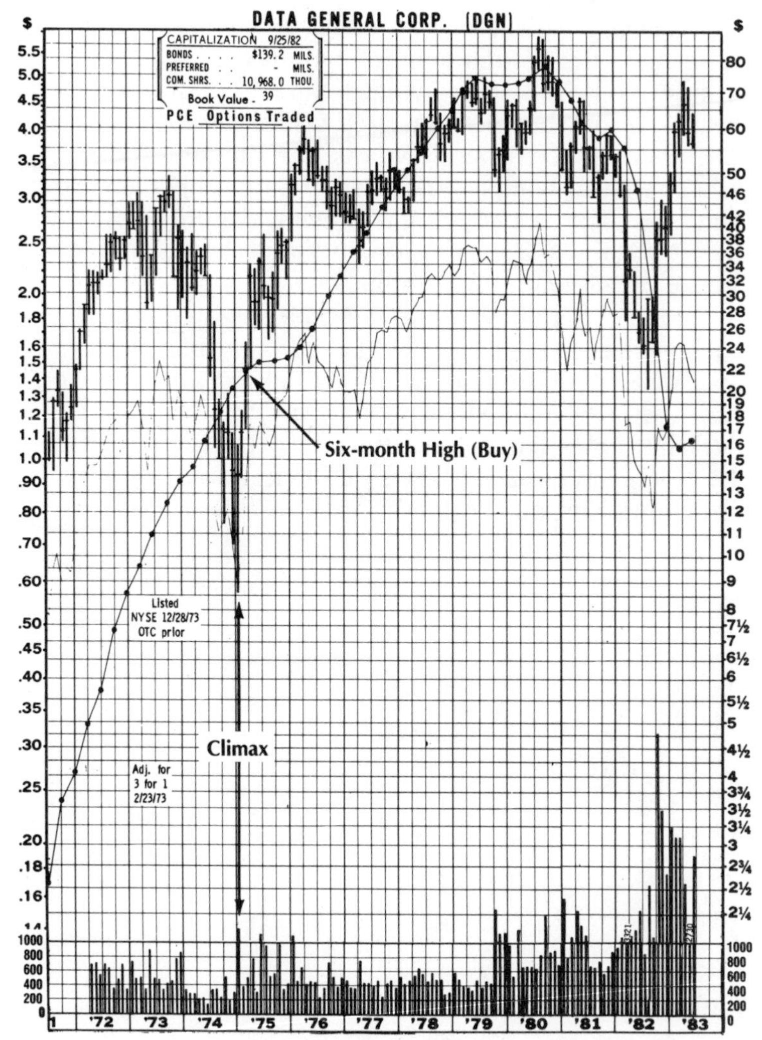

Climax: Even as the rally of 1975 began, Data General continued to dive, with huge monthly ranges in price and suddenly higher volume. When you see such price swaths accompanied by large volume, you will do well to suspect that the climax, the orgasm, of the sellers has arrived. Watch closely now, for as prices begin to climb off the climax they do so with great rapidity—the sellers have been completely "discharged" from the situation. As in the vee, when a stock has lost 90 percent of its value and is still earning well, you should consider the bottom complete when a new six-month closing high has been reached.

8

Screen Five: There Must Be a Technical Turn

If you've seen a classic bottoming pattern in a stock that has passed through all the previous screens, you can put your finger on the button. But you can't *press* the button until you see technical evidence that the stock has not only stopped falling but also has begun to rise in a way that predicts further rises in the future.

It's the weather vane principle again. You don't want to commit your precious capital until you're really sure which way the wind is blowing. First a bottom pattern, then a turn pattern, then all systems are go.

There are several major price patterns that have a high predictive value when they follow or complete a bottoming pattern. Because we are looking more closely at what's happening to the stock *right now* (as opposed to the past five years), we switch to weekly basis charts. Again, you can subscribe to these charts or use them in a library, or look at your broker's or banker's charts. As with the bottom patterns, you can also derive the same essential information numerically from easily available statistics published in the newspapers and by Standard & Poor's.

Basically, all our technical turn patterns are ways of seeing that there is sudden or clearly accumulating buying interest in the stock. The charts are like the footprints of large investors with important knowledge about the company, or who are beginning to take the first bites into a new investment darling. Only when we see evidence of solid buying will we join in. We'll climb on the bandwagon, but only when we see that the band has arrived and is getting ready to play.

The Volume Building on Rising Prices

No matter what the pattern, it is always going to show rising prices, and it is almost always going to show increasing volume of trading. We want to see increasing activity in the trading of the stock with an upward bias in prices. We want to see the buyers cleaning out the sellers of all the sellers' unwanted inventory. We want to see that buyers are there and ready to buy every time the price dips a little and that they are ready to buy at ever increasing prices as well. Historically, with very few exceptions, rising prices are accompanied by rising volume in every trading market in the world. There can be expansive, avaricious buyers around if there is low volume, but if the volume and the prices both pick up, you know there *must* be covetous souls with their hearts set on this love object.

Rising volume and rising prices together will look like this on a chart:

⟶

In all three of these charts, notice how prices generally tend to advance on rising volume and decline when volume falls. Of course, there are exceptions, but *rising volume makes rising prices more credible.*

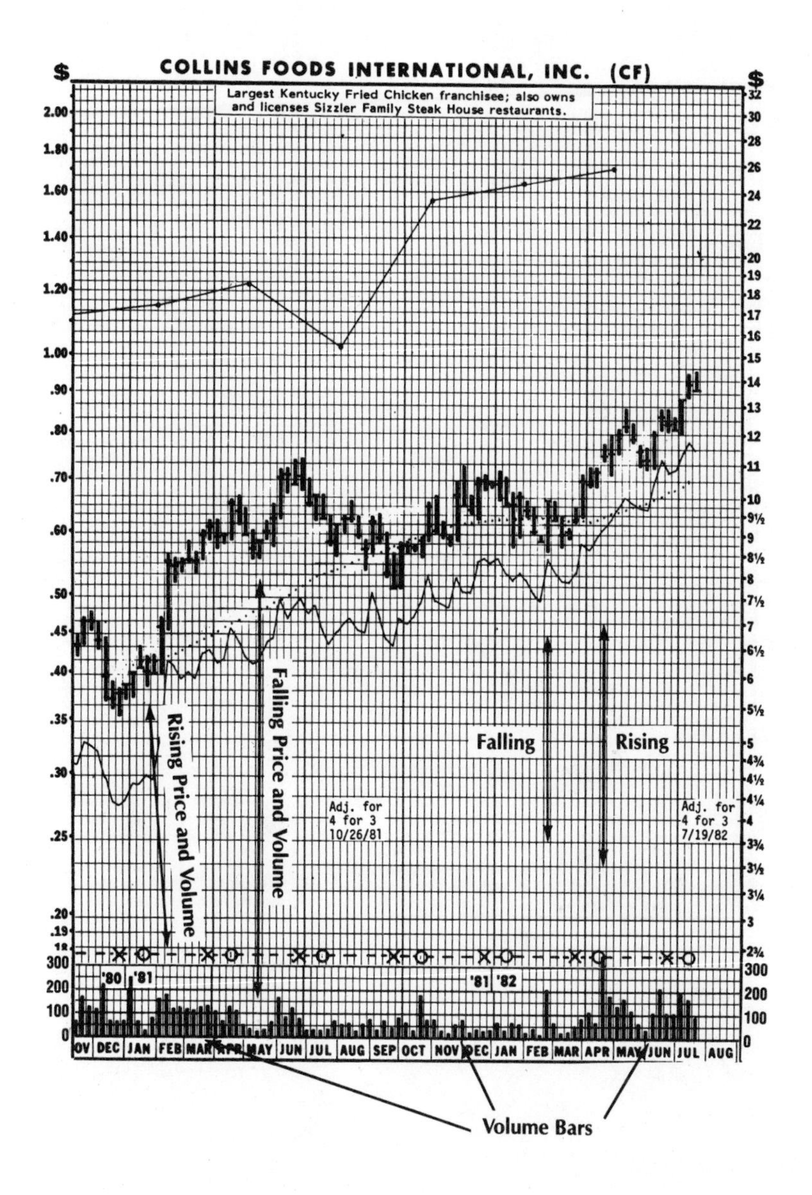

COLLINS FOODS INTERNATIONAL, INC. (CF)
Largest Kentucky Fried Chicken franchisee; also owns and licenses Sizzler Family Steak House restaurants.
Rising Price and Volume
Falling Price and Volume
Falling
Rising
Adj. for 4 for 3 10/26/81
Adj. for 4 for 3 7/19/82
'80 '81
'81 '82
Volume Bars

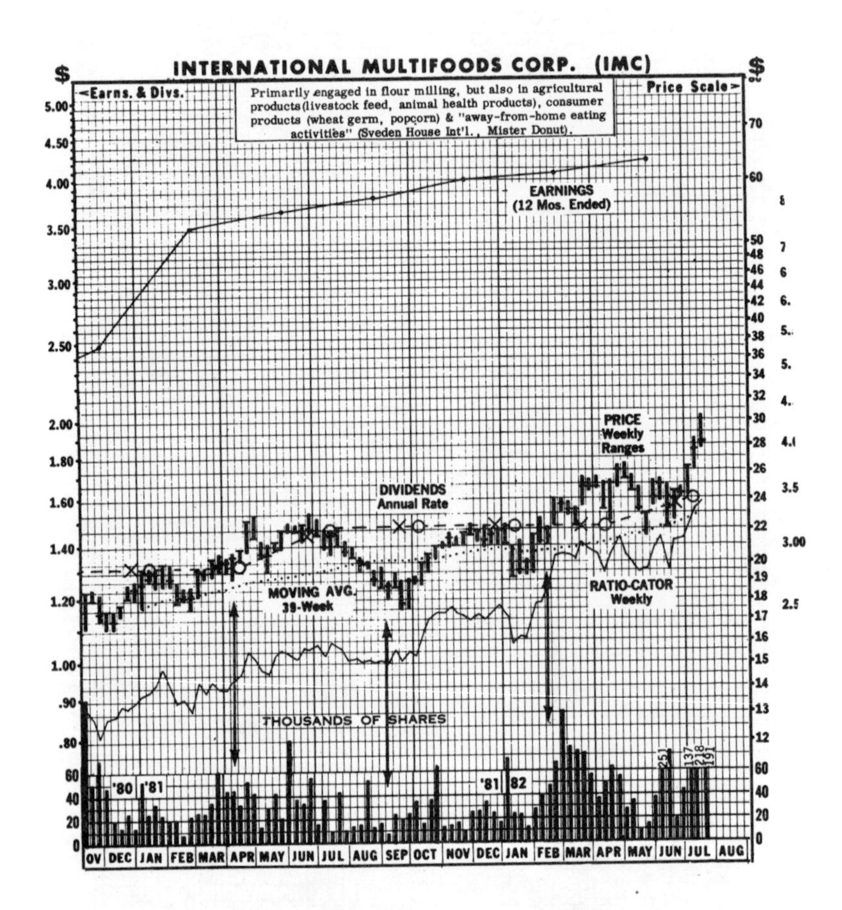

INTERNATIONAL MULTIFOODS CORP. (IMC)
<Earns. & Divs.
Price Scale>
Primarily engaged in flour milling, but also in agricultural products (livestock feed, animal health products), consumer products (wheat germ, popcorn) & "away-from-home eating activities" (Sveden House Int'l., Mister Donut).
EARNINGS (12 Mos. Ended)
PRICE Weekly Ranges
DIVIDENDS Annual Rate
MOVING AVG. 39-Week
RATIO-CATOR Weekly
THOUSANDS OF SHARES
'80 '81
'81 82
OV DEC JAN FEB MAR APR MAY JUN JUL AUG SEP OCT NOV DEC JAN FEB MAR APR MAY JUN JUL AUG

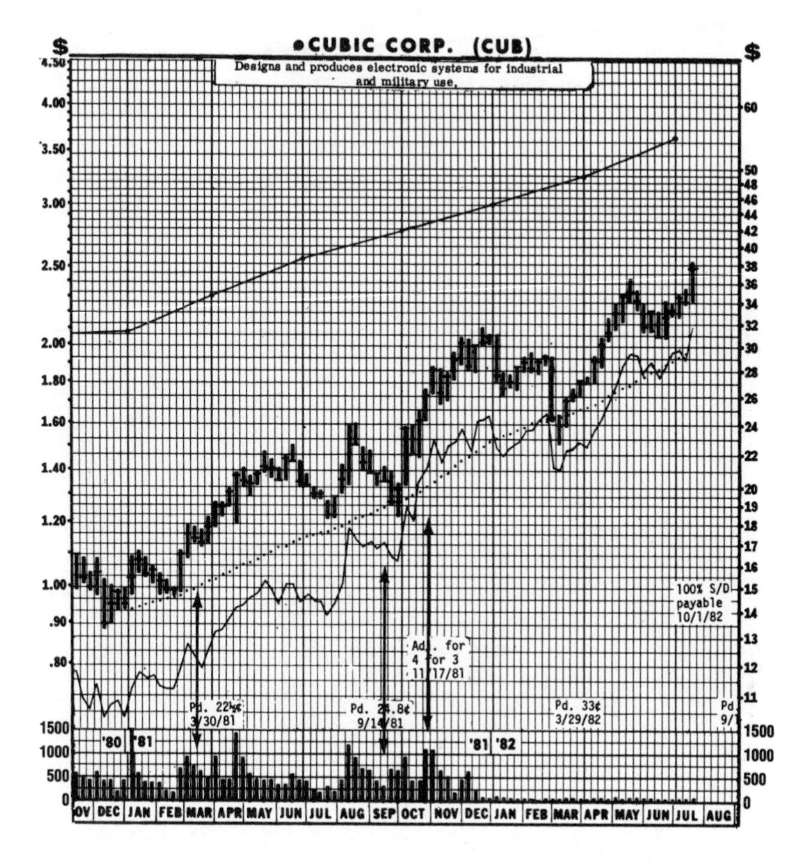

CUBIC CORP. (CUB)
Designs and produces electronic systems for industrial and military use.
Pd. 22½¢ 3/30/81
Pd. 24.8¢ 9/14/81
Adj. for 4 for 3 11/17/81
Pd. 33¢ 3/29/82
100% S/D payable 10/1/82
'80 '81
'81 '82
NOV DEC JAN FEB MAR APR MAY JUN JUL AUG SEP OCT NOV DEC JAN FEB MAR APR MAY JUN JUL AUG

The Second Run

Just as the second rally is the confirming rally in a double bottom, the second run is the best run in most upswinging, turn-showing movements. In this case we look for *any* sign of big buying. You might see a couple of inexplicable price spikes, then a fallback to the prior price levels, then a movement upward again. As soon as you see the upward movement, you buy. There might be a little wiggle downward that is met by voracious buying,

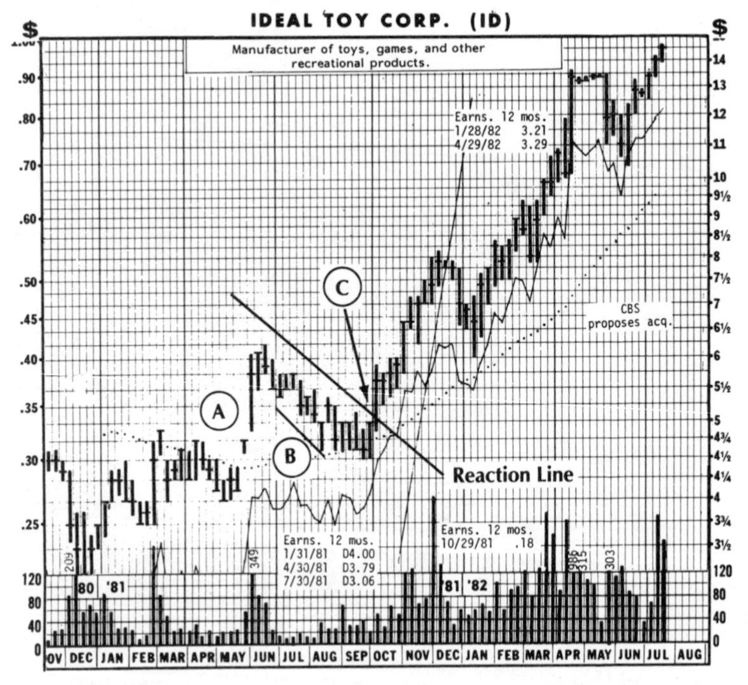

The second run is my favorite time to buy. Often you can buy at close to the first-turn signal price, but the last diehard sellers are flushed when you wait for a small correction, and buying at the second run point tends to be a more efficient use of capital over time. To ascertain that a second run is

sending the stock sharply higher. As soon as the stock falls back a bit, then begins to climb again, you should buy.

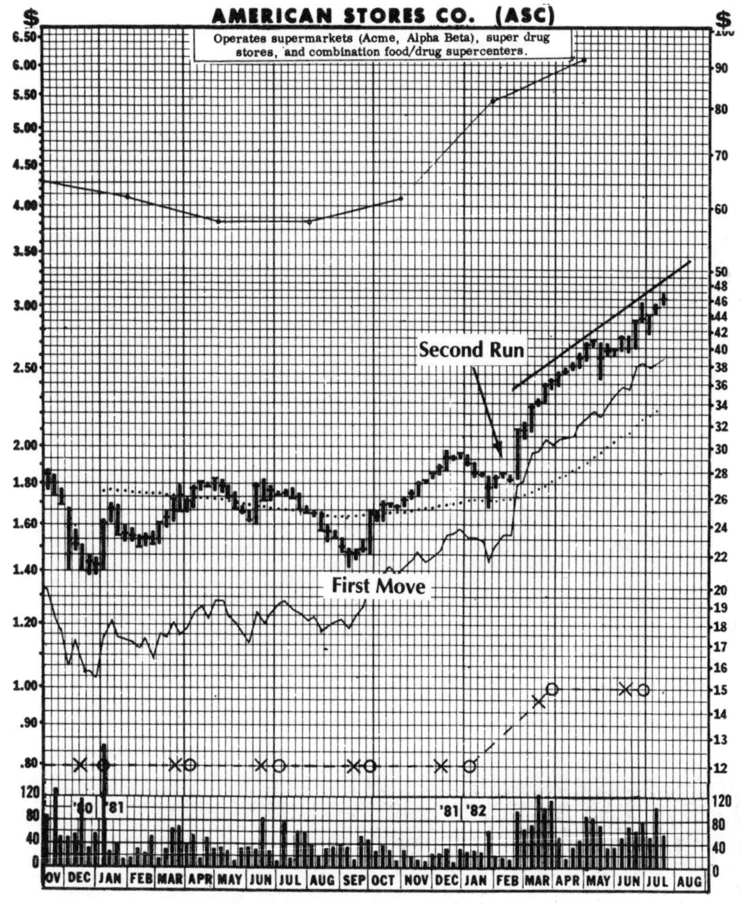

occuring, be sure your buy point is placed *after* the downtrend line of the reaction has been broken (C). So there's a three-step process: (A) an upmove from the bottom, (B), a temporary short-term decline, (C), a break of the decline downtrend line, signaling a purchase.

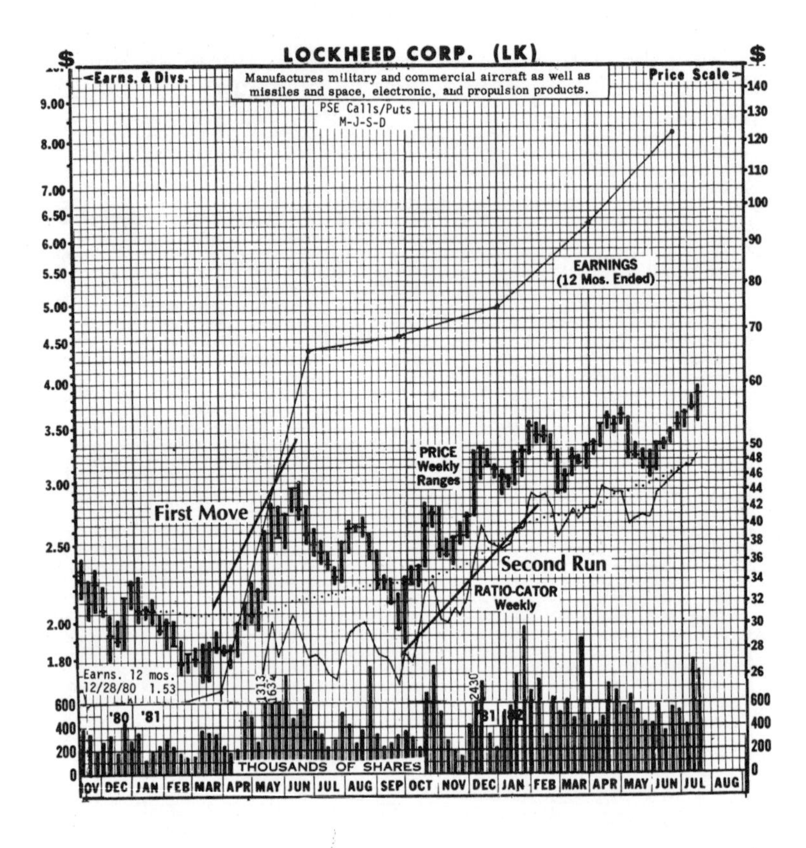

The Standard Breakout

The best signal that a new trend of upward prices after a bottom has begun is what is known as an upside breakout. Breakouts can take many forms, but all are characterized by the same essential principle. Prices have been flat or slowly trending upward for several months (remember, this pattern is valid for us only *after* a long-term bottom has appeared). Then there is a sudden surge of buying, which lifts the prices *clearly* above the previous highs of the preceding period. A three-month period of "congested" prices is sufficient for determining that a breakout has occurred. You should not jump right in on a sharp price move until it has proved itself—until it has shown that it is not merely a one-week aberration. I like to see prices jump sharply and *stay* at their new, higher level, well above the previous highs, for three or four weeks. This shows that the buying is sincere and serious, not a temporary imbalance of orders. And it usually

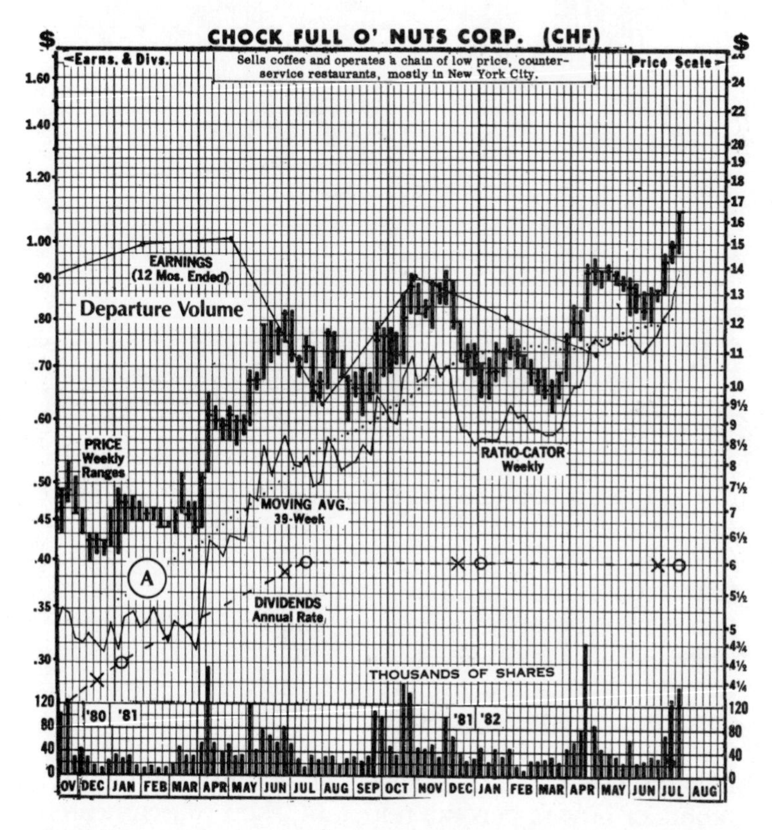

Breakouts can take many forms. In general, they are characterized by a sudden change in the quality and quantity of price movement, and by a penetration or departure on the upside from the thirty-eight-week moving average (A).

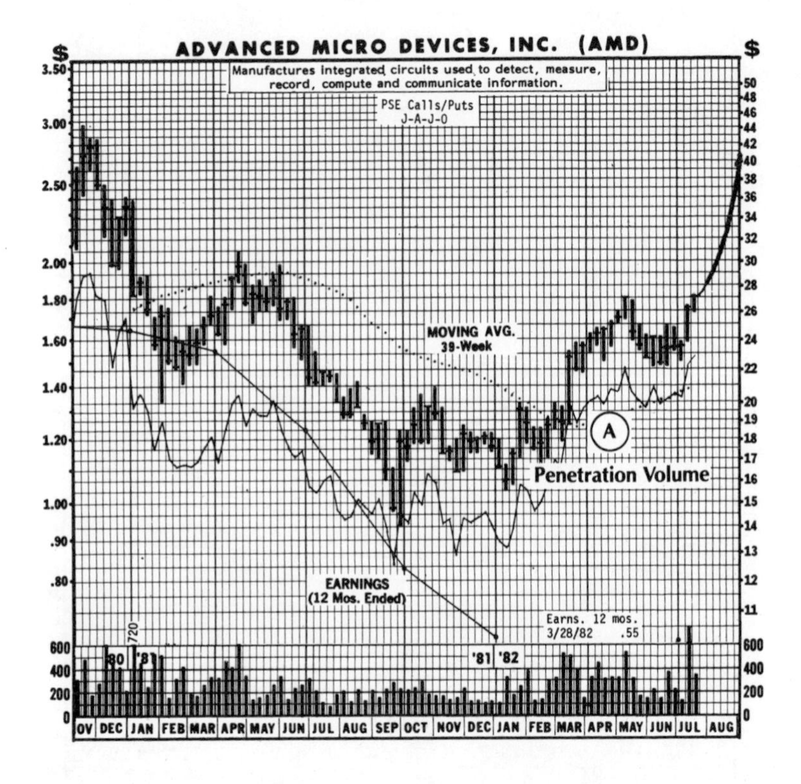

shows there is some change brewing for the stock and/or the company.

Sometimes stocks will jump and keep on going. Feel free to pass these by. You can't always be right on the spot when the action heats up, and it is better to pass than to risk opening a position in which the buying support is far below the present price. You need to be sure there are plenty of other buyers around near your price to protect against a fall. Too, sharp moves often are followed by a pullback as sellers enter the market to take profits or buyers become reluctant; then you can catch the stock on the all-important *second run*, which is almost always longer and stronger than the first upmove. Wait for the pullback. Then, when you see prices begin to rise again, invest.

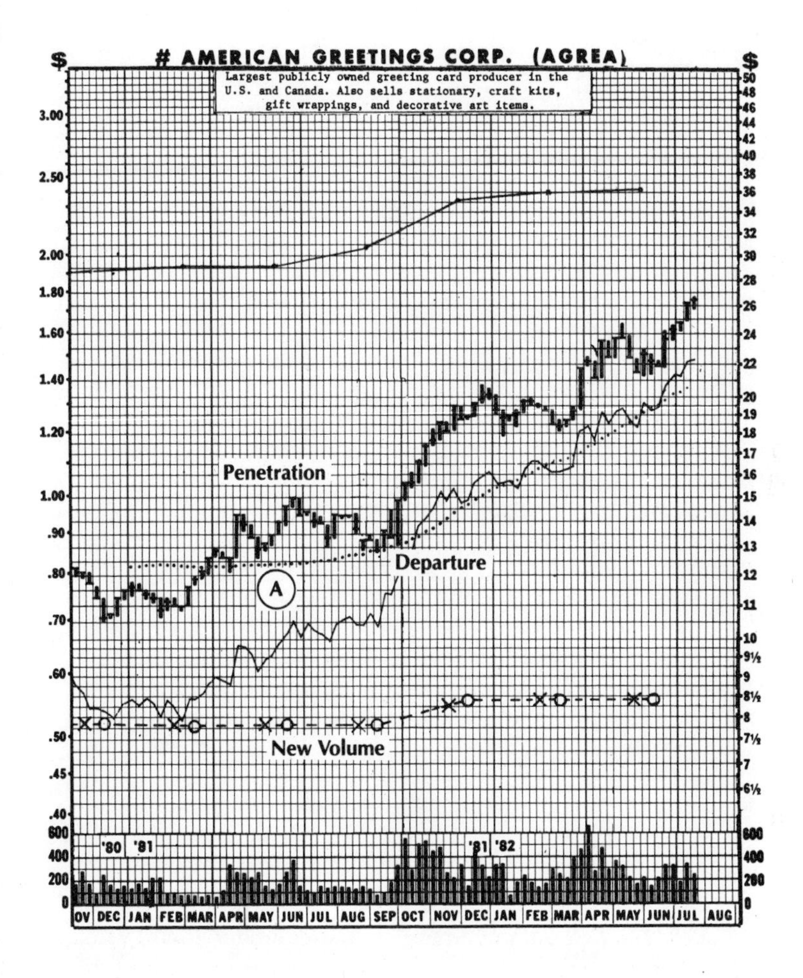

There's one kind of breakout where you don't have to wait. This is a price pattern that I discovered—indeed, wrote an entire book about, *The Momentum-Gap Method*. For our purposes, we will look only for a certain kind of momentum-gap, one I call in the book a "sure thing" pattern. When you see this pattern, the probabilities for future price gains are astounding—90 percent of stocks gain well over 50 percent in the following eight months.

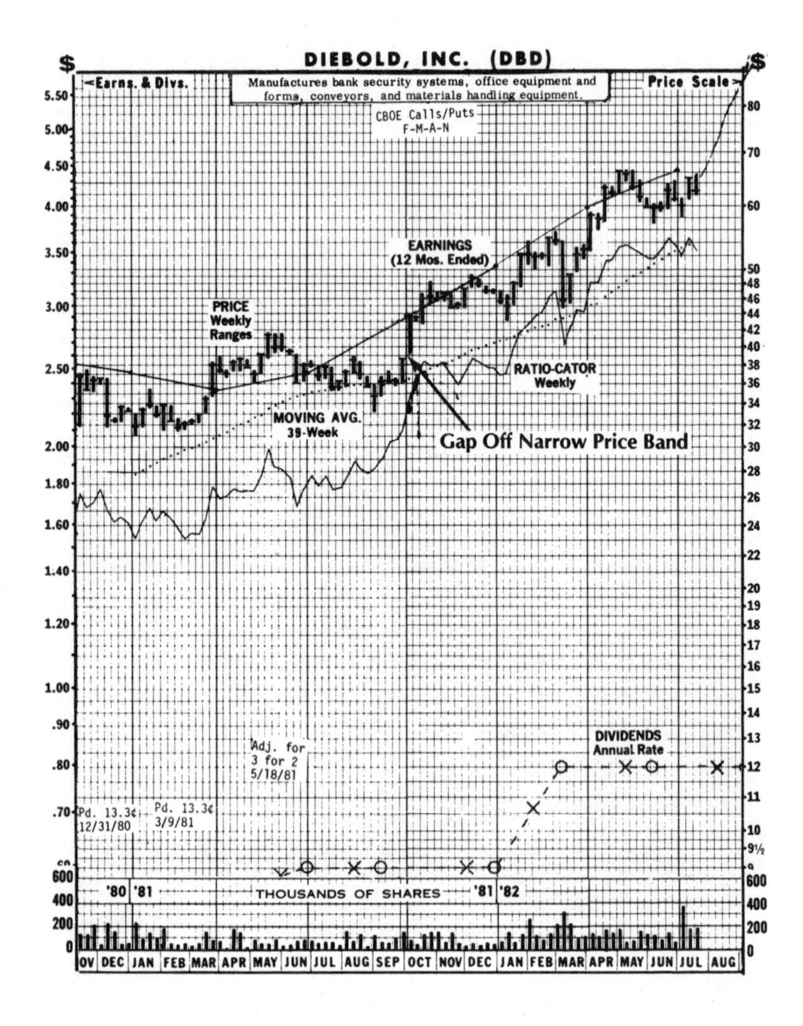

The "sure thing" momentum-gap appears also off a flat base of prices. You need to see at least three months of virtually unchanged pricing (a 10 percent range of closing prices is the most you can accept), but the longer the stock has been stuck in stasis, the better. Suddenly you will see a gap between the bars on the price chart—this

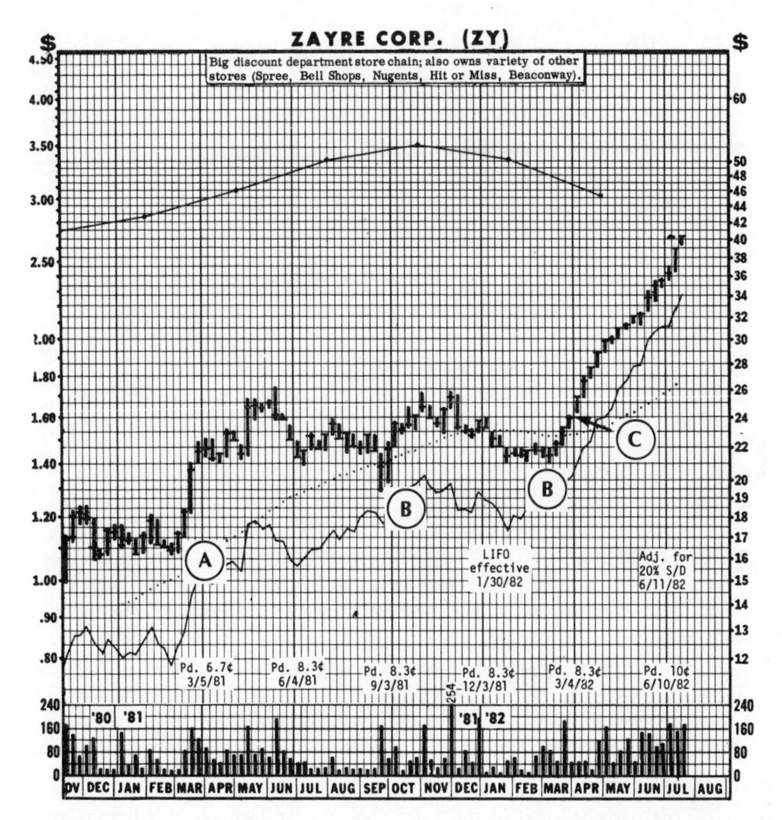

Gaps from a narrow band of "locked" prices are a most positive sign. Sometimes, as in the case of Zayre, you can get your whole "turn-kit" working for you. The stock had a volume breakout in March 1981 (A). Then it stayed flat and subsequently provided a second-run opportunity in September and then again in March 1982 (B). The March 1982 second run was *also* a sure thing, momentum-gap (C). The stock followed through smartly on these patterns even as the overall market kept falling.

means the low of the week in which the gap appears is higher than the high of the preceding week. The gap shows that buyers simply cannot wait to get into the stock. They are practically slavering to buy. It is the premier breakout pattern, and if you see it, you'd better buy without delay. Here are some examples of "sure thing" momentum-gaps.

(If you are interested in obtaining a copy of *The Momentum-Gap Method*, send $30 to:

Lowell Miller
Box 549
Woodstock, NY 12498

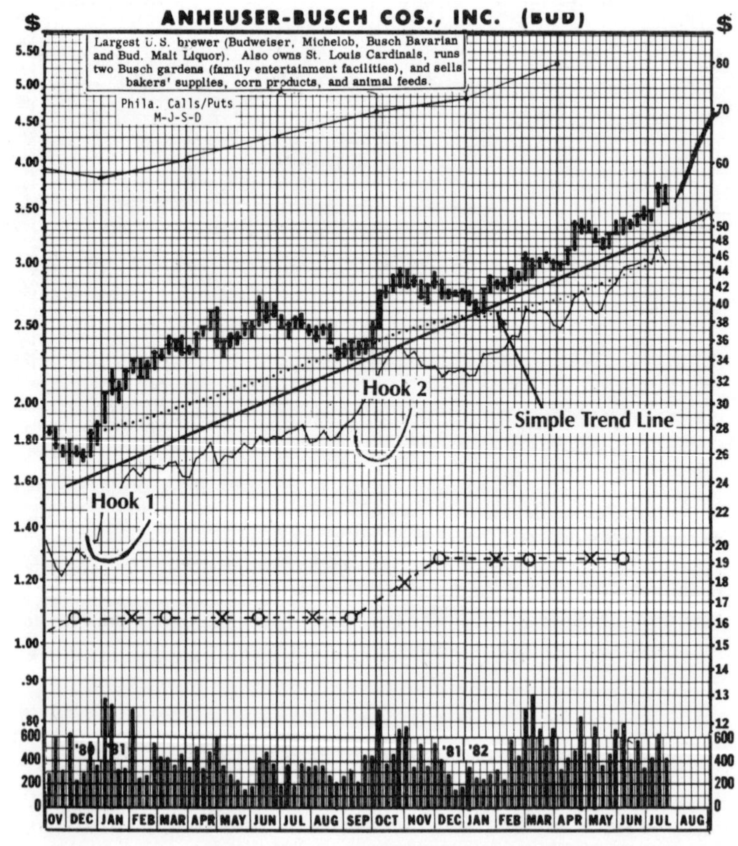

Anheuser-Busch was buyable on the two-hook approach in September 1981. Note that the two-hook trend line is very much like the second run—only no breakout-type action is required.

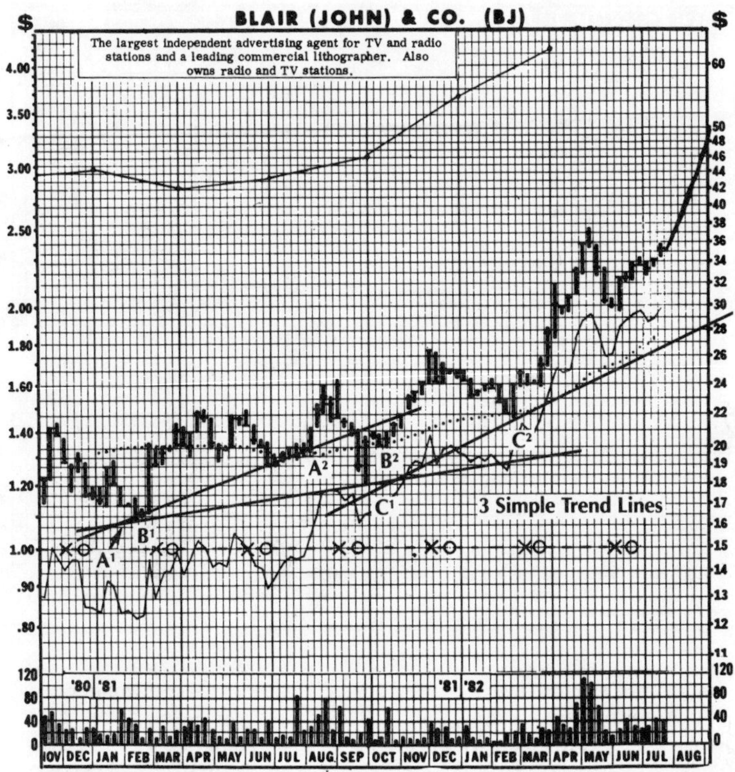

John Blair shows several possible buy-points using the two-hook approach—each prior to the price-volume burst in April that went contrary to the general market.

Two Hooks Make a Trend Line

Another pattern I favor involves the creation of a simple trend line by observing two "hooks" in the weekly price pattern. A trend line shows you the rising levels at which buyers will come into the market and buy (for a stock that is trending upward; the reverse is true for a stock trending downward).

This pattern is a kind of cousin to the double bottom, but no bottom is required to make it a legitimate signal, and the second decline *must* end at a price level *higher* than the first one. What you'll see is a rally, then a

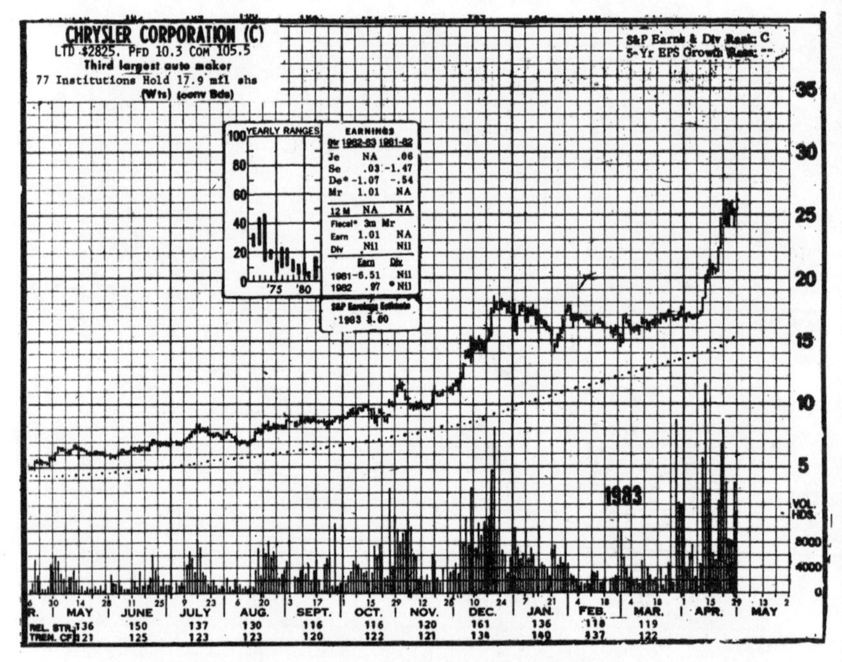

In this daily basis chart of Chrysler, note how, in early 1982, as the stock rises above the forty-week moving average, each increase in volume alsc shows an increase in prices. And when volume decreases, prices *don't* decline—a positive sign. When the volume bars look as if you're getting closer and closer to New York—you know, the prices are always higher once you get to New York—pick up that bargain-basement stock. Chrysler, buyable though without earnings because of its size, was the *best-performing stock on the New York Stock Exchange in 1982*. What a difference a change in management (to Lee Iacocca) can bring.

pullback to a level higher than the one the rally started from, then a new rally. This is the typical pattern of all rising stocks, so if you see it early after a bottom pattern has appeared, you have a clear sign that the stock has begun a new uptrend. It's sort of like seeing a mini double bottom after seeing your main, long-term double bottom. When the two hooks appear, you can draw a line connecting the bottoms (see the chart) that will give you a very good idea of what to expect in terms of the jiggles, the inevitable ups and downs as the stock progresses upward. You can see quite clearly the kind of dips to expect if the stock is in an uptrend, and, as you'll learn in the chapter on selling, you can also see when and where to sell your position.

The Idealized Situation

You've probably noticed that all the patterns that show us a turn upward is in progress have common features. In each we want to see flat or gently rising prices after one of the long-term bottom signals has appeared. Then we want to have some evidence that the area of previous prices is being left behind.

Bear these principles in mind, for reality is never so neat that it will provide for us the exact pattern we are looking for every time. These patterns *are* patterns because they continually appear and reappear in stocks, and when they do, they provide consistently predictable results. But the patterns aren't mystical tea leaves—they're predictable because they're graphic representations of substantial underlying realities relating to the dynamics of the buying and selling in the market. Once you realize that, you will also realize that a pattern may not precisely fit what you have seen before but may well "speak" to you of the underlying market reality. But act only if it shouts. There's no need to jump the gun—the market is full of irrationally created bargains and is always making new ones.

The essential principles behind the patterns I've shown have some corollaries you should keep in mind:

- *Never buy a stock when it is going down.* Stocks travel in trends, remember. If a stock is going down, it could always go down some more.
- *Don't chase a stock.* The likelihood is that it will pull back and give you a chance to buy it at a better price. When you see it begin to rise a second time, you know the uptrend is real.
- *Always be certain the bottom pattern has appeared before you accept the trend-turning pattern.* In effect, the turn patterns *complete* the bottom pattern.

Your investment candidate has now passed through the fivefold screen and you're ready to invest in what is undoubtedly the best potential for profit with the lowest risk available anywhere.

But some questions must surely remain in your mind:

What if I find several stocks and I have only the money or the desire to invest in one of them? How do I choose?

How long do I hold my position? When can I expect my biggest profits?

When should I sell?

What about the overall market? Won't the Dow Jones Industrials Average affect how my stock does?

Is there such a thing as a *more perfect* Perfect Investment?

Is this really a low-risk technique? How low? How much can I make?

The remainder of this book is devoted to answering these questions and to providing you with tricks that can make your profits even larger and more certain. It might interest you at this point to turn to Chapter 15, "The Perfect Investment Record, 1970–80," to see just how dazzling the profits from this method can be. And be *sure* to pay close attention to Chapter 11 on selling. Buying at the right price and the right time is undoubtedly the best thing you can do for yourself as an investor, but all too many investors overlook the crucial importance of correct selling, only to see their intelligently gained profits dissolve when not converted into real dollars.

PART THREE

THE INVESTMENT PROCESS

9

Plus Factors

This chapter will focus on a group of features that will help you distinguish which stocks are best of those successfully passed through the fivefold screen. (Sometimes, when the whole market is low, there are more stocks than you need, and the plus factors become more important. At other times there are only a few good candidates, so the plus factors are of less interest.) These factors bring extra confidence that the underlying company is not only sound but also ready to resume its prior earning power and its prior status as a stock many buyers want to own. One or more plus factors in a stock certainly strengthens the case that its low price is irrational.

Dividend Reinstatement or Increase

At some point we simply must rely on corporate management to know more about the true state of a company than anyone else. If management begins to pay a dividend when it hasn't before, or reinstates a dividend that had been cut, or raises the existing dividend, we have no choice but to infer that those closest to the company feel its fortunes are improving and will continue to improve. Few management acts would demonstrate such poor judgment as a dividend increase or reinstatement that is followed in short order by a cut. (This virtually never happens for stocks that have passed the fivefold screen.)

To provide a new dividend attraction a company must have the money to pay out, and it must see more money coming in the future to continue the practice. No matter what the stock market is saying about the company through ill treatment of its stock, a positive change in the dividend picture is one of the most favorable signs you can see. Further, the dividend gives you extra insurance against interim declines in the share price, since the payout can, in effect, make up for a loss.

As dividends increase, the stock may soon be perceived by investors as an *income* instrument in addition to a potential capital gains vehicle. Obviously, the higher the dividends go, the more attractive the stock becomes on the basis of income, or yield. Yield-oriented investors—a large group in the marketplace—love to see a company that increases its dividend regularly. Let's say a stock pays a dividend equal to 5 percent today. If you hold the stock for five years and the dividend continues to go up, the yield based on the original price at which you bought the stock might be 20 percent or more. And that's excluding the capital gains likely to accrue from owning a Perfect Investment stock showing this plus factor.

The logic of this position is sound, but the practicalities are sounder. All it takes is a glance through a chartbook. You will see very clearly that stocks of companies that have been in the investment doghouse begin to light up when a dividend is added, reinstated, or increased. They outperform all other stocks in general, and other crashed stocks in particular.

Here are two good examples. See how the price begins to move after the dividend news, well in advance of the earnings increases. Management makes its dividend policy long in advance because it knows, long before other investors do, that the company has bright prospects.

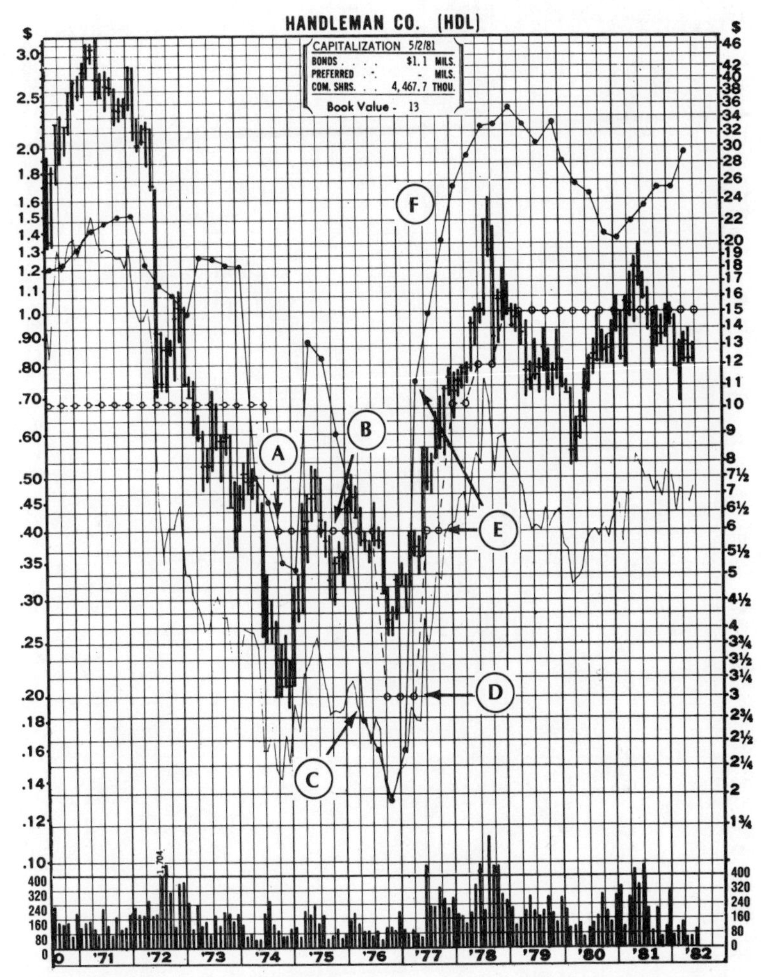

Handleman Co. (a large wholesaler of records) shows us how management's dividend policy can provide insight into the company's true fortunes. In 1974, with earnings in a severe decline, the dividend was reduced (at A). Though earnings appeared to rebound in 1975, the dividend was not restored to its former level or even raised, a tip-off that perhaps the company was not yet out of the woods (B). Earnings subsequently headed south again—management knows the state of its own house (C), forcing yet another cut in the dividend (D). The next upturn in earnings, however, in 1977, saw management confirm the brighter prospects with a dividend increase (E). This time we could invest confidently, having heard management's "message" about the future. And indeed this stock did triple within two years, as earnings continued to power ahead (F).

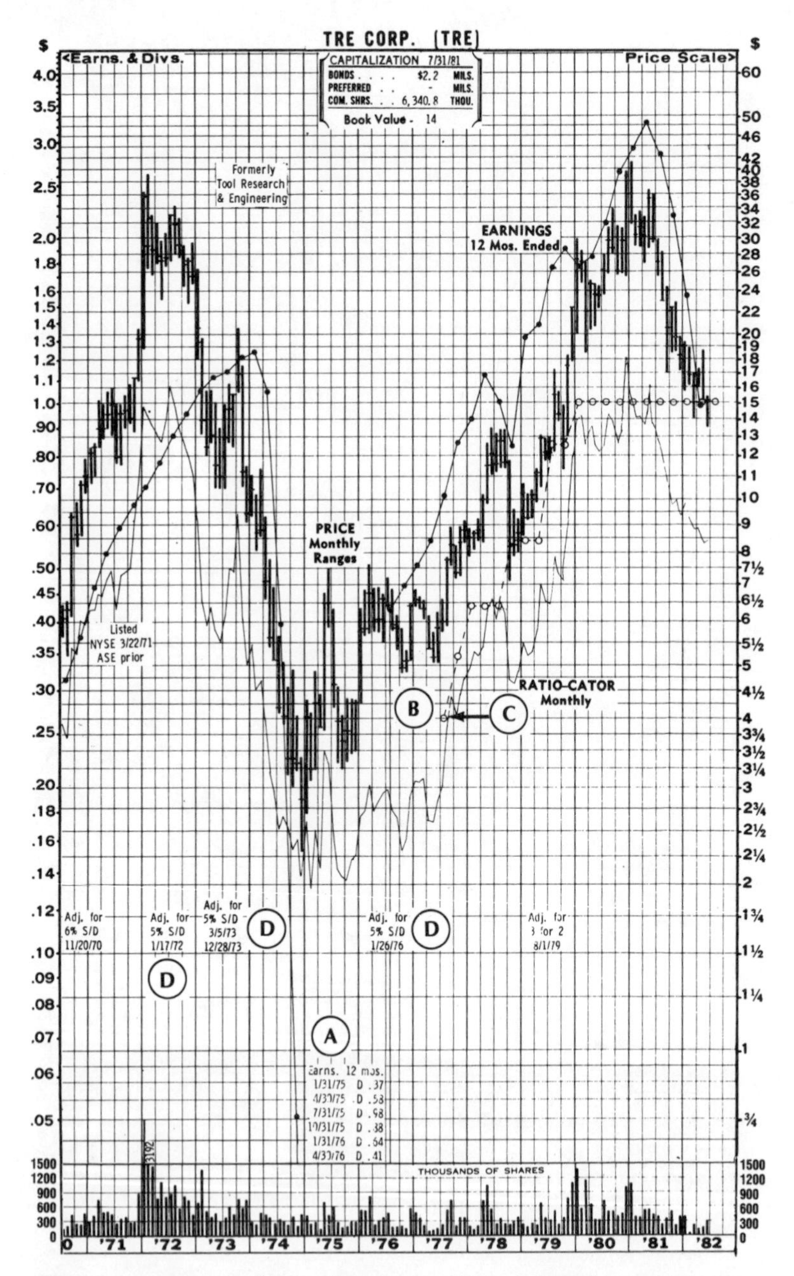

TRE (an aerospace supplier) suffered losses during 1975 and part of 1976 (A). Was the company in dire trouble, or was it restructuring to make more money in the years ahead? When earnings appeared in 1976, investors remained skeptical and stock went nowhere (B). However, when the company demonstrated its own confidence in its future by paying a cash dividend for the first time (C)—it had previously paid stock dividends (D)—the market became a believer. Management's confidence proved well founded, and the stock responded with a sevenfold gain.

Price Earnings Ratio and the Earnings Vee

The ratio of stock price to corporate earnings per share is one of the most examined factors among all investments, and yet it is one of the trickiest. Sleepy, conformist investors tend to use the price-earnings ratio (PE) as a simple rule of thumb to predict what a stock price *should* be. If the average stock has a PE of 9, for example, and a given stock earns one dollar per share, in theory it "should" sell for nine dollars per share. The problem is that earnings per share are not nearly as predictable as most investors and "authorities" would like to believe, and any PE must inevitably be based on future as well as past earnings, for investors always invest on real or imagined future prospects. Further, the PE ratios that investors are willing to "assign" to different kinds of stocks are always changing. Some of the glamour stocks once sold for PE ratios of thirty, forty, even fifty times earnings (Remember our candy store? If you buy a business at fifty times earnings it will take you a mere fifty years to recover your money if earnings stay flat. Some deal!) but now sell at eight or nine times earnings.

In general, because earnings are so unpredictable and because the ratios investors will accept are so malleable, the PE ratio is a fairly useless concept for us. Is a company with no earnings and billions in assets worth zero? That would be the response if you looked only at PE.

When PE ratios are exceptionally low—far below the average of all stocks or, better yet, at an absolutely low level from the point of view of an investor who would be interested in buying the entire business—a somewhat different perspective emerges. We return again to the candy store concept, to the apartment building. When a stock has a very low PE it makes the underlying company attractive as a business investment: In effect, *a low PE (say, six times earnings or less) becomes a kind of undervalued asset*. The company's capacity to earn money has been given short shrift by investors. Often you'll see substantial companies with solid book values selling at three to five times earnings. *That's as cheap as a candy store that has virtually no assets as all!*

Indeed, many studies have shown that over long periods of time stocks with *low* price-earnings ratios consistently outperform the overall market as well as stocks with high PE ratios.

Sometimes a PE is low compared with the previous year's earnings because investors know that next year's earnings are going to take a dive, so the PE is not really that low in a forward view. But just as often the PE is as low as it is simply because the stock is out of favor with investors, or because the company had troubles in its recent past—for any of the less than rational reasons we've discussed throughout this book.

One thing is certain: There's just as much chance of a company with a high PE turning up with bad earnings in the following year as there is for one with a low PE. At least the one with the low PE has some flexibility, for the PE can't get much lower. Any company with a PE of two or three or four and genuine earnings is going to be bought out quickly. It's a better deal than a candy store.

So if you see a low PE (under six, and the lower the better), consider it a plus factor. The PE has nowhere to go but up. If the stock is recovering, as we believe, then the stock must move similarly.

My favorite use (my only use, really) of PE is what I call the earnings vee. When an earnings vee appears, it means that investors were willing to assign a much higher PE to a stock *within the past year* and that the stock has declined sharply but the earnings have either stayed flat or risen. On a chart, the trend of earnings and the trend of prices separate and go in radically different directions. As you can see in the following chart, investors demonstrate their essential irrationality by paying a higher price for lower earnings, then paying a lower price for higher earnings less than twelve months later. Sooner or later investors have to wake up and start bidding up the price of the stock, or one day it will be selling for a share price equal to its earnings per share.

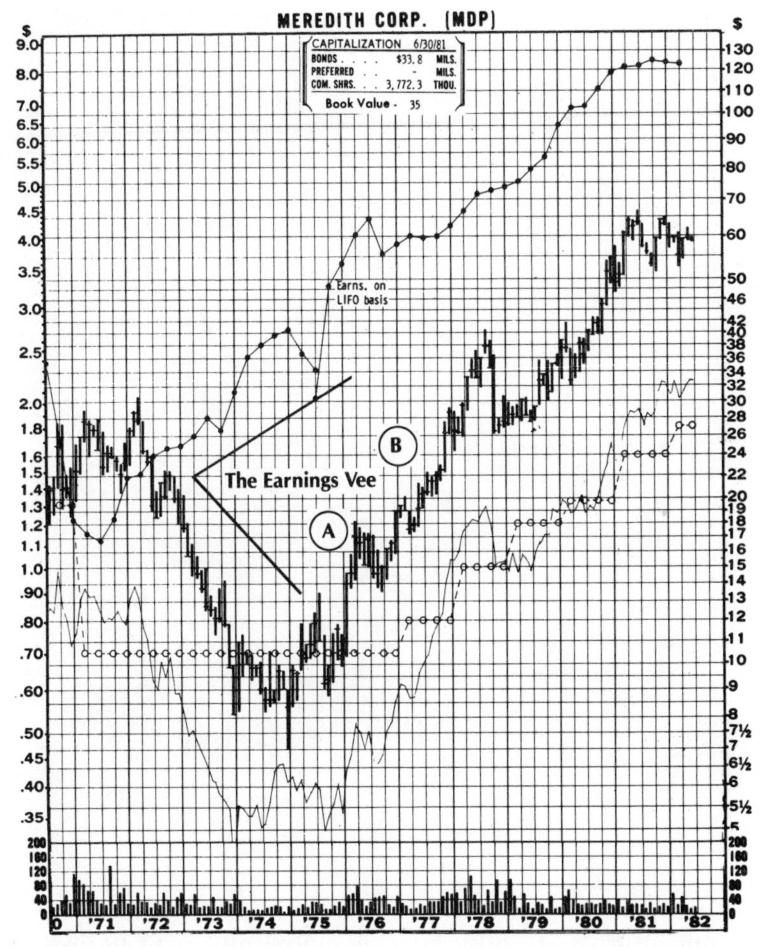

An earnings vee can result from increased earnings, decreased stock price relative to earnings, or both. Meredith is one of the strongest publishing companies in the country, but it ran into problems around 1970, with a resultant decline in earnings and a dividend cut. In 1971, though, investors still thought enough of MDP to pay roughly twenty times earnings for the stock. As the company turned around, the market went lower, and investors simply ignored the news. By December 1974, MDP was selling for only 2½ times earnings. If you bought the whole company then, you would have recovered your entire capital in less than three years and still owned all the assets and earning power! When an earnings vee becomes intense, share price and earning power are so out of whack that even a decline in earnings won't necessarily hurt the share price (A and B). Earnings can't go up and share prices go down forever. Sooner or later, the stock catches up. Just watch the charts.

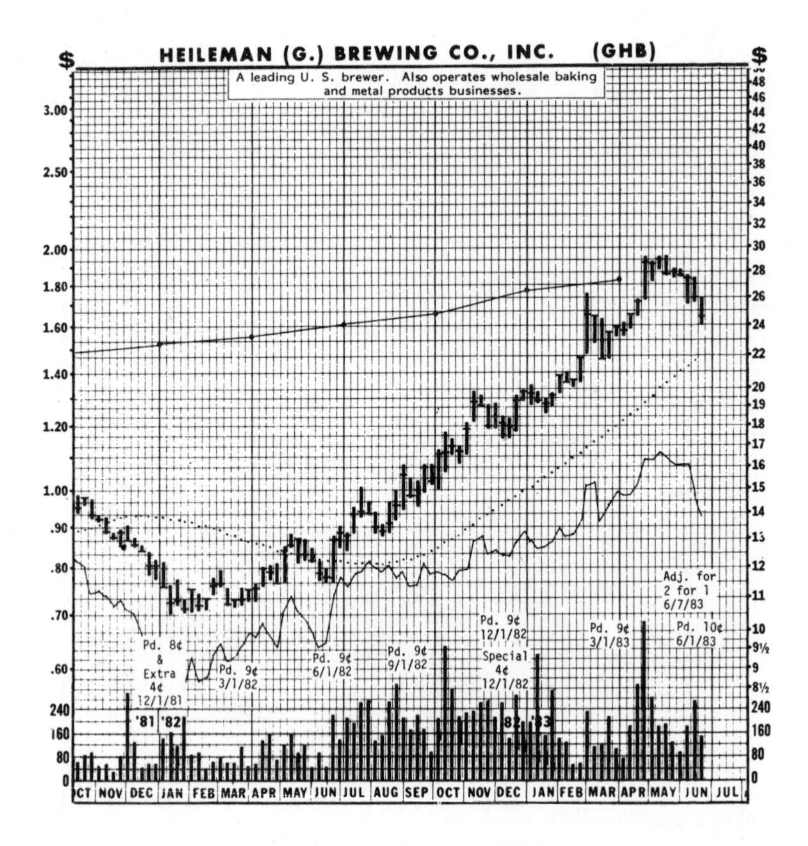

When you see an earnings vee you're actually seeing a kind of price pressure cooker. Something's got to give, and most often it's the stock price pushed upward. Surprisingly, declining stock price as an indicator of a future earnings drop does not seem very accurate. You see the sharp earnings drops in the stocks that have already been bid to the sky. When investors are *already* scared, it seems their fears are typically unfounded.

Indeed, many's the time I have seen a mild earnings decline at the chronological end of an earnings vee only to see the stock *still* move upward, because the PE was so low to begin with that the lower earnings were more than discounted in the excessively low stock price.

Insider Purchases

Reports of insider purchases of stock (insiders are management and directors and their families) are published each week in *Barron's* as well as in some chart services and advisory services. It's a good idea to keep track of this kind of activity, for here you will see the people responsible for a company put their money where their mouths are. Glowing annual reports are as nothing compared to the purchase of ten thousand shares. That shows knowledge and belief that the stock is a good investment. Small purchases of a thousand shares or less don't really tell you much—it could be an executive exercising a stock option—nor do sporadic purchases by one or two individuals. But when you see substantial buying over a period of several months by many insiders in a company, you can be certain your analysis of a Perfect Investment is on solid footing. After all, they know the truth about the value of assets and the potency *now* of the company's intrinsic earning power.

Some investors like to construct entire investment strategies based on the activities of insiders, but such an approach simply won't work. Use this factor as a plus factor, however, and you'll find that it tends to single out the best future performers from among the system selections.

What about insider sales? These are much less reliable as an indicator. Sales of stock are often needed by executives to pay taxes, make gifts, send Junior to college. *Heavy* selling of large blocks by many insiders, though, might show you the rats leaving the ship. If one of your candidates shows lots of insider sales, look for another with plus factors instead.

Outsider Purchases

If you follow the business papers or the business section of your local paper you'll often see reports of large block purchases of one company's stock, usually by another company. These aren't takeovers, but the establishment of positions on the order of 5 or 10 percent of the stock outstanding. Often they are the prelude to a takeover, though, or future big buys. If your stock is a Perfect Investment on the bargain counter, it's really nice to know that your judgment has been confirmed by a heavyweight investor with armies of M.B.A.'s and all the information anyone could possibly get on his or her side. Outsider purchases are a most attractive plus factor, for these are most often made by investors who view the company the proper way—not for a stock trade but as the purchase of an entire business.

If you don't follow these items, your broker is easily able to get the information about block purchases—or existing block holdings, for that matter—from his quote or databank machine. Even discount brokers have this capability.

One more point about outsider purchases: The lower the level of ownership of the stock by banks, pension funds, and mutual funds, the better. You want them to *become* buyers, *after* you buy, to push the stock price higher.

Momentum Industries

Some of the best Perfect Investments are stocks that have had recent temporary troubles but are well positioned in rapidly growing industries. Frequently stocks in these industries are expected by greedy-eyed investors to do much better than is reasonable. Then when they turn up with earnings that are merely well above average instead of spectacular, the stock is dropped like a hot potato and the crash psychology develops. The company's still good; in fact, it's better than most because it's in an industry where the market and the profits are easier to come by than in many others. When the company gets back on the track or begins to perform up to expectations, investors go crazy to buy in to this renewed "hot stock." Once again they see earnings rising to the sky—and the stock price with it. Unconsciously, investors begin again to use the same logic that underlies the entirety of this book: "We paid X dollars per share for this company a few years ago, and it looks like a good company again—it must be worth at least that much if not more today."

There is a constant falling off and rebounding today in most of the technology industries. If you see a Perfect Investment stock in one of these growth areas, you're much more likely to have a winner; look for computers, electronics, communications, health care and drugs, media, defense. I'm also fond of banks and financial companies. Though their stocks are not perceived as glamorous, it seems to me that the financial industry has been a growth industry since the beginning of time. In general, keep in mind that our economy has increasingly become service-oriented and that service-oriented companies will have an easier time making money in this environment than manufacturers.

Market Leadership

It is axiomatic in the world of business that the rich get richer and the market leaders have significant advantages over the competition. Companies that are the biggest in their industries—ideally these companies will have monopoly or quasimonopoly positions—are able to squeeze the smaller competitors by offering better prices, better distribution and service, spending more on research and development to generate new and better products, and finding funds more easily in times of financial crisis. If an industry turns poor for a while, the smaller companies go down first, not the larger ones. The larger ones are larger precisely because they have

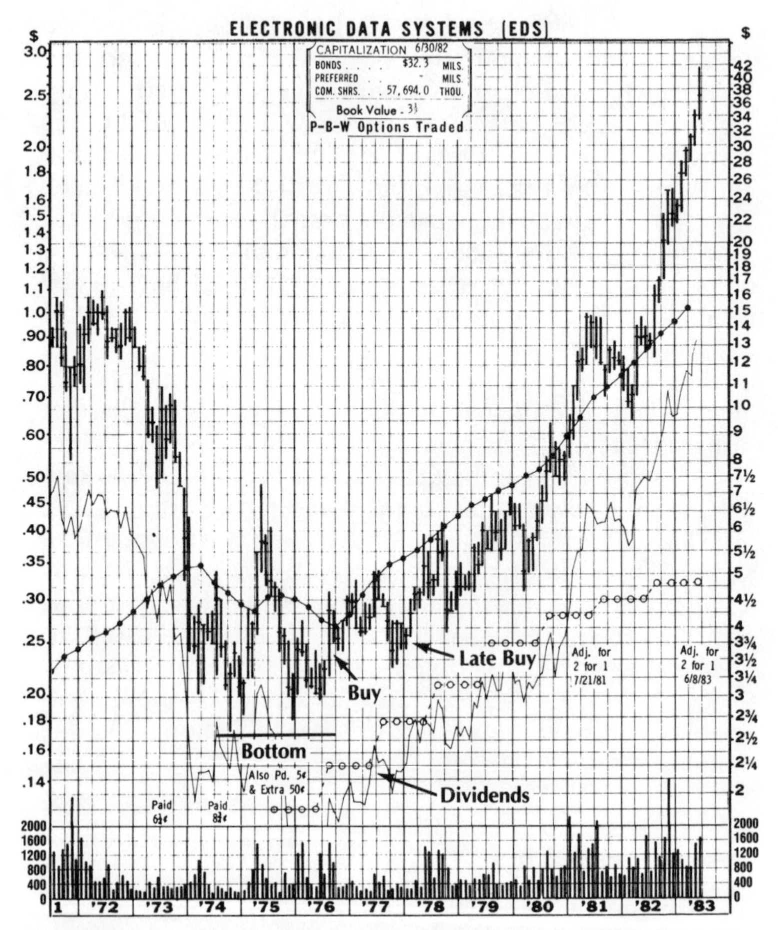

Electronic Data Systems was one of the highest of the high fliers during the late 1960s and early 1970s—manic investors grossly overpriced it. When earnings slowed in growth rate, the stock plunged to almost 10 percent of its former value. As a pioneer in computer data processing, however, EDS was clearly positioned in a momentum industry. By 1976, despite apparently weak earnings, the company felt strong enough to pay dividends and to increase them yearly. Upon the completion of a massive double bottom in late 1976, one had to expect that the company had a bright future and was now as underpriced as it had once been overpriced. If in doubt, there was a good "late" opportunity to buy in 1978, after its third straight dividend increase with ample evidence of the sort of growth that might be expected from a company in a momentum industry solidly in place.

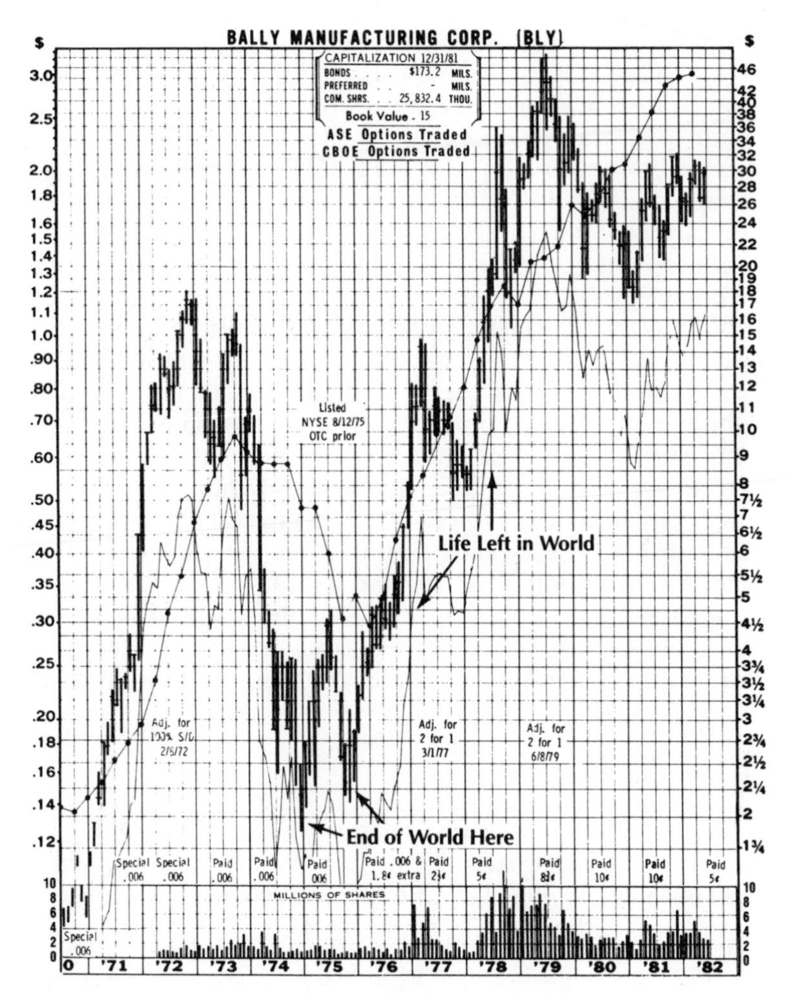

When investors dumped Bally Manufacturing, they must have assumed the death of slot machines, for Bally is by far the dominant company in the gambling machine field, as well as in nongambling arcade games. How Wall Street could have such a low opinion of the gambling industry is as mysterious as it is ironic. In any event, by moving up some 2,000 percent from its low, Bally showed the explosive power an investment in an industry leader—bought when it is being shunned—can have.

demonstrated the ability to survive hard times. Assuming you are sure that the industry involved is not suffering from obsolescence, always award a gold star to any company whose dominance in its market means that competition is the least of its problems. That's why, for example, Marine Midland was such a clear and solid investment. In virtually all of its locations it was the only bank or much the biggest bank in town. It could deal with its problems internally, without having to worry about its market being stolen by some outfit leaner and hungrier. Polaroid used to be the best stock on the block. But now Kodak has taken half the market for instant photography, and Polaroid will never become the hot number it once was unless it can develop (to coin a phrase) a new gimmick without competitors. A utility company in temporary crisis gets a plus factor here too, such as Con Edison in the mid-1970s. After all, a utility has the only game in town, and we can't live without it. Imagine what a terrified mess *any* utility would be in if they actually had to compete and provide service as efficiently as possible! Dominance gives you more room for mistakes.

Special Futures

Here you have to become what's known as a macro or inferential economist. You've got to look into the crystal ball of societal and governmental and economic trends to

→

The cost of new housing in this country has risen so fast that many experts estimate that only two families in ten can afford to buy a new house today. What about the other eight? As the contours of the housing industry change, the demand for prefabricated or manufactured housing would seem promising and potent. An important producer of such housing, Fleetwood is well positioned to benefit from this change in consumer purchasing patterns. Remember, though, this story is not enough on which to base an investment. All the Perfect Investment criteria must be met, so that you can be sure you are at the *beginning* of an upward cycle in the stock price, not somewhere in the middle or at its end. In January 1981, upon the completion of the head-and-shoulders bottom, we saw a nice technical point at which to buy. But the company was in deficit then—you would have had to wait until May 1981 at about 5.

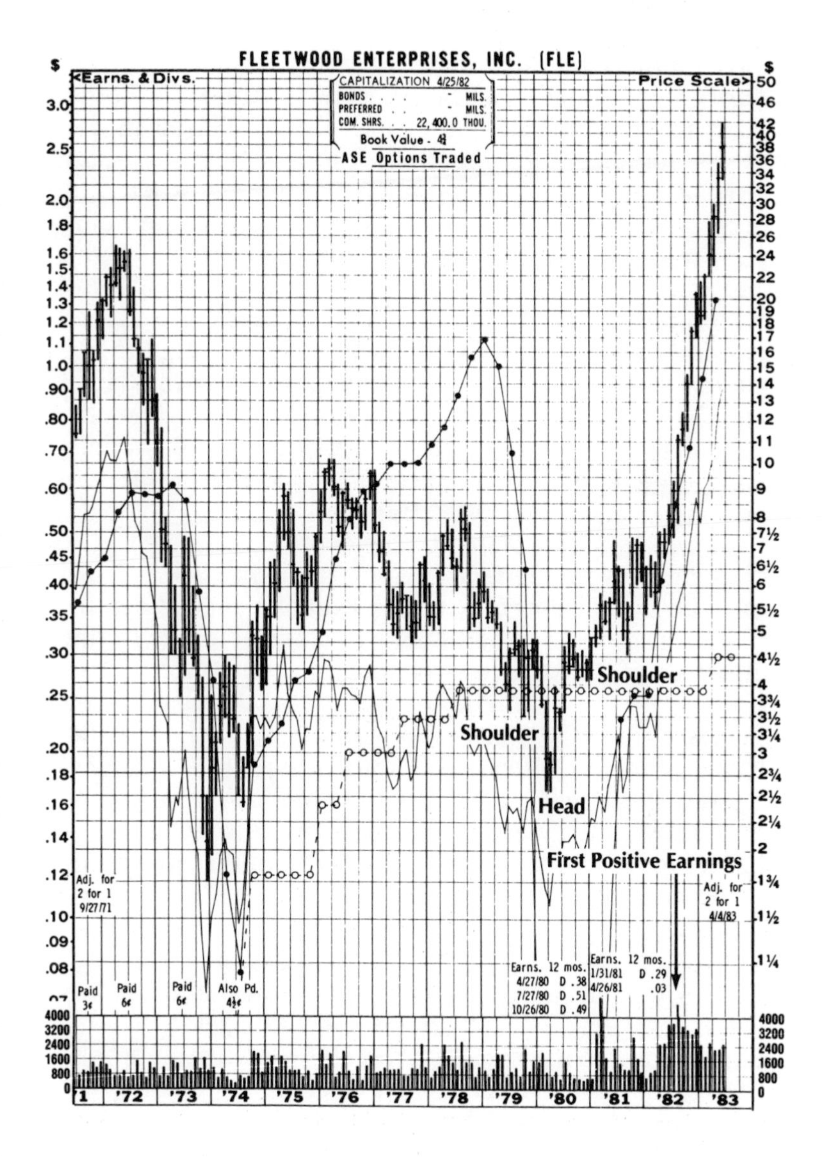
FLEETWOOD ENTERPRISES, INC. (FLE)
Earns. & Divs.
Price Scale
CAPITALIZATION 4/25/82
BONDS . . . . - MILS.
PREFERRED . . - MILS.
COM. SHRS. . . 22,400.0 THOU.
Book Value - 4¾
ASE Options Traded
Shoulder
Shoulder
Head
First Positive Earnings
Adj. for 2 for 1 9/27/71
Adj. for 2 for 1 4/4/83
Earns. 12 mos. 4/27/80 D .38 7/27/80 D .51 10/26/80 D .49
Earns. 12 mos. 1/31/81 D .29 4/26/81 .03
Paid 3¢
Paid 6¢
Paid 6¢
Also Pd. 4½¢
'71 '72 '73 '74 '75 '76 '77 '78 '79 '80 '81 '82 '83

spy an emerging environment that will prove extraordinarily helpful to the Perfect Investment candidate. If the company you are looking at is heavily involved in defense, for example, you know there are better than normal chances of its earnings improving when the defense budget is being sharply increased. If your company makes ice cream and suddenly all over the country people are eating ice cream like maniacs, the environment is favorable. If your company explores for oil and gas and the government passes a law increasing the tax shelter for oil and gas exploration, you can be more certain that your company is going to be able to raise the capital it needs. Likewise, if war breaks out in the Middle East, that domestic producer you have your eye on becomes somewhat more attractive.

The special environmental factors that mark a positive change for your Perfect Investment candidate can be innumerable. They cannot yield a suitable investment by themselves but are useful tools in conjunction with the entire set of Perfect Investment rules. One caveat: These special futures should be real, not speculations or guesses. If there's a bill pending in Congress that should have a positive effect, wait until it's passed. If lower interest rates will be a big help to your company, wait until they actually begin to come down. Use insight but not imagination. In the world of investment, dreamers are losers.

Cash Growth

The growth of a company's reserves of cash and equivalents (marketable securities) is the most golden of the plus factors. To me it is the surest sign—no matter how ill things may look otherwise—that you are making an investment in a fundamentally healthy company that will be attractive to other investors.

What does the growth of cash and equivalents tell you?

It is a key measure of the *quality* of earnings. Earnings, as I've mentioned more than once, can be very tricky indeed. All too often the reported figures are what I call "accountant's earnings" rather than a real measure of the profitability of the company. Many arcane factors go into the computation and reporting of earnings—depreciation, tax-loss carry-forwards, extraordinary (one-time) gains and losses, the booking of expense and income in different fiscal years, provison of special reserves, etc. These kinds of factors, plus managements' customary desire to show high earnings on their quarterly statements, make earnings too slippery, too *mendacious* for any investor to rely on.

But changes in cash and equivalents can give an investor a good sense of whether reported earnings are genuine or an accounting chimera. When a company's cash and equivalent balances are rising *without a concomitant rise in debt*, you can feel reasonably well assured that the company is actually making money. You can be deceived by statements about profit and loss, but you cannot be deceived by cash.

Interestingly, a study of thousands of companies, comparing their profit performance to the growth or decline of cash and equivalents (after factoring changes in long-term debt), shows the following general results:

1. Increased earnings plus increased cash usually result in higher future earnings.
2. Decreased earnings plus increased cash usually result in higher future earnings.
3. Increased earnings plus decreased cash usually result in a subsequent earnings decline.
4. Decreased earnings plus decreased cash usually result in a decrease in book value, a decrease in future earnings, and prolonged profit problems.

In each case, the sharper the change, the more likely the indicated result. Thus, for example, when you see a stock that fits all the other Perfect Investment rules and that also begins to show a marked increase in its cash and equivalents, you can *expect* with considerable certainty that both earnings and dividends will shortly show significant increases. It is the rare case indeed in which,

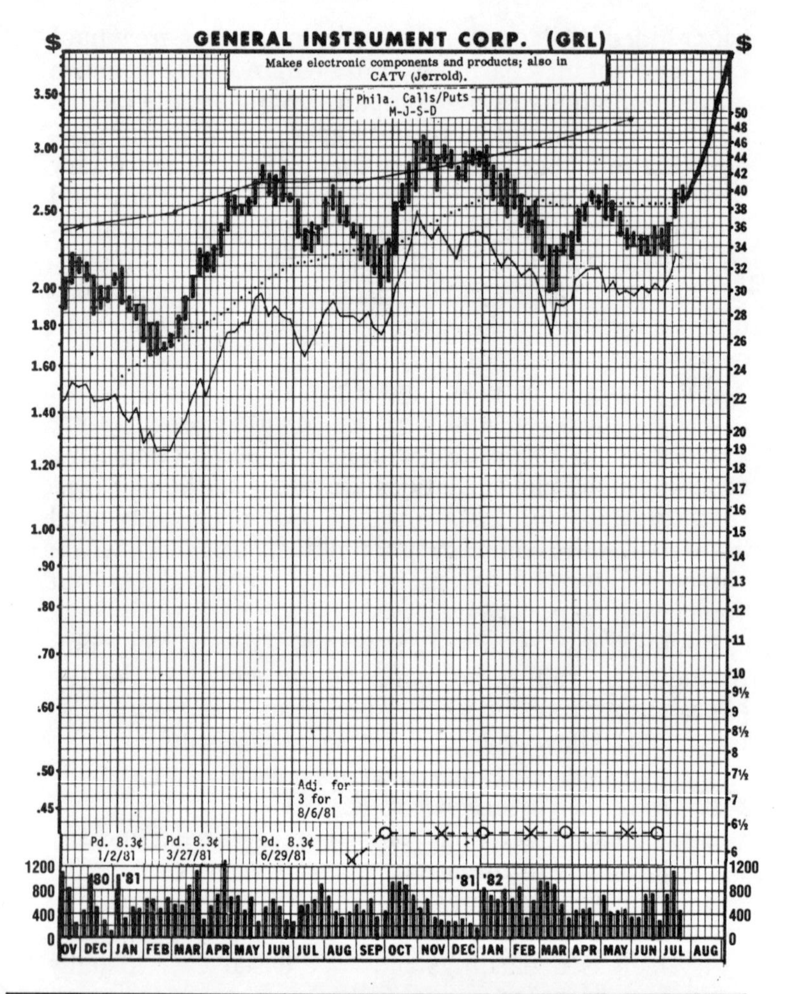

COMPANY	YR. END		CAPITALIZATION BONDS MIL. $	PFD STK MIL. $	COMMON SHS (000)	WORKING CAPITAL Millions $ CASH & EQUIV.	CURRENT ASSETS	CURRENT LIAB.	BK VAL $	SALES MIL. $	NET INC. MIL. $
GENERAL INSTRUMENT	*Feb	'80	44.7	12.1	29,066.1	129.6	421.3	152.0	14	825	68.1
		'81	39.6	-	30,880.1	141.5	505.6	193.9	16	957	90.0

EARNINGS & DIVIDENDS PER SHARE	1978	1979	1980	1981	1982		QUARTERLY EARNINGS J-F-M	A-M-J	J-A-S	O-N-D	QUARTERLY DIVIDENDS J-F-M	A-M-J	J-A-S	O-N-D
EARN.	1.41	1.97	2.49	3.01		'81	.65	.65	.75	.80	.166	.083	.10½	-
DIV.	.469	.233	.30	S .377		'82	.81	.90			.21	.10½		

whatever the cause, this increase in cash position does not shortly translate into higher earnings—the yardstick watched by most investors—which will draw buyers to the stock.

Be sure your cash figure is realistic. You will find changes in this position listed in annual and quarterly reports, in information services such as Value Line and Standard & Poor's, and in chart services such as the Securities Research *Red Book* of weekly basis charts (shown below, and available from the company by subscription or by single issues, or in most libraries). First look at the cash and equivalents figure to see if it has increased. Then check the long-term-debt figure. If it too has increased, you must subtract that amount from the increase in cash position, for the cash could merely be the proceeds of new debt financing awaiting investment (the company receives cash for its debt). If the long-term debt has decreased, that is *an excellent, most positive sign,* for an increase in cash combined with a decrease in debt means that the company has been able to pay off some of its debt *and* hold more cash than it did before. The actual cash increase, then, is much greater—the shown increase *plus* the debt repayment. As a final check, be sure the increases and decreases in current assets are in balance, or in favor of the assets. If there is a net decrease, the cash position is likely to be eroded in making up the difference.

←

General Instrument shows us an example of "clean," reliable earnings. Looking at the bond column, we can see that GRL was able to retire $5 million of debt. Its cash hoard still *rose* some $12 million, while current assets grew far faster than current liabilities. Sales and book value both increased, as have dividends. All these factors make the growing earnings look very legitimate. You'd really have to be an accounting magician to fudge this group of numbers. By the end of 1982, GRL reached over $60 per share.

10

What About the Market?

No one can predict where the overall market is going to go on a long-term basis. Anyone who claims he or she can is an egomaniac, a fool, or both. Anyone who actually does predict the future course of the market over several years has been lucky.

Who can know if war will break out? Who can know if OPEC will pop the price of oil again, or, for that matter, if OPEC will collapse and prices return to 1960s levels? This year the Federal Reserve Board has loosened the credit ropes and interest rates are falling, which usually is good for stocks. Will the Fed tighten up next year? Who knows? Who knows who will be on the board in two or three years? Will the President be shot? Will it matter to the market? Will investors pay twelve times earnings for stocks next year, or only seven?

The key issues that make for up or down stock markets are imponderables. The most imponderable of all—the level of expectations and confidence of the group of stock market investors—is beyond all possibility of measurement into the long-term future. All this notwithstanding, the streets of the investment world are crowded with experts who are certain that the Dow Jones Industrials Average will reach 2,000 within two years, or 500 by summer. I even have a T-shirt from one such expert (a former songwriter) who has calculated, for the edification of his four thousand advisory service subscribers, that the Dow "should," by all reasonable analysis, reach

3,420 by 1985. Who knows? Maybe it will. And then there are the brokers. With brief exceptions—most commonly when the market is about to make a major bottom—brokers are always bullish. Of course they are. They want you to buy stock so they can get a commission. Brokers have a million reasons why the market is going higher. When it doesn't, they quickly come up with new reasons why it will go higher after this latest bout of "profit-taking" or "correction."

Prediction of the long-term market has become a mini-industry of quintessential nonsense, satisfying the need of investors who rightly feel they don't know what's going to happen to get an "answer" to this mystery. The "experts" provide relief from anxiety, provide hope, provide a rationale for investors to separate themselves from their cash. Men with titles get quoted in the most prestigious newspapers. Readers say, "Ah, *here's* an authority I can believe in."

A typical example occurred yesterday and today, as I write this chapter. The market is in the midst of its most hysterical rally ever, trading over one hundred million shares a day as each institutional money manager becomes afraid of losing his job as the market runs away and blasts his clumsy millions at the stock of the moment. For now, the stock of the moment happens to be IBM. Yesterday the market was up "only" about 9 points, when IBM announced third-quarter profits up 36 percent—at a time when most companies are reporting lower earnings. As reported in *The New York Times*, this news goosed the market, and stocks rose to close up 35 points. "Analysts say the strong showing of IBM's third quarter gave investors hope that the economy is turning around," said the *Times*. "An analyst from Bache Halsey Stuart said that with IBM in the lead, since it is the favorite of nearly all institutional managers, there's no telling how high the market can go from here."

That was yesterday. Today the stock market dropped 28 points. What was the "reason" for this decline? "Investors were disappointed in the third-quarter report of IBM yesterday," said the *Times*, "as many analysts were expecting substantially higher earnings."

And, as Kurt Vonnegut has said, so it goes.

What's a poor investor to do?

First of all, you must pay *no* attention to news about the stock market, and even less attention to commentary on that news. Nowhere is yesterday's news as old as it is on Wall Street.

Even when the news is clearly important, such as the OPEC oil embargo or the outbreak of war, *you must not invest based on the news*. It will only make you poorer. It seems to me that more money is lost by investors acting based on news than any other factor. The problem lies in interpreting the investment *meaning* of any development. When OPEC put the squeeze on our oil supplies, an astute investor might well have realized that the price increase in crude oil would vastly raise the value of domestic oil companies' reserves in the ground and would prove incentive for much new drilling that would boost the revenues of the oil-drilling and service companies. *But such an astute investor might well have gotten wiped out as the market—and the oil-related stocks with it—continued to fall until 1975*. Only then did investors realize the implications of a new world of oil pricing, and oil stocks that had gotten killed in the market slide snapped back sharply, reaching new highs that were more than ten times the price of their lows.

News in the market means nothing for the overall market or for individual stocks until prices change as a reflection of how investors feel about the news. In short, don't try to be too smart. Forget about staying one step ahead of the pack, forget about prescience or brilliance or the genius to peer into the future.

There is only one truth for the Perfect Investor: Sooner or later intrinsic value will be recognized by investors who are ignoring it now. A stock won't be given away forever. When you know how to tell if a stock is likely a superbargain and you can see that the emotional selling of it has subsided, and you can see that buyers are once again interested in buying, you no longer have to be concerned about whether this world event is an opportunity or a danger, whether that article in *Fortune* means you'd better buy or sell, whether *Forbes* thinks your stock is for sharpies or schmucks.

So first of all, as far as the general market is concerned, forget the media, forget events, forget investment advisers, forget what the experts are quoted as saying, and forget what your broker or anybody's broker thinks about the direction of prices more than a few months hence. (It *is* possible to predict prices a few months into the future with reasonable accuracy, but that's a game for traders, not investors; for professionals, not part-timers.)

Of all stocks, Perfect Investment stocks probably are least subject to the magnetic pull of the general market. Even in the pits of 1973–74 there were Perfect Investment stocks moving upward against the worst bear market since the Great Crash. And stocks that were *becoming* perfect investments went determinedly downhill in their own private crashes through the bull markets of 1975 and 1976.

Still, it should be clear to anyone that declining stocks decline more in bear markets, rising stocks rise faster and farther in bull markets, declining stocks are propped up by general bull markets, and rising stocks are hampered in their ascent when the investor environment is emotionally contractile, fearful, and bearish.

Though you can't predict long-term trends in the stock market, there are, still, some legitimate conclusions to be drawn from the past history of the rises and falls of the averages. Ideally, of course, you want to buy low, when the market is also low, and sell high, when both the market and your stock are high. Your risk is theoretically lower when the market is unlikely to drop, and theoretically higher when the market has plenty of empty space below it. The age-old question immediately arises: What's high and what's low?

We already know what's low for a stock. We have a formula for determining when its assets, its earning power, have been emotionally and irrationally undervalued at the moment by most investors. We know that within five years investors were willing to pay five times as much for essentially the same company (even a smaller, less valuable version), so we can rest as certain as certain can be in the market that we've spotted a bargain. We know when a stock is low, and that's all we need to know, for the stock can go in only one direction from there: upward.

The market's not the same. Rarely will you see the market being "given away" at the same low levels that can occur with an individual stock. Investors can shun one stock for others, but there's a single stock market, and the asset values it represents as a whole, as an average, are not often permitted to waste away unwanted. In 1974 the market came close for a few months, but the bargain counter in the averages was open only for a blink and quickly closed down as investors realized the absurdly cheap levels that had been reached.

Still, there are historical high and low valuation standards for the overall stock market. If the market is high by historical standards, the probabilities favor an imminent decline. If the stock market is low by these yardsticks, the odds are much better for a subsequent rise than a further fall. Obviously, your Perfect Investment stocks will do better if *both* the market *and* your stock are low when you buy, and if you have the discipline to limit yourself to times in the market cycle when the two are "in synch," you'll likely have better and more consistent results. But you don't *have* to include the market level in your calculations. A Perfect Investment is still a Perfect Investment even if the averages have just hit their all-time high. In general, the best time to buy is when everyone says the market is going *even lower* and all your friends swear they are getting out of the market for good. If there's talk of depression in the air and collapse of the banking system, so much the better. These things never happen when people are expecting them.

Below are some of the high and low valuation standards of the market. They are only historical, you should bear in mind, and "new history" can be created at any time. But market history does have a way of repeating itself, as you may have noticed from seeing, for example, so many double bottom patterns in the stock charts. One important point: You never can call the market "high" or "low" based simply on the physical number of the Dow Jones Industrials Average (or any other average). One day the market could be cheap at 3,000. The only way you can compare any now to any then in the stock market is through ratios.

BOOK VALUES

Over the years the market has generally seen its highs when the stocks of the Dow Jones Industrials Average sold for 1.7 times book value, and low points in the market have been marked when these stocks sold for less than book value.

INTEREST RATES

In the new world we seem to have entered it is difficult indeed to place an absolute high or low level on interest rates. It is clear, however, that rising interest rates are the single most ominous factor for stock prices, and falling rates—as evidenced in the historic rally of 1982—can do wonders for stock prices. Interest rates are among the "trendiest" of all economic numbers. When they are rising, don't try to outguess the future and predict a turn—wait for at least the first downtick. Rates have a great deal of inertia—if the most recent move was up, the probabilities are highly in favor of the next move being up as well, and vice versa. Rising rates help create the bargains you're looking for. A guess, and it is only a guess, is that over the next five years the highs in T-bill rates will be 15 percent and the lows will be 5 to 6 percent.

DIVIDEND YIELD

When the average yield on stocks is 3 percent less than that of long-term government bonds, the bonds become more attractive to large institutions on a risk/reward basis, and income-oriented money tends to move out of stocks. During the 1970s, when stock yields reached the 5 to 6 percent level, it proved time for a rally.

PRICE-EARNINGS RATIO

When the PE for the Dow Jones Industrials Average is below 10, it is on the low side. When it is above 15, it's getting kind of rich. These are tricky figures, though, for strong impending earnings can drop the PE, while a recession can make it soar overnight. Try to use an average of last year's, this year's and next year's projected earnings to arrive at the current multiple. If the average for the Dow stocks is $100, a market average of 1,500 (fifteen times earnings) would be quite high based on investor actions over the past decade, and a market low of 700 to 800 would be about as low as you could expect.

SYNCHRONICITY OF AVERAGES

Most studies have shown that in order to expect a market advance or decline to continue, the three key Dow Jones Averages—Industrials, Utilities, and Transportations—should all be moving "in gear." Seen over a period of a couple of months, they should all be going up, or all be going down. I would add that you can't get a truly strong market unless those averages *and* the broader-based market averages (Standard & Poor's 500, New York Stock Exchange Composite, Value Line, Zweig Unweighted) are moving in tandem.

ELECTION-YEAR CYCLE

The market tends to move up in the year before a presidential election, and continue up in the election year itself. Since World War II most major gains in the overall market have occurred during this time. Why it should be so is beyond me—perhaps investors always think things will get better—but you should not ignore so consistent a pattern.

AVERAGE LENGTH OF BULL MARKETS

Students of cycles claim that bull markets last around four years, but in my view the really powerful upward price changes in the market last only two years. Whatever the case, if a bull market has been going on for two years when you're about to invest, you might want to think twice about doing so.

AVERAGE LENGTH OF BEAR MARKETS

Here again I differ with the cycles observers. Although they feel bear markets last eighteen months to two years, the radical downward price changes seem to me to last, typically, for about twelve months. Much depends on how you measure a market. I suppose. As a Perfect Investor you should certainly begin making up your shopping list when the market's been going down for a year.

TECHNICAL PATTERNS

The overall market doesn't often make classic double bottoms the way individual stocks do. Most often the market will squeeze out all sellers with a frightening decline. Then it turns on a dime and moves upward while all the analysts are scratching their heads. In other words, look for a vee. In the overall market, *do not trust any rally that does not show greater volume than the prior decline*. Rising prices on new historically high volume are an almost sure sign of a bull market for at least the next six months, as in January 1971, 1975, 1976, March 1978, and August 1982.

GROUP INDICES

Similar to the synchronicity of the Dow Jones Averages, researchers have found that at least 70 percent of all the industry groups, as groups, must be in an uptrend if a bull market is to be sustained.

CONTRARY SENTIMENT ADVISERS' RATIO

Investment advisers hate to be wrong, so they tend to follow trends. What seems to happen is that the greatest majority become "believers" in the current trend just as it is about to end. The more bullish the advisers are as a group, the less faith you should have in the market. When most have nothing but bad things to say, there are no more sellers left and the market is ready for an upturn. *Investors Intelligence,* a service that surveys advisers, keeps track of the numbers; *Barron's* often reports their findings. This may seem like a nutty indicator to people who are used to following the crowd, but it's really one of the best.

MOVING AVERAGES

I'm fond of moving averages, such as the thirty-eight-week average shown on the weekly charts in the Technical Turn discussion. Most brokers have charts showing the relationship of the Dow or broader market indices to their two hundred-, forty-, and ten-day moving averages (a moving average just shows you the average price over the time period selected, and the way the price-for-time is moving). It's much better for you as a buyer if the market is above its two hundred-day moving average, and much worse if it's below.

NEW HIGHS AND LOWS

In a real bull market, you'll see increasing numbers of new highs and stable levels of new lows. Watch out if the former starts to decline and the latter increase.

ADVANCE/DECLINE

No bull market will last unless there are consistently more stocks advancing than declining. The reverse is true for a bear market. Often changes in the advance/decline ratio presage changes in the subsequent price levels.

CASH LEVELS

You'll often see reference in *Barron's* or other business periodicals to the amount of cash held by investing institutions. This is a very important number, because they are the main buyers, and if they don't have cash, they're not going to be buying. At market lows institutional cash can reach 15 percent of their total assets (it sometimes goes even higher). When that cash gets put into the market it produces a buying infusion of *billions*. Low cash doesn't necessarily mean the institutions will become sellers (they have a reputation for buying at tops, too), but high cash levels really start to burn in their pockets.

INDEX OF LEADING INDICATORS

Ignore.

HOUSING STARTS

High starts are bullish; low starts, bearish. This is one of the better long-term market indicators.

These indicators are a help, but they only help one get a sense of where the market is *at present*. Few can foresee the future well enough to know where the market will be in three or five years. That is why you must rely, for long-term investing, on the secure knowledge that you have bought your stocks as cheaply as stocks can ever *be* bought, by anyone, at any time.

SELECTED BUSINESS STATISTICS

SEASONALLY ADJUSTED WHERE APPLICABLE – SHADED AREA DENOTES RECESSIONS/DEPRESSIONS

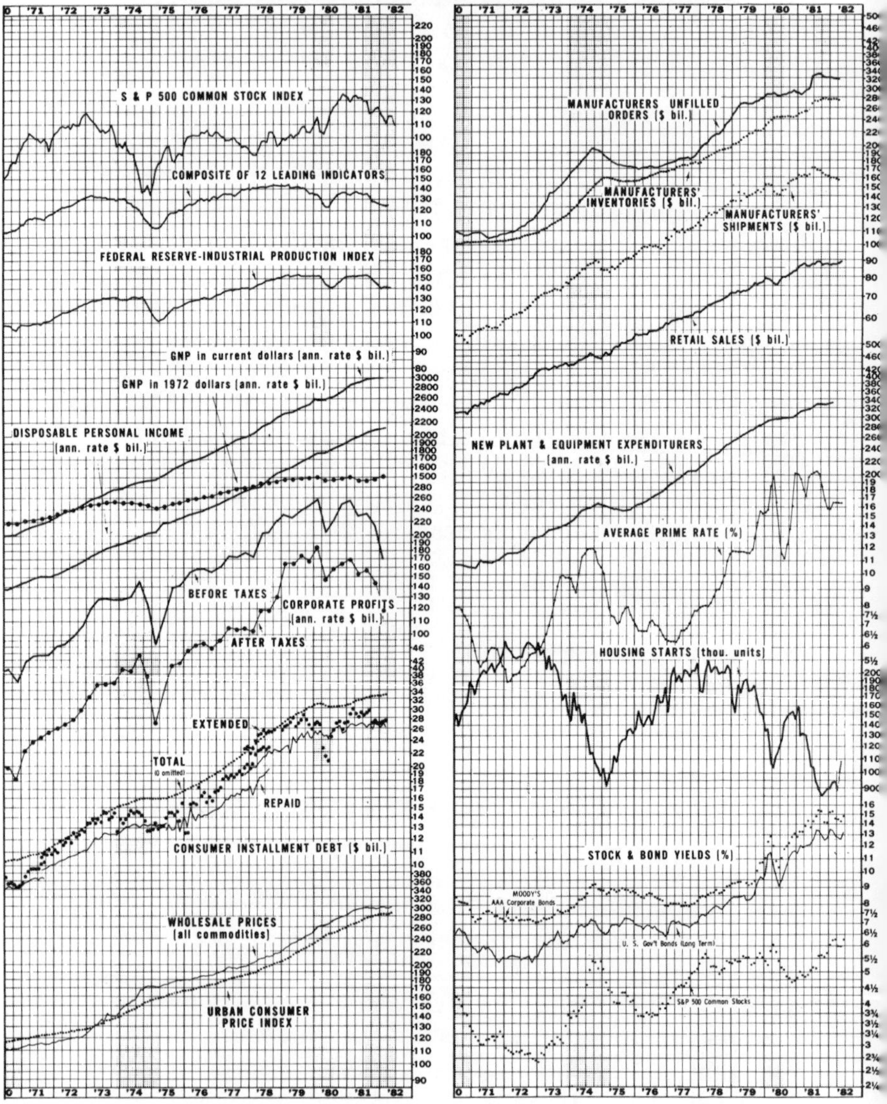
S & P 500 COMMON STOCK INDEX
COMPOSITE OF 12 LEADING INDICATORS
FEDERAL RESERVE-INDUSTRIAL PRODUCTION INDEX
GNP in current dollars (ann. rate $ bil.)
GNP in 1972 dollars (ann. rate $ bil.)
DISPOSABLE PERSONAL INCOME (ann. rate $ bil.)
BEFORE TAXES
CORPORATE PROFITS (ann. rate $ bil.)
AFTER TAXES
EXTENDED
TOTAL (0 omitted)
REPAID
CONSUMER INSTALLMENT DEBT ($ bil.)
WHOLESALE PRICES (all commodities)
URBAN CONSUMER PRICE INDEX
MANUFACTURERS UNFILLED ORDERS ($ bil.)
MANUFACTURERS' INVENTORIES ($ bil.)
MANUFACTURERS' SHIPMENTS ($ bil.)
RETAIL SALES ($ bil.)
NEW PLANT & EQUIPMENT EXPENDITURERS (ann. rate $ bil.)
AVERAGE PRIME RATE (%)
HOUSING STARTS (thou. units)
STOCK & BOND YIELDS (%)
MOODY'S AAA Corporate Bonds
U. S. Gov't Bonds (Long Term)
S&P 500 Common Stocks
'71 '72 '73 '74 '75 '76 '77 '78 '79 '80 '81 '82

11

Holding and Selling

All our sins come from sloth and impatience,
and sloth comes from impatience.
—Franz Kafka

You've got to know what the act of investing does to your mind and emotions, and maintain an awareness of it, if you want to succeed as an investor. This does not apply just to stocks. There is a mind-set without which you cannot succeed in investments of any kind—real estate or gold or fine paintings or American antiques. The *lack of awareness* of the necessary mind-set is the precise phenomenon that produces the bargains you are buying as a Perfect Investor—so it's clear that you've got to become stronger—more perfect, you might say—than the average investor who has been fearfully dumping stock into your hands.

As I discussed at some length in Chapter 2, the act of investing produces a psychic energy excitation. There is no sense trying to deny this excitation, or pretending you're immune to it. Even if you hold only one stock (perhaps especially so), you are going to be subject to the oscillating inner emotions of covetousness and anxiety. You need to accept the fact that this happens as a natural part of the investing process and not hide from it.

Indeed, we're talking about the basic problem of all investing. Once it's recognized as a problem, though, like any problem, you can then begin to think about solutions.

Long-term investors are more subject to energy charges that produce anxiety than covetousness. Covetousness provides the initial stimulus that results in action—the action of buying a stock. There is not much anxiety involved in buying a Perfect Investment stock—at least there should not be, because you as an investor know right from the start:

1. The probabilities of the stock going much lower are as minimized as humanly possible.
2. The stock at its low price represents purchase of a portion of the company that issued the shares at a true bargain level relative to the company's potential earning power.
3. Historically, stocks that meet the Perfect Investment criteria are 97 percent more likely to go higher than not.

You invest in Perfect Investment stocks with the confidence of a real-estate investor—knowing that you've bought a bargain and that if you hold on to it long enough the market eventually will recognize if not its true value, at least a much higher value.

But as a long-term investor, you have to *hold* or there won't *be* any long term. To *hold* an investment means *not to sell,* most assuredly. But it also means *to hold yourself.* Holding yourself for the long term—that's really the essence of successful investing. You choose the stock as your object. In choosing your object you create a kind of union between yourself and the object: For as long as you own the stock you are identified in part by the statement, "He (or she) is an owner of XYZ Corporation." You may be many other things, but you are that as well. Like the lover who cannot be perceived as a lover without simultaneously perceiving the object of his love, once you own a stock your mind and your property fuse in an indistinguishable unity. Like the lover, as long as you maintain the relationship you are going to have to tolerate the energy excitations of the ups and downs that your life with the stock will inevitably see. When things don't go your way and you become afraid that the relationship is going to harm you, you will experience *anxiety*. You must be *aware* that you are experiencing anxiety—in a stockholding as in all of life—in order to prevent the anxiety from controlling you and forcing impulsive actions.

Against the natural anxieties that develop as you hold your stock, you must hold yourself. That doesn't mean that you shut your eyes and wish you weren't feeling anything. You've got *to let yourself feel the anxiety*, experience it as an interesting natural phenomenon, feel it while maintaining a kind of psychic distance and observatory state. It is only when we try to *avoid* the feelings within that we feel compelled to take frantic actions we imagine will provide relief.

That's probably the major problem for investors—selling often appears to be the easy route for relief from anxiety. Anxiety is like the monster that waits on the darkened stairs when you are a child. The more you fear the "thing" that hides on the stairs, the more you feel the need to cry so that someone will come and turn on the lights—to relieve you of your anxiety. It's true with any feeling. The more we're afraid to feel it, the more frightening the feeling itself becomes . . . until it has become such a monster of the psyche that we become capable of doing rash, self-destructive things to avoid coming face to face with the feelings. Rather than experience the occasional anxiety that comes from holding a stock for a while, many investors will rashly sell before the time is right.

There is a series of rules that tell you when the time is right for selling, but you've got to get yourself that far first. You've got to establish your position and hold it until the selling signal appears. You've got to toss your hat into the ring and leave it there. This is the only way to reap really big profits. The system will get you what you want, but you've got to follow its rules.

Once you've permitted yourself to feel your anxiety,

you can begin to apply some tricks to reduce it and tolerate it better. Go ahead, tell yourself how you really feel. *Articulate it.* Break the superstition. Say, "I'm afraid I'm going to take a loss." Say, "I'm afraid I'm going to lose all the profits that I waited for so long." Say, "I feel as if I can't hold out any longer even though I know the stock is still cheap and rising." Say, "Maybe I should be content with a few points and move on." Let yourself know it when you feel negative, when you've contracted around your energy excitations. *Just don't do anything stupid.*

The venting itself is the first step toward relief, the relief that you need so that you can stay the course on your systematic program to attain long-term gains. Take out the dirty laundry so you can wash it.

Once you know you're uptight, there are some ways to reduce and tolerate anxiety. *The whole goal is to make it easy for you to be patient.* Patience is profit for the long-term investor. This is a race won by tortoises, not hares, and the tortoises win big.

1. Review Past History:

The first important thing you've got to do to reduce anxiety and develop patience is to freshen your realization of the value of this system. Turn in this book to the full record of the 1970s and examine it. Get a good sense of how much money you can make, either with one individual stock or through making Perfect Investments as an ongoing program. The worst thing in investing is to feel lost, that you're without a road map to profits. And go beyond the record in this book. Take a copy of your latest chartbook (go to the library or your broker if you haven't got one) and see how all the Perfect Investments have done over the past few years. Get in tune again with the cycle of decline and renewal, how stocks that are given up for dead by investors magically come to life again. Restore your confidence that the approach really works, and that it works because it is governed by rules that have to be followed.

2. *Keep Away from the Jiggles:*

As a long-term investor you don't want to know how the stock did today, nor yesterday, nor tomorrow. The closer you get to the daily fluctuations of the market and your stocks, the more miserable you're going to be, for each jiggle of prices—up or down—restimulates the energy excitation within you. *You don't need to know the prices, for the selling rules go into effect automatically.* Nothing in the market goes straight up or straight down. There are always short fallbacks during a rise, always short rallies during a decline. If you pay attention to every rise and fall, you're going to be a nervous wreck by the time you finally cash in for your profits, and you're going to be asking yourself if the ordeal was worth it. Things don't have to be this way. Investing can actually be a very pleasant and entertaining affair—though short-term traders in the market would never believe it. Avoid the newspaper, avoid the business section; most of all, *avoid the stock tables*. Don't rush for the paper in the morning just because you own some stock and its price happens to be reported each day. Forget it. A half point up, a half point down—it'll put sweat on your face and accomplish nothing. You know why those businessmen you see on the train are always poring over the stock tables on the way to work every morning? Because they have no confidence that the stocks they own are going to go up in time.

I know it's hard to keep away. We all tend to be fans, we become fans of our investments, wanting to know how the stock is doing in the standings after each day's battle against the other "teams," wanting to know if our stock won the World Series or was eliminated from the league. But this impulse needs to be controlled. You're not a fan. You're a cold-eyed, intelligent, methodical, long-term investor. You buy what others don't want right now. You're apart from the crowd, by the nature of what you're doing. So don't join in with the crowd when they shove their noses inside *The Wall Street Journal* seeking magical clues to the future. The clues aren't there. Market losers are the people who haven't learned that yet.

Just as important in keeping away from the jiggles is making yourself scarce to your broker. Brokers are the ultimate jiggle watchers. Not only do they see the jiggles in the paper, they've also got their computer screens jiggling at them all day long. They want to phone you and say, "Hi. Your stock just jiggled up." They phone because they want you to sell and take your profits. If you do, they'll get a commission on the sale and one on your next investment. They'll call if it jiggles down, too. Same reason.

Don't call your broker to ask him what to do. Follow the rules of your system. It's better than anything your broker's got. If your broker phones, tell him your ulcer just acted up. If he leaves a message, don't answer it. If he tries to give you a tip, tell him you're going to change brokers if he ever gives you a tip again. If he's got information about one of your holdings, accept only something in writing—*in the mail.* You're best off using a discount broker who won't bother you and will charge you less than half of the big-name brokers' fees for the same execution service.

Ask no one for advice. No one but you will be making your Perfect Investments, so no one else will know exactly what criteria are important. The worst confusion you can have is the application of someone else's criteria to your system, which may have totally differing premises. Some investors, for example, buy only when a stock hits a new yearly high. What are they going to know about superbargains? Investment advisory newsletters aren't much help, either. Each one has its own pet theory of investing, each one looks for different characteristics to predict the future price course of a stock.

So you'll find no help there. You'll find no help anywhere, really. You're on your own and all alone. Holding on.

And hold on you must. All the really great stock market fortunes have been made by investors who saw the wisdom of holding on to their positions until the positions were ripe. The great "gunslinger" managers of the mutual funds of the 1960s are gone now—their short-term trading could not hold up when the market got too high. All the legendary speculators lost it in the end, no matter how well they might have done once in a buying or selling panic.

Hear what master investor Jesse Livermore, who rose to fame in the 1920s and 1930s, had to say on the issue:

"After spending many years in Wall Street and after making and losing millions of dollars, I want to tell you this: It was never my thinking that made the big money for me. It was always my sitting. Got that? My sitting tight . . . Men who can be both right and sit tight are uncommon. I found it one of the hardest things to learn. But it is only after a stock operator has firmly grasped this that he can make big money."

Holding: Year One

As I've stressed throughout this book, Perfect Investments are long-term investments. Every effort should be made to hold your stock for at least twelve months, to obtain the more favorable long-term capital-gains stock treatment. If you sell after eleven months you might pay as much as 50 percent in tax on your profit. If you hold for twelve months or longer, your maximum tax is only 20 percent. Although it can be foolhardy to hold on to a declining stock simply to get the better tax treatment, your net after-tax gain can be much larger on a smaller long-term vs. a larger short-term gain. At a 50 percent tax rate, for example, a 100 percent short-term taxable gain yields an after-tax net of 50 percent. Under the long-term rates, on the other hand, you require only a 62.5 percent gain to net the same *after-tax* 50 percent gain.

A glance at the Perfect Investment record will show you that the average *best* gain (over twelve months) for the group of stocks is 19 percent greater than the average gain at the end of twelve months precisely. (Sometimes the best gain is the same as the end-of-twelve-months gain.) Given the impossibility of knowing exactly when the top in a stock has been reached, a policy of holding, initially, for at least twelve months rates a clear priority.

But what about the handful of stocks that are terminal cases? Do we hold them to the bitter end?

Of course not. As I mentioned in the discussion of bottoming patterns, the price action of the stocks is the best indication of the accuracy of our overall analysis. You don't have to worry, as a rule, about buying stocks that are headed for bankruptcy because you don't *get* a bottoming price pattern in those companies. The rally or double bottom that you require before you'll invest simply doesn't appear in those stocks.

One or two, though, will inevitably slip through the net. Perhaps a positive change in the company's fortunes is suddenly canceled out by new problems, or by a surprise rise in interest rates. How long can you hold on to a company if the stock isn't performing well? How much patience do you really have to have?

The record of Perfect Investment stocks answers our questions.

No Perfect Investment stock declined below the low of the bottom pattern during the first twelve months. That is, if there was a vee, the stock did not go lower than the low of the vee. If a double bottom, the stock did not go lower than the *first* low of the double bottom. In fact, it is very rare for a stock to move lower than the second low of the double bottom—the one closest to the buy point.

Taking this characteristic of Perfect Investment stocks into consideration, the holding rule for the first twelve months becomes clear:

Hold your stock for the first twelve months no matter what happens, unless the stock declines below the bottom pattern low.

Remember that only 3 percent of Perfect Investment stocks show any decline at all if they've been held for twelve months. What we're trying to accomplish with this broad loss parameter is to set up an environment in which the very short-term up-and-down jiggles in the stocks—which simply are part of the game—can be tolerated with a low anxiety level. We don't want to exit from a perfectly good stock merely because its price begins to bounce a bit. In almost every case a dip is going to be followed by a rally. In the few cases where the dip goes as far as the rule allows, the rally isn't going to be worth waiting for. You're better off redeploying your cash elsewhere.

On the day you buy your stock you should establish your stop-loss. You can place a stop-loss order with your broker—the stock will automatically be sold when it hits the stop-loss point. This is the best way to ensure you don't get emotional and sell too quickly or refuse to do so when the time to act draws near. You can, as an alternative, keep the stop-loss point in your head and keep track of the stock on a regular basis. But don't you have better things to do than keep track of stock prices? And don't you have better things to put in your head? The more automatic an investment strategy, the better.

See also Chapter 14, wherein I discuss the limitation of risk through the use of options.

Holding and Selling: After the First Twelve Months

The first twelve months are seen as primarily a holding period—giving the stock a chance to consolidate the buying momentum that has become evident and allowing it some latitude to develop the almost inevitable price appreciation. The goal, in fact, for the first twelve months is to *avoid* prematurely selling the investment.

After the first twelve months our relationship evolves from one characterized by "holding on" to a quest for the appropriate time to sell. We want to preserve the gains that have already appeared but not "leave too much on the table" in the form of further gains that may materialize.

We are no longer concerned with the tax benefits of long-term capital gains. While there is considerable benefit in holding for twelve months, the tax advantage does not increase for any period beyond twelve months—unless, of course, you never sell at all. (Some investors have followed this policy, buying cheap and never selling at all, with success. Please feel free to do it if it suits your psyche.) Since the tax issue has been resolved, our attention now turns to other problems, such as: What is the best point at which to sell to obtain the highest possible annual returns?

The key word in that question is *annual*. While it gives you a great feeling to pick a stock that goes up, say, 200 percent in five years, the feeling is mere egotism and doesn't address the reality of making profits in the market. The only true measure is your annualized return over a number of years, or, better yet, your compounded return. Compounded return is the net gain on original capital plus the net gain on the reinvestment of all gains and dividends.

In the case of Perfect Investment stocks we can see that the average stock is up 53.57 percent at the end of twelve months and 84.45 percent after twenty-four months; 84 percent is better than 53 percent, right?

Wrong. On a purely statistical basis, the gain in the second twelve months is only 31 percent (84 percent less 53 percent) vs. a gain of nearly twice that much in the first twelve months.* Seen this way, the second year of holding is only half as good as the first year.

The obvious conclusion—again, on a statistical basis—is that you will show far better profits over the long term if you sell everything after twelve months and buy new stocks to replace those sold.

That's not an unacceptable policy, but you must remember that statistics are not the market; they only provide a way of measuring the market. The investing task would be a great deal simpler if we had only to deal with numbers, with averages, but that's not our fate. We cannot ignore the numbers, but we also can't afford to ignore the fact that the numbers are the result of market processes and that the market—the investing environment—is different year after year.

The statistics tell us what we can expect, on average, but they don't tell us enough about what is happening *now*. Is this a time that is pulling up the average or dragging it down? Often the same stock that pulled up the average last year is weighing it down right now. We cannot simply look at the probabilities if we wish to maximize profits; we must defer to the real world of stock trading as well. After the first twelve months, clearly, our goal is going to be to *stay invested* in stocks that are continuing to go up and to *sell* stocks that have stopped rising. We need the big gainers to boost our average performance, and we'll also boost performance by cutting the dead wood. Since the movements of an individual stock—as opposed to our total group—are only roughly predictable, it is to be expected that some of the stocks we hold further will perform disappointingly and that some we cut will prove to be big gainers. Taken in toto, however, it is quite possible to exceed the statistical

*Based on starting capital. However, after twelve months your capital has already increased by 53 percent, so the additional gain or compound gain is only about 20 percent in the second year.

average substantially by instituting selling rules that have some built-in flexibility (as opposed to mechanistic formulas such as "sell all stocks after twelve months").

On the other hand, much depends on the level of involvement you want or are able to have in the market. If you want to remain as utterly detached as possible, sell after twelve months. Bear in mind that this policy will result in some years in which you are completely uninvested.

The best approach for the average investor who wants to maximize profits and cut slow movers is the *simple trend line*.

A simple trend line merely takes the last two declines in an upward-moving stock and connects them with a line. This line is extended into the future to establish an upward trend and its degree of momentum. As you can see in the following chart, the creation of a trend line is, in effect, a decision to hold the stock as long as the momentum of its ascent does not decrease. As long as the stock continues to gain as much in price over time as it has in the recent past, it will not fall below the trend line. When it does fall below the trend line, the probabilities of a resumption in its price trend are severely decreased. There's no "scientific" reason for this: It's just what happens in the market—probably because many investors consciously and unconsciously utilize simple trend lines as an investment decision tool.

Making Trend Lines

You need to use judgment and common sense in making trend lines; then, when you've made your decision, you must stick to it with discipline. Trend lines are a sound approach for maximizing profits, but not when you second-guess yourself.

The two factors that influence the way you'll make your trend line are the nature of the bottom pattern and the progress of the stock.

When the stock shows a double bottom or a vee with

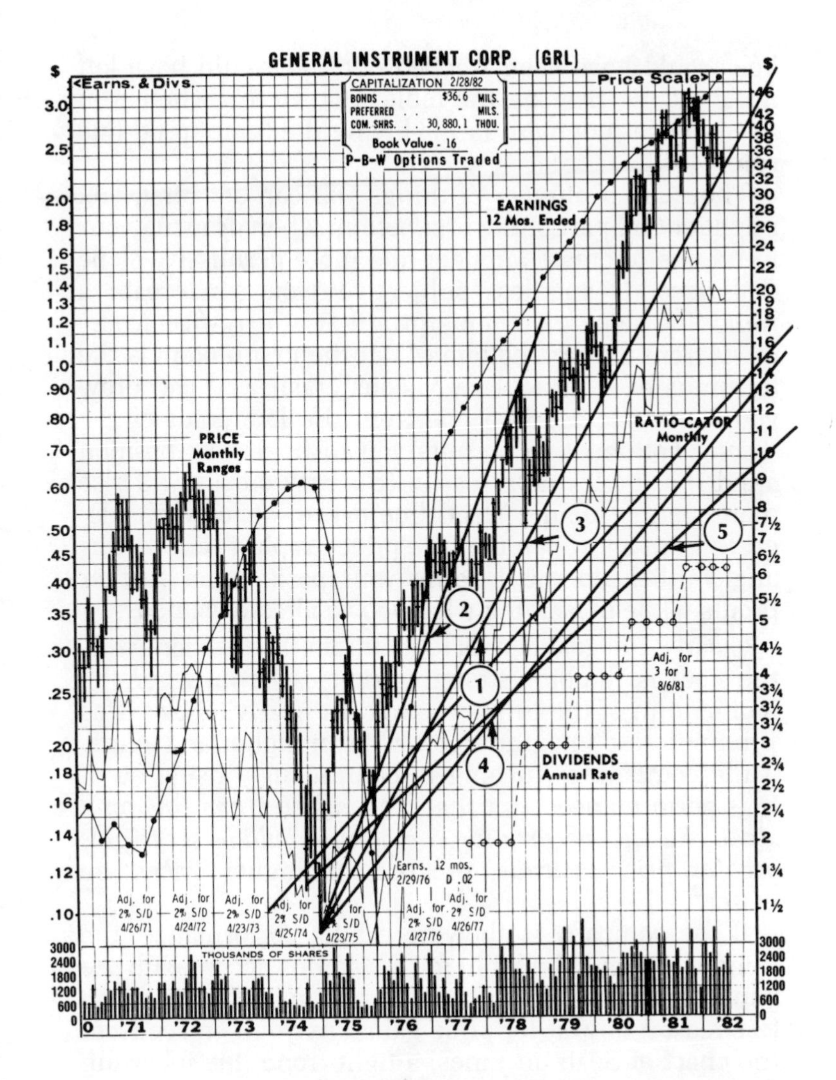

some kind of correction, the first trend line (which you set *after* the first year) is relatively easy to create.

In the chart of General Instrument you can see that the pair of bottoms in the bottom pattern (December 1974 and December 1975) sets the coordinates for a trend line that includes the entire rise of the stock (1). But what if the second bottom had been much higher?

You would have been stopped out and would have left much of the rise "on the table" (2). Here's where you need to use judgment in modifying the basic trend-line rule.

There are a number of things you can do. First, you might cut off part of the first bottom when drawing your trend line to create a milder and more permissive slope (3). Second—and less subjective—you can create a trend-line slope that runs upward at a *forty-five-degree angle* from the first bottom (4). If the first bottom is the terminus of a particularly vicious crash, you can draw your forty-five-degree slope from the low point of the *second* bottom; this permits you to hold your position amid the jiggles more easily (5). Few stocks will rise more sharply than a trend line drawn at forty-five degrees from a low point on the price graph. A line at this angle will keep you holding your position for further profits while preserving what you've already gained.

Clearly, the goal here is to maintain the position while the stock is climbing strongly, and close it out when the momentum of the run is waning. In nearly all cases, as you might assume, the stock will run higher and longer if the company is turning in continuously rising earnings performances. For that reason, the *trend line on a stock of a well-performing company should be set to give greater price latitude;* the odds of higher prices are better.

If the company is showing erratic performance, the trend line should be set in fairly rigorous accord with the pattern of prices. There is more risk in such a stock, so less reason to wait for price gains. As you can see from the chart of Seatrain Lines, a tight trend line following the important bottoms (1) managed to keep you in the stock until it had hit almost its exact peak price. When earnings started to fall away again, you were elsewhere.

As time goes by you need to let the stock "talk" to you and tell you where to put the trend line. The double bottom in Searle gives us no real clues as to how to set the trend line after year one, so the forty-five-degree-

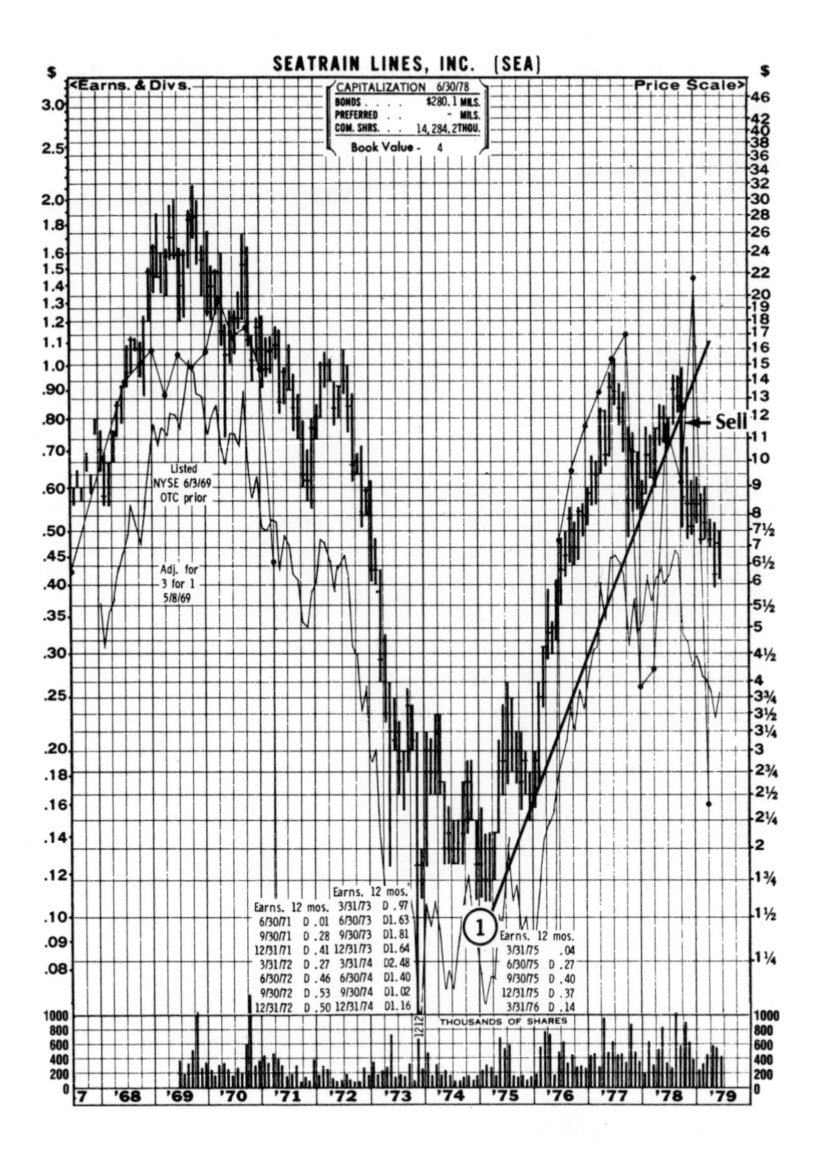
SEATRAIN LINES, INC. (SEA)
<Earns. & Divs.
Price Scale>
CAPITALIZATION 6/30/78
BONDS . . . . $280.1 MILS.
PREFERRED . . - MILS.
COM. SHRS. . . 14,284.2THOU.
Book Value - 4
Listed NYSE 6/3/69 OTC prior
Adj. for 3 for 1 5/8/69
Sell
Earns. 12 mos.
6/30/71 D .01
9/30/71 D .28
12/31/71 D .41
3/31/72 D .27
6/30/72 D .46
9/30/72 D .53
12/31/72 D .50
Earns. 12 mos.
3/31/73 D .97
6/30/73 D1.63
9/30/73 D1.81
12/31/73 D1.64
3/31/74 D2.48
6/30/74 D1.40
9/30/74 D1.02
12/31/74 D1.16
1
Earns. 12 mos.
3/31/75 .04
6/30/75 D .27
9/30/75 D .40
12/31/75 D .37
3/31/76 D .14
THOUSANDS OF SHARES
'68 '69 '70 '71 '72 '73 '74 '75 '76 '77 '78 '79

angle approach seems most appropriate, especially since Searle is showing modest, albeit not stunning, signs of recovery (1). By 1980 we started to see some fairly wide—nervous-making—swings in price, as investors were definitely of two minds about Searle's prospects. Then, in October 1980 we saw an extraordinary volume spike (2), which is very reminiscent of the action at a climax bottom, telling us that further declines are unlikely. A new trend line connecting that bottom with the one prior, or a new trend line set at forty-five degrees from that bottom, is the appropriate change point (3 and 4).*

As you can see, each stock presents a somewhat different challenge. You can never expect to discover the exactly right trend line that will permit you *all* of the gains and none of the premature sales. If you use a forty-five-degree angle and reset your line as significant reactions occur, you'll nearly always keep the best performing stocks and eliminate the weaker ones.

Remember: If you set your trend lines and use them religiously, you will *never* get caught holding stocks in a major downturn, numbed by the evaporation of profits and not knowing what to do.

Don't go running to the charts every month to revise your trend-line stop-loss points. After one year, find your trend line and stick to it. Make a change only if there's been a significant decline and then a renewal of price increases. At most, other than that, you need only review your trend lines every six months or every year.

In a way, the selling rules (and, by definition, the holding rules) boil down to a pair of very simple principles:

---

1. **Hold your stock for twelve months.**
2. **Continue to hold until a simple trend line is broken. Then sell.**

---

*The forty-five-degree-angle approach works with "semi-log" charts, such as the Securities Research Charts used in this book, but it may not work with other charts, such as Mansfield, when scale changes are made to accommodate major price moves.

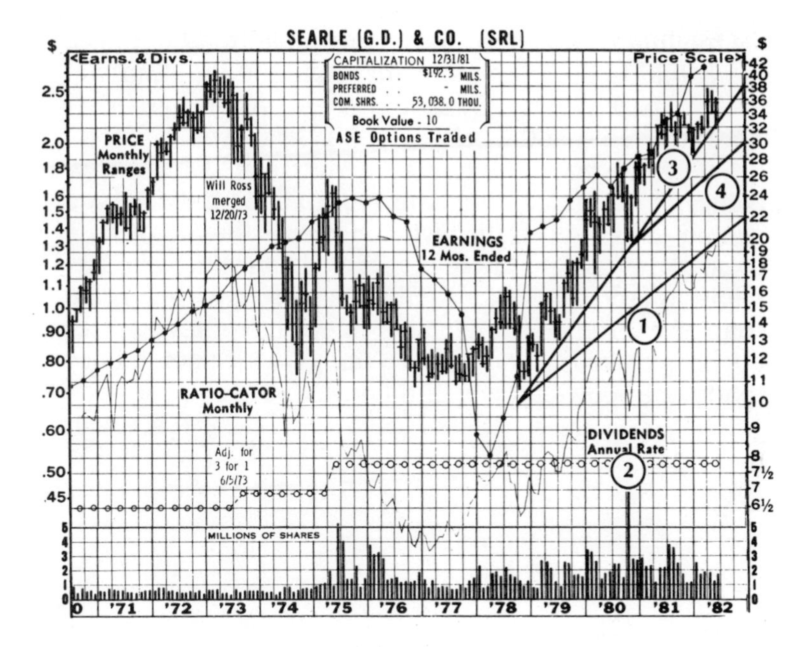

If it suits your psyche, you can sell after twelve months, or after twenty-four months. If you'll look at the record, you'll see that on a statistical basis the annualized returns decline the longer you hold the stock beyond twelve months, though the annualized rate difference between one and two years, 53 percent versus 42 percent, still is not so great considering that you will have no more stocks losing money after two years than after one year. I think it's worth the extra effort to follow the trend lines, though. Often you can stay with a stock as it rises straight up for years and years. And you'll get out of one when its day in the sun is over. I have tried all kinds of combinations of factors to computer-model a profit-maximizing approach superior to the simple trend line after twelve months. Nothing is better equipped to deal with a wide variety of stocks, each with its own price characteristics. In this case, the simplest parameter has proved to be the best.

PART FOUR

MASTERING THE SYSTEM

12

Two Perfect Investment Stocks: Start to Finish

Now that we have been through the rules and rationale of Perfect Investing, you may find it instructive to review the thought process. Here we will examine two companies whose stock suffered from the mass mentality of the market and whose true values reaffirmed themselves when investor fear simply could not be sustained any longer in the face of corporate facts.

Few stocks could be a more obvious selection than Bandag, Inc. Bandag has a unique process for retreading tires—their product lasts nearly as long as a new tire at about half the cost and is popular with truckers as a cost-saving device. Their market is permanent, and they are by far the leader in the field—they've got the "franchise." Now, tire retreading may not seem like a very glamorous field to you, but in 1973 Wall Street valued this company at nearly $500 million—it's something more than a garage on the highway. In 1973 investors paid a whopping forty times earnings for the company—its earnings had grown in a straight upward line from $.25 in 1970 to $1.40 four years later. They evidently knew the trick for making money. Investors respected that—so much so, indeed, that during the 1973–74 crash, Bandag's shares hardly budged in price. In large part this was due to the company's ability to continue earning at its torrid clip even during the recession.

But in 1975 the pace of earnings growth flattened out a bit. Investors who had been lovers of the stock, high and expansive, felt slapped and betrayed. Their dreams of constantly doubling earnings to infinity were suddenly dashed rudely. Though the overall market had become expansive and filled with the pleasure of rising prices and profits during 1975 and 1976, Bandag's supporters became fearful of news that might be worse than a mere slowing down of growth. They sobered up about the high price-earnings multiple. If the damn company can't double earnings every year, what am I doing holding shares at forty times earnings?

The selling continued. Analysts announced, in ominous tones, that Bandag's patents were running out and that the company would die without them. They conveniently forgot to mention that Bandag had nearly all the important customers in its business and that the entry "ticket" for competitors was steep—it requires equipment and trained workers in addition to a process (patented or not) to come up with a finished product. And how many competitors would come rushing in against a company whose earnings were *slowing*? In my opinion, Bandag had matured from an exciting growth company to a solidly entrenched industrial business. That's just the point at which "oversexed" growth investors are heading for new things, young and blond.

Bandag went on my watch list. A few brief rallies could do nothing to stem the overall downturn in prices, until by 1977 Bandag had dropped to 25 percent of its former value, and the Perfect Investment lights began to flash. At precisely the 75 percent decline point the stock began to rally, as stocks often do in such a situation.

Meanwhile, during the decline Bandag had shown the kind of liveliness and resiliency I like to see. Like any sane person, I don't want to invest in a company that's on the way to oblivion; I want live meat cheap. Earnings

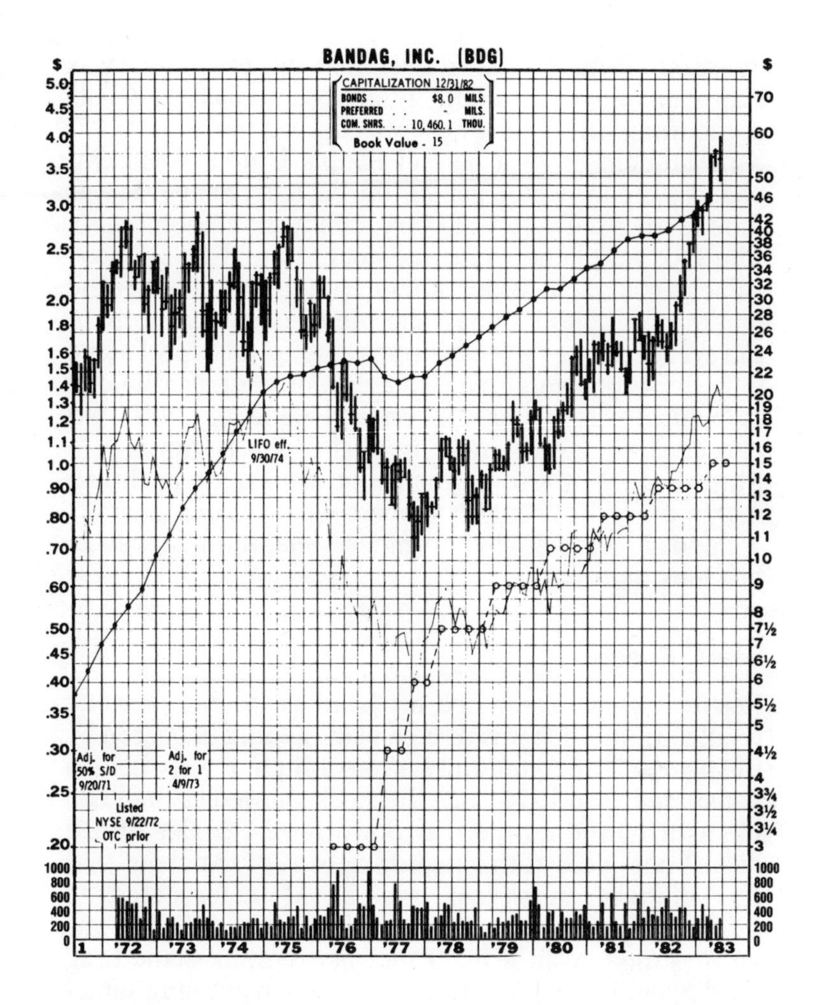

showed only two mild quarterly declines during the entire two-year stock price crash and had not declined at all from their level when the stock sold four times higher. Indeed, by late 1978, earnings were *twice* what they were at the peak in 1973. Book value had risen 50 percent, from ten dollars per share to fifteen dollars per share. Dividends were instituted in 1976 and had steadily risen, until the dividend yield on the stock was approximately equal to the interest being paid on T-bills at the time. An earnings vee was developing.

In January 1979 a perfect double bottom was completed with an upside gap off the second decline. It was time to invest. There was, very simply, no reason not to. The risk was gone from the stock. It sold below book value and at about seven times earnings—well below the market multiple. Further, the pre-election-year rally in the overall market was beginning, so I could expect some help from the overall environment for equities. Bandag rose nicely, resisting the price decline of 1982 and participating handsomely in the boom beginning in August 1982. My investment had tripled on an initial maximum risk of roughly 30 percent.

Bandag had risen, by the end of 1982, right back to its previous high.

Sears, Roebuck & Co.

For five years I scratched my head as the number one retailer in America was treated with nothing but scorn by the investment community. From a high of forty dollars per share in the 1976 rally, the stock showed virtually no life as it moved all the way down to just under fifteen dollars per share at the beginning of 1981. At about that time the teller in my local bank asked me for a stock to buy with a small inheritance she'd received. Sears was on my mind. Wait a bit, I told her, I think something good's coming up. (You think twice when advising someone at the bank—even a teller.) I began some research and reminded myself to be patient.

The stock had declined to just a hair above 35 percent of its former value. Ordinarily that hair would have disqualified it, but since the overall market had clearly been up during this time, especially during 1979–80, I availed myself of the extra 5 percent option. Even though earnings had slacked off in 1980, the company still was earning more per share than it had in 1976, when the price had begun its decline. And dividends had increased all during the slide. At $23, the book value was way above the share price, and the book had to be understated, for much of Sears' assets were in real estate and in Allstate Insurance investment holdings that were booked at cost.

Sears didn't look like an impending corporate casualty to me. The real question was whether it would keep stumbling along or find a way to resume the kind of growth it had seen in its past, thus gaining a higher PE multiple from investors with increased optimism. Sears had been working on improving its merchandising, but would that be enough in a world increasingly dominated by discounters?

More important, its happy experience with Allstate Insurance had convinced Sears to diversify into the financial services field—and diversify in no small way. Management announced that the company intended to become a major factor in this field, and with the purchase of Coldwell Banker and Dean Witter Reynolds, Sears had overnight become a leader in both the real-estate and the securities businesses. In other words, there was "life." It was no longer just department stores and a place to get tires.

I knew these facts from general reading in the business press—Sears was closely watched if not warmly perceived—and from a perusal of Standard & Poor's data sheet (pages 188, 189). It appeared to me that Sears had already spent the money necessary to change the efficiency and character of its business, and with a PE ratio of 7 and a dividend yield of 10 percent, it would be very hard to lose money in the stock. Assuming its diversification and new efficiencies worked well, it seemed to me the stock would have to double at the very least.

On the monthly chart I saw an excellent double bottom formation indicating an end to the selling. It was a particularly notable bottom, since there was a "climax" of heavy trading volume right at the lowest price point, implying that the last of the sellers had bailed out. Shortly thereafter even heavier volume appeared as

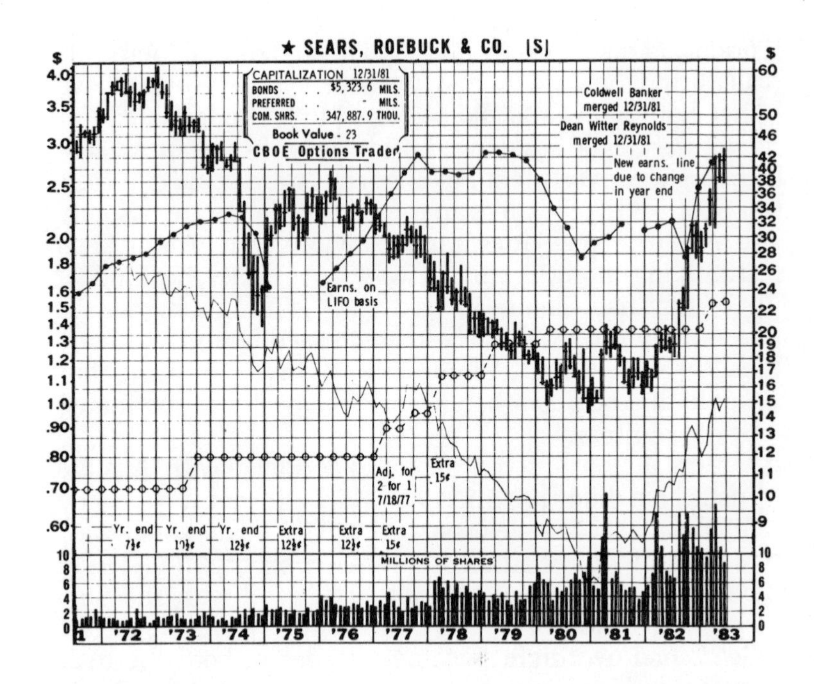

prices began to move upward; the buyers were arriving.

Looking for a turn pattern, I moved over to the daily basis charts (though I could, of course, have used the weekly basis charts). There I saw a nice momentum-gap in March 1982, three months after the merger of Coldwell Banker and Dean Witter Reynolds. By then the big money had concluded Sears's new direction was indeed promising. After many weeks of flat prices, the stock suddenly jumped out of its trading range, and the stage was set for a sustained move. Should I wait for the second run? I thought not. Such a big company selling for so little, such a high dividend!

I went back to my teller, "Well, here I am a year later," I told her, "and it's finally time for you to buy a stock." I had her invest in Sears, and I invested for myself and my family. I'd rarely seen an investment with so little risk, and I was sure the profits would take care of themselves.

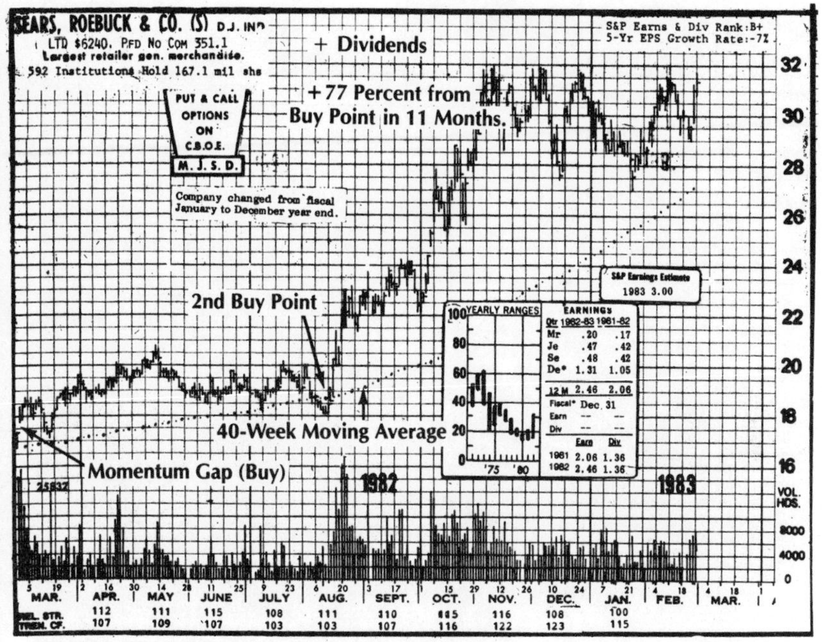

Reprinted courtesy Standard & Poor's Corporation

When the boom hit in August there was no need to look frantically for stocks. The position had already been taken, at a very good price. I was content to sit back and let the updraft do its work. It is no coincidence, I think, that as stocks were generally being revalued upward, Sears—previously selling for an irrationally low price—became a leader. By the end of the year, *Sears had proved to be the best-performing stock among those that are components of the Dow Jones Industrials Average.* Twelve months from the buy point the stock had doubled. The weak, as they say, shall become the strong.

Sears, Roebuck 2002

NYSE Symbol S Put & Call Options on CBOE

Price	Range	P-E Ratio	Dividend	Yield	S&P Ranking
May 25'82 19½	1982 20¾-15¾	9	1.36	7.0%	B+

Summary

Sears is a diversified general merchandise, insurance, real estate and financial services company. The company acquired Dean Witter Reynolds Organization (a leading factor in the securities industry) and Coldwell, Banker & Co. (a real estate broker) at the end of 1981. Various policies have been adopted to lift profitability in retailing, and contributions from diversified operations should expand over the longer term.

Current Outlook

Earnings for 1982 are estimated at $2.40 a share, versus the $2.06 of 1981.

Dividends should continue at $0.34 quarterly.

The major merchandise group should experience a recovery trend during 1982, aided by a profits improvement program. Income contribution from Allstate should remain significant, with some increase likely for the year. Profits from financial services will be bolstered by the acquisition of Dean Witter Reynolds, and the real estate group now includes Coldwell, Banker. Larger total income is expected.

[4,5]Total Revenues (Billion $)

Quarter:	1982	1981	1980-1	1979-80
Mar.	6.44	5.84	5.47	3.63
Jun.		6.66	6.00	4.25
Sep.		6.83	6.46	4.53
Dec.		8.03	7.26	5.10
		27.36	25.19	17.51

Revenues for the March, 1982 quarter rose 10.3%, year to year. Costs rose less rapidly, but after much higher interest expense and smaller capital gains, the pretax loss was $6.8 million, versus the year-earlier loss of $62.6 million. After substantial tax credits in both periods, net income rose 35.2%, to $71.4 million.

[4]Capital Share Earnings ($)

Quarter:	1982	1981	1980-1	1979-80
Mar.	0.20	0.17	0.19	0.47
Jun.		0.42	0.42	0.60
Sep.		0.42	0.43	0.67
Dec.		1.05	0.88	0.80
		2.06	1.92	2.54

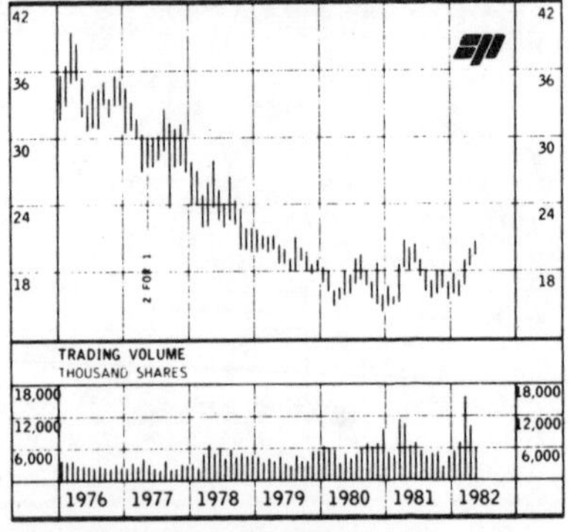

Important Developments

Apr. '82—In the March quarter, the Merchandise group cut its loss to $23.2 million, from $62.9 million a year earlier, on a sales gain of 3.5%. Revenues of the Allstate group rose 10.1%, but net income rose only 1.8%. The Dean Witter Financial Services group lost $10.2 million, while the Coldwell Banker group had a nominal profit. Net realized capital gains and other income totaled $29.1 million, down from $45.2 million a year earlier.

Mar. '82—The chairman looked for continued improvement in merchandising operations. The mid-year tax cut and slowing of inflation in energy and food costs should contribute to strengthening sales in the second half of 1982.

Next earnings report due in late July.

Per Share Data ($)

Yr. End Dec. 31[1]	[2]1981	[6]1980	1979	1978	1977	1976	1975	[2]1974	1973	[2]1972
Book Value	**22.74**	24.38	23.53	21.98	20.27	18.61	16.72	16.60	15.87	14.38
Earnings[3]	**2.06**	1.92	2.54	2.86	2.62	2.18	1.65	1.63	2.16	1.96
Dividends	**1.36**	1.36	1.28	1.27	1.08	0.80	0.92½	0.92½	0.87½	0.80½
Payout Ratio	**66%**	71%	50%	44%	41%	37%	56%	57%	40%	41%
Prices—High	**20⅞**	19⅝	21⅞	28⅛	34⅝	39⅝	37⅛	45⅛	61⅝	59¾
Low	**14⅞**	14⅜	17¾	19¾	27	30¾	24⅛	20¾	39⅛	48⅝
P/E Ratio—	**10-7**	10-7	9-7	10-7	13-10	18-14	22-15	28-13	28-18	30-25

Data as orig. reptd. Adj. for stk. div(s). of 100% Jul. 1977. **1.** Yrs. ended Jan. 31 of fol. cal. yr. prior to 1981. **2.** Reflects merger or acquisition. **3.** Bef. spec. item(s) of +0.02 in 1972. **4.** Quarters ended April, July, Oct. & Jan. prior to 1981. **5.** Net sales prior to 1980-1. **6.** Reflects merger or acquisition and accounting change.

Standard NYSE Stock Reports
Vol. 49/No. 105/Sec. 24

June 2, 1982

Standard & Poor's Corp.
25 Broadway, NY, NY 10004

2002

Sears, Roebuck and Co.

Income Data (Million $)

Year Ended Jan. 31[1]	Revs.	Oper. Inc.	% Oper. Inc. of Revs.	Cap. Exp.	Depr.	Int. Exp.	Net Bef. Taxes	Eff. Tax Rate	[4]Net Inc.	% Net Inc. of Revs.
[2]1981	**27,357**	**2,277**	**8.3%**	**[6]348**	**295**	**1,537**	**[3] 660**	**1.5%**	**[5]650**	**2.4%**
[7]1980	25,195	2,081	8.3%	368	279	1,150	[3] 698	12.2%	606	2.4%
1979	17,514	1,336	7.6%	372	218	634	[3]1,029	21.3%	810	4.6%
1978	17,946	1,423	7.9%	324	209	527	[3]1,264	27.1%	922	5.1%
1977	17,224	1,267	7.4%	262	196	356	[3]1,194	29.8%	838	4.9%
1976	14,950	1,304	8.7%	229	170	264	[3]1,076	35.5%	695	4.6%
1975	13,640	1,234	9.0%	282	166	279	[3] 915	42.9%	[5]523	3.8%
[2]1974	13,101	1,135	8.7%	411	149	381	[3] 816	37.3%	511	3.9%
1973	12,306	1,248	10.1%	401	127	277	[3]1,113	38.9%	680	5.5%
[2]1972	10,991	1,104	10.0%	352	120	148	[3]1,030	40.4%	614	5.6%

Balance Sheet Data (Million $)

Jan. 31[1]	Cash	——Current—— Assets	Liab.	Ratio	Total Assets	Ret. on Assets	Long Term Debt	Common Equity	Total Cap.	% LT Debt of Cap.	Ret. on Equity
1981	**1,171**	**NA**	**NA**	**NA**	**34,509**	**2.0**	**[8]5,837**	**8,269**	**15,547**	**37.5%**	**7.8%**
1980	787	NA	NA	NA	28,054	2.7%	[8]3,382	7,689	12,495	27.1%	8.0%
1979	284	10,256	6,261	1.6	16,422	5.2%	2,474	7,467	10,161	24.3%	11.2%
1978	225	9,676	5,926	1.6	15,262	6.1%	2,040	7,092	9,336	21.9%	13.5%
1977	237	9,642	6,059	1.6	14,746	6.1%	1,990	6,524	8,687	22.9%	13.4%
1976	223	8,201	5,039	1.6	12,712	5.7%	1,564	5,937	7,672	20.4%	12.3%
1975	277	7,454	4,807	1.6	11,577	4.6%	1,326	5,302	6,769	19.6%	9.9%
1974	192	7,248	4,896	1.5	11,339	4.7%	1,095	5,241	6,444	17.0%	10.0%
1973	198	6,772	4,393	1.5	10,427	6.9%	981	4,993	6,034	16.2%	14.3%
1972	233	6,207	3,877	1.6	9,326	6.9%	916	4,515	5,449	16.8%	14.3%

Data as orig. reptd. **1.** Of fol. cal. yr. **2.** Reflects merger or acquisition. **3.** Incl. equity in earns. of nonconsol. subs. **4.** Bef. spec. item(s) in 1972. **5.** Reflects accounting change. **6.** Net of curr. yr. retirement and disposals. **7.** Reflects merger or acquisition and accounting change. **8.** Incl. current portion of lt. debt. NA-Not Available.

Business Summary

Sears operates through four major business groups: Sears Merchandise group, Allstate Insurance, Coldwell Banker Real Estate and Dean Witter Financial Services.

Merchandising is the largest segment, with 1981 sales of $20.2 billion mainly derived from over 850 retail stores and catalog operations. Included is $1 billion from credit operations and a slightly lesser amount from international operations in Central and South America, Spain, Mexico and Puerto Rico, and in Canada through 40% owned Simpsons-Sears.

The Allstate Insurance group had revenues of $6.8 billion in 1981 of which $5.9 billion was from property-liability insurance, $737 million from life-health insurance, and the balance from consumer finance services.

The Coldwell Banker group invests in, develops, and operates real estate and offers mortgage banking, employee relocation and mortgage guaranty insurance. Activities also include real estate brokerage and related services following the late 1981 acquisition of Coldwell Banker.

First quarter 1982 revenues were $129 million.

The Dean Witter group (acquired at 1981 year-end) engages in securities brokerage and trading, domestic and foreign investment banking, mutual fund and money management, savings and loan and related services. First quarter 1982 revenues were $300 million.

Dividend Data

Dividends have been paid since 1935. A dividend reinvestment plan is available.

Amt. of Divd. $	Date Decl.	Ex-divd. Date	Stock of Record	Payment Date
0.34	Aug. 11	Aug. 20	Aug. 26	Oct. 2'81
0.34	Nov. 10	Nov. 18	Nov. 24	Jan. 4'82
0.34	Feb. 8	Feb. 11	Feb. 19	Apr. 2'82
0.34	May 17	May 24	May 28	Jul. 2'82

Next dividend meeting: mid-Aug. '82.

Capitalization

Long Term Debt: $5,566,300,000.

Capital Stock: 350,000,000 shs. ($0.75 par). Institutions hold about 41%. Shareholders: 359,095.

Office—Sears Tower, Chicago, Ill. 60684. **Tel**—(312) 875-2500. **Chrmn & CEO**—E. R. Telling. **Pres**—A. R. Boe. **VP-Secy**—C. W. Harper. **VP-Treas**—R. F. Gurnee. **Investor Contact**—R. Greer. **Dirs**—W. O. Beers, A. R. Boe, E. A. Brennan, A. V. Casey, D. F. Craib, Jr., E. M. deWindt, L. H. Foster, R. M. Jones, A. J. Melton, Jr., N. Pace, C. W. Poulson, C. B. Rogers, J. Rosenwald II, D. H. Rumsfeld, E. B. Stern, Jr., E. R. Telling, A. M. Wood. **Transfer Agent**—Co's. Office. **Registrar**—First National Bank of Chicago. **Incorporated** in New York in 1906.

13

Quick Review of Perfect Investment Rules

- ***There must be a crash.*** Measured from its previous five-year high, to qualify under this rule a stock must meet *one* of the following criteria.
  A. *Decline to 20 percent of its former value.*
  B *Decline to 25 percent of its former value if:* Earnings have declined less than 25 percent from the five-year high point to the crash low.
  C. *Decline to 30 percent of its former value if:* Earnings or dividends have increased from the five-year high point to the crash low.

  or

  Earnings have declined less than 25 percent from the five-year high to the crash low and the company was formerly valued in the market at over one billion dollars.
  D. *Decline to 35 percent of its former value if:* The stock is a component of the Dow Jones Industrials Average.

  or

  The stock is a utility.

  or

  The stock was formerly valued in the market at its five-year high at over two billion dollars.

The company is a bank and ranks in the top two hundred in size nationally.

Option: Raise all percentage figures by 5 percent if the overall market has been rising during the stock's decline.

- ***The stock must pass the fivefold screen.***

A. *There must be assets.* At the time of purchase the stock should be selling for less than the stated book value per share. An exception may be made if off-balance-sheet or undervalued assets can reasonably be inferred.

B. *There must be "signs of life."* Only the fact of earnings is *required* as a "sign of life."

Maintenance of the dividend all through the crash.

or

The company must have shown earnings in its most recent quarter. *Exception:* Prior market value over one billion dollars.

or

Rising sales support earnings status.

or

Evidence of efforts at corporate change (sales of assets, replacement of management, new bonds, joint ventures, etc.).

C. *There must not be obsolescence.* Especially avoid one-product companies in highly volatile areas and fad companies. Also avoid companies whose major operations are in unstable foreign countries.

D. *There must be a technical bottom.* Examples of technical bottoms are given. Investors with technical expertise may deviate from these patterns; all others should require the appearance of at least one of the listed bottoms.

1. Double bottom.
2. Vee plus six-month high after 90 percent decline.
3. Vee plus flag.
4. Vee plus correction.

5. Vee plus gap.
6. Reverse head-and-shoulders bottom.
7. Saucer or congested.
8. Climax.
9. Saucer plus gap.

E. *There must be a technical turn.* Weekly price movements are viewed to confirm the completion of the bottom pattern and the commencement of a new trend.
   Volume buildup with rising prices.
   Second run.
   Breakout patterns.
   Momentum-gaps.
   Two-hook trend line.

- ***Plus Factors—to screen multiple candidates further.***
  Dividend reinstatement or increase.
  Price-earnings ratio of 6 or less.
  Earnings vee.
  Insider purchases.
  Outsider purchases.
  Momentum industries.
  Market leadership.
  Special futures.
  Cash growth.
- ***Holding and selling rules.***

A. Place first stop or mental sell point just below the crash low. Keep it there for at least twelve months.

B. *Create a trend line by connecting the two most recent low points, or create a trend line at a forty-five-degree angle from the crash bottom. Revise yearly or after significant corrections. Sell when prices fall below trend line.*

Option: Buy according to rules, keep stop at crash low, never sell.

Option: Sell after twelve or twenty-four months.

14

Portfolio Management and Further Risk Reduction

Successful investing requires more than simply picking good stocks.

Though 97 percent of Perfect Investment selections are profitable after two years, the degree of gain can be stated only as an *average*. When you are dealing with averages, of course, you find that some stocks perform well above the average and others do not do nearly as well. For your own return on capital to match the average gains for the total sample, you will need considerable *diversification* in your portfolio.

If you hold only three or four stocks, you just might pick the three or four best performers, in which case your average return would far exceed what's to be expected. On the other hand, you might as easily pick the three or four worst performers, perhaps even including, God forbid, a loser. Although the system provides outstanding investments, there is no way to know in advance which will ultimately prove the best and which the worst.

For that reason, you *must* spread your capital over a number of issues if you want to ensure a consistent year-by-year pattern of profits. Computer studies of the total sample here indicate that the soundest policy is the broadest diversification possible. Selected groups of stocks, chosen on the basis of industry group, arbitrary sequence in the tabulation, buy-price level, alphabetical order, etc., all produced the same result: The greatest consistency of return was achieved through the broadest possible diversification.

You should have *at least ten stocks in your portfolio.* Due to the generally low price level at the buy points, even a small portfolio of twenty thousand dollars can hold one hundred shares of each of ten stocks. Indeed, ten stocks is a *minimum,* and *twenty or more stocks is a far more statistically comfortable level.* Obviously, the greater your capital the more easily you can diversify, but small investors should not hesitate to buy odd lots of less than one hundred shares to achieve diversification and to spread risk.

Since the goal is to attain maximum return on total capital, diversification must be *dollar-weighted.* The idea is not to hold one hundred shares of ten or twenty stocks, but to have *equal dollar amounts* invested in a large number of issues. Think of your portfolio as containing so many *dollars' worth* of each stock, rather than so many shares. Otherwise you will be overweighted in favor of stocks whose buy-point price is higher, and there is neither any logical nor any statistical reason to do this. If you decide to hold twenty stocks, for example, that means that *no more than 5 percent of your funds are to be invested in one company.*

Don't be fooled into overweighting by the glowing "case" you can make for a particular company, or the beautiful way it fits the Perfect Investment system model. *You never know which stocks are going to do better or worse,* and the less second-guessing you do, the less emotional involvement you're going to have in your positions.

Aside from reducing the risk of an underperforming portfolio or of picking one of the rare losers, one of the best reasons for diversification is its soothing emotional effect. If you have only a few stocks and one or two have remained stagnant, it becomes difficult to hold on. You begin to question your judgment. You begin to question the strategy itself. You see other stocks going up, and you feel like a chump. You see another Perfect Investment stock appear: Should you sell what you've got and switch to that one? You should know by now that cool, calm, confidence, and patience are the keys to investment results. Diversification is one of the best ways to keep yourself relaxed.

Let's say you've got ten stocks. Nine of them remain static, but one goes up 1,000 percent. Your total capital doubles. On the other hand, let's say you've got only three stocks, and they don't include the one that went flying. You *see* the one that soars, but you don't own it. You start to tap your foot on the floor. "I shouldda, I shouldda," you're saying, your composure and your mind slowly dissolving away. . . .

Having already said that you can't predict which stocks will do best as a group, let me now contradict myself. The more "plus factors" a stock has, the more likely it is to do well. Still, you cannot always buy this kind of stock—there are periods in the market when you may have to wait years for one to appear, and few investors have that much patience (or is it masochism?).

One more important point about diversification: *Don't rush to get your portfolio fully invested.* Just because you've decided to invest no more than, say, 5 percent of capital in each stock, don't feel that it's urgent to become fully invested in twenty stocks. You must keep calm and wait for stocks to appear. Anxiety over becoming fully invested tends to lead to "stretching" of the rules and to acceptance of stocks that don't quite fit.

Further, we know that a rising market is helpful for Perfect Investment stocks, and we also know that the exact stage of the market at any given time is often difficult to determine (except in hindsight). These stocks characteristically appear after the market has made a low and become scarce near market tops. Therefore, by passively waiting for investments to appear rather than chasing them, we can also *reduce the risk of entering the market an an inappropriate time.*

Remember, you're never going to lose money when it's parked in T-bills or a money market fund, and when the market for these stocks is right you'll become fully invested automatically.

Controlling Risk through Options

Many though not all major stocks now have exchange-listed puts and calls traded on them. For the uninitiated, puts give you the right to *sell* a stock at a certain price within a certain period of time, and calls give you the right to *buy* a stock at a specified price within a certain time period. Each put or call has a strike price—the price at which you can buy or sell the stock. Options run for three, six, or nine months, go up and down as the stock goes up and down, and can be bought back anytime before the expiration of the time period. (Options can also be sold, but that is irrelevant for Perfect Investing.)

As a rough rule of thumb, options sell for about 10 percent of the stock price. Option prices vary depending on how long they are, the opinions of buyers and sellers in the market, and how close the strike price is to the present stock price. You can find tables listing options in *The Wall Street Journal* and many daily newspapers. Most brokers will have a booklet explaining exactly how options work, or you can write to the exchanges for information (American Stock Exchange, Chicago Board Options Exchange, Philadelphia Exchange, etc.). If you don't already know about options, come back to this section when you do. It's important.

Put Insurance

You can limit your risk in advance, at the moment you invest. Since puts give you the right to sell stock at a certain price, puts *increase* in value as a stock declines.

If you have purchased both stock and a put on the stock, you will have a profit on the put even if the stock goes down. For example, if you buy a Perfect Investment stock at 20 but are concerned because the first stop-loss point is at 12, you might want to buy a put at the same time. Prices will vary, but you can expect to pay at least $300 for a put on one hundred shares with a strike price of 20. If you bought one hundred shares of stock and a put on those shares, your total cost would be $23 per share. If the stock goes down to 17 at the expiration of the put, the put would be worth $300 (20 strike price less 3). Upon selling the put you would have a total loss of $3 per share—the loss on the stock. If the stock declined to 12, however, the put with a strike of 20 would be worth 8. You would have a gain of 5 on the put and a loss of 8 on the stock, for a total loss, again, of 3. Indeed, no matter how low the stock might go, you could never lose more than $3 per share, or 15 percent of your investment.

There is a cost. If the stock rises to 23 at the time the put expires, your gain of 3 on the stock would be offset by a loss of 3 on the put, which is now worthless. In other words, to obtain the "insurance" of a maximum loss of 15 percent on the stock, you have to give up the first 15 percent of profits. Beyond that point—that is, above 23—you will retain all the profits and sustain no additional loss on the put.

Also remember that any gains on the put will be short-term capital gains—less attractive than the long-term gains you're seeking, but more attractive than losing capital.

This put strategy is most useful when you're unsure. Appropriate times to employ it might be when you find a Perfect Investment stock though the market has already had an extended rally, when you're investing in one of the vee bottoming patterns, when the company has been showing losses and you're not sure if the recently reported earnings are "for real."

The extra cost of put insurance, I think, can be justified only by special circumstances. In general, the low loss levels of this system do not warrant the use of puts as a standard policy.

Zero Risk through Calls

Options are often seen as a speculative vehicle, but there are many ways to use them as conservators rather than riskers of capital. Options are speculative only when accompanied by greed. With a call you can participate in the upward movement of a stock while paying only 10 percent of the value of the stock. And your loss is limited to the amount you put up. But option speculators don't use options in this straightforward fashion. They take the money that would be required to buy one hundred shares of stock and buy calls on a thousand shares instead. Naturally, small movements in the stock price are magnified by ten, and speculators make or lose fortunes in a matter of weeks.

There is an extremely sensible way to use calls, though, and reduce your capital risk to zero. Let's say interest rates have risen strongly and the market has therefore taken a tumble. Rates on one-year paper go to 15 percent. Then Perfect Investment stocks begin to appear and you want to put some money in the market.

Instead of investing in the stocks, you could decide to buy a note that pays you 15 percent. You now know that over the next year on your hundred thousand dollars of capital you'll be getting fifteen thousand dollars in interest.

Rather than buying one hundred thousand dollars' worth of stock, you can buy, over the course of the year, fifteen thousand dollars' worth of calls on Perfect Investment stocks. Your capital remains intact, because you can't lose more in an option than you put up. But you still control at least one hundred thousand dollars' worth of stock with your fifteen thousand dollars' worth of options (actually, it's likely you'll control even more than one hundred thousand dollars' worth of stock). If the stocks perform according to the script, you'll make just about as much as you would had you invested all your capital. If it's a bad year, you've still got your capital in hand to take advantage of opportunities next year.

What's the catch? Time. If you buy a nine-month call, the clock starts ticking the moment you make your purchase. You don't have the leisure to wait, say, thirteen months until the stock is really rolling. Profitable action must occur in those nine months. Further, you can't get long-term capital-gains treatment—with a maximum tax of 20 percent—on options transactions. So your calls will have to do better than outright stock purchase to get the same after-tax gain.

The value of this approach is more psychological than economic. If you're frightened of the market, or frightened of losing your capital, or insecure about using a system developed by someone else, you can at least get your foot in the water without too much anxiety this way.

Note that not all stocks have options. Also, if you decide to buy calls, buy only calls that are "in the money"—where the stock price today is higher than the call strike price. *And buy calls on only the number of shares you would have bought had you bought the shares outright.*

15

The Perfect Investment Record, 1970–80

The following record includes all qualifying Perfect Investment stocks charted by Securities Research Company that appeared from 1970 through the end of 1979. Securities Research Company covers a universe of 1,105 leading stocks—mostly New York Stock Exchange-listed companies with a smattering of the more important American Stock Exchange and over-the-counter stocks. There are, of course, several thousand additional stocks, mainly smaller companies, but this list represents a clearly valid statistical sample.

Over the years the Securities Research list changes in composition as a result of mergers, corporate growth, and interest in different industries, so some stocks you see listed may not appear in current editions of their chartbooks. Brokerage commissions were not included in the tabulations, but neither were dividends, which often can add 10 to 20 percent to a stock's gain over three years.

I did not include the simple trend line selling method in this tabulation—as simple as it is, it's also, ironically, extremely cumbersome to program into a computer. Suffice it to say that the trend line approach will definitely improve your overall results.

Most important, *this record does not include stocks that met the first qualification—the crash—in 1974.*

Often a single good year can make a system appear much more effective than it really is. A system should, of course, perform well in extraordinary times, but it's far more important that it do well in ordinary, expectable periods. Although the 1973 decline was what you might call an expectable bear market (there are always going to be some fairly severe downturns), the one in 1974 was exceptional. In 1974, when we thought New York City was going bankrupt and we'd be buying gasoline by the pint, the decline was a bear panic that ranks among the worst in history. The record would be much improved by including stocks that qualified in 1974, but we wouldn't learn how well this strategy works year in, year out during the kind of markets one can expect to prevail. Stocks that qualified in 1973 may have gone yet lower in 1974 before a buy point was eventually reached—often as late as 1975 or 1976—but stocks that came *close* to qualifying in 1973 weren't included even if the 1974 market then pushed them within our limits.

You may be curious about just how well you can do when conditions have been optimum. As a sort of exercise in titillation, I've included a separate list of stocks that qualified under the crash criteria in 1974 *and* continued to show higher earnings than ever before. Just the best ones, in other words (for a time when you have the luxury of choosing only stocks with no underlying company problems). These stocks were "bought" the moment they hit a six-month high. Now, you're not going to come across such investing "locks" very often in your life as an investor, but I think you'll find it instructive to see what can happen when they do appear. Perhaps this exercise will help you realize that a panic is not a crisis but an opportunity.

One of the most interesting and exciting features revealed by the record is the extremely strong performance of stocks picked in 1973 and the first half of 1974.

They went completely counter to the overall market, showing solid gains and little or no weakness. They displayed the ideal characteristic of any investment strategy—they were stocks that moved in the predicted direction *no matter what the rest of the market was doing.*

Summary of Results

Total number of stocks selected	194	
Number of stocks profitable after one year*	186	(95.9%)
Number of stocks profitable after two years*	188	(96.9%)
Number of stocks profitable after three years*	175	(90.2%)
Average gain after one year	53.57%	
Average gain after two years	84.45%	
Average gain after three years	102.33%	
Maximum average gain within one year (best price)	72.66%	
Maximum average gain within two years (best price)	99.32%	
Maximum average gain within three years (best price)	131.55%	
Maximum average gain within five years	249.28%	
Number of stocks doubled within one year	74	(38.1%)
Number of stocks doubled within two years	132	(68%)
Number of stocks doubled within three years	159	(82.9%)
Number of stocks doubled within five years	178	(91.8%)
Number of stocks tripled within three years	82	(42.2%)
Number of stocks tripled within five years	116	(59.8%)

*Unchanged stocks are deemed losses for purposes of these figures.

These figures are based on stock purchases made for all cash. If you used 50 percent margin, for example, they double. The average annual first-year gain, for example, would then be 107.14 percent, rather lofty for these ugly ducklings that nobody wants.

A glance at the following distribution chart of the appearance of Perfect Investment stocks over the decade will show you there's a definite rhythm to the investing process. You load up when things are low, you move into cash when prices are high. Can you be patient? Can you follow the rhythms of the market? Can you dance when the music plays, and sit when it's quiet? Or will you dance in silence?

The numbers below the Dow Jones prices (A) show you how many selections appeared in that year. Remember, there are actually about four times as many actively

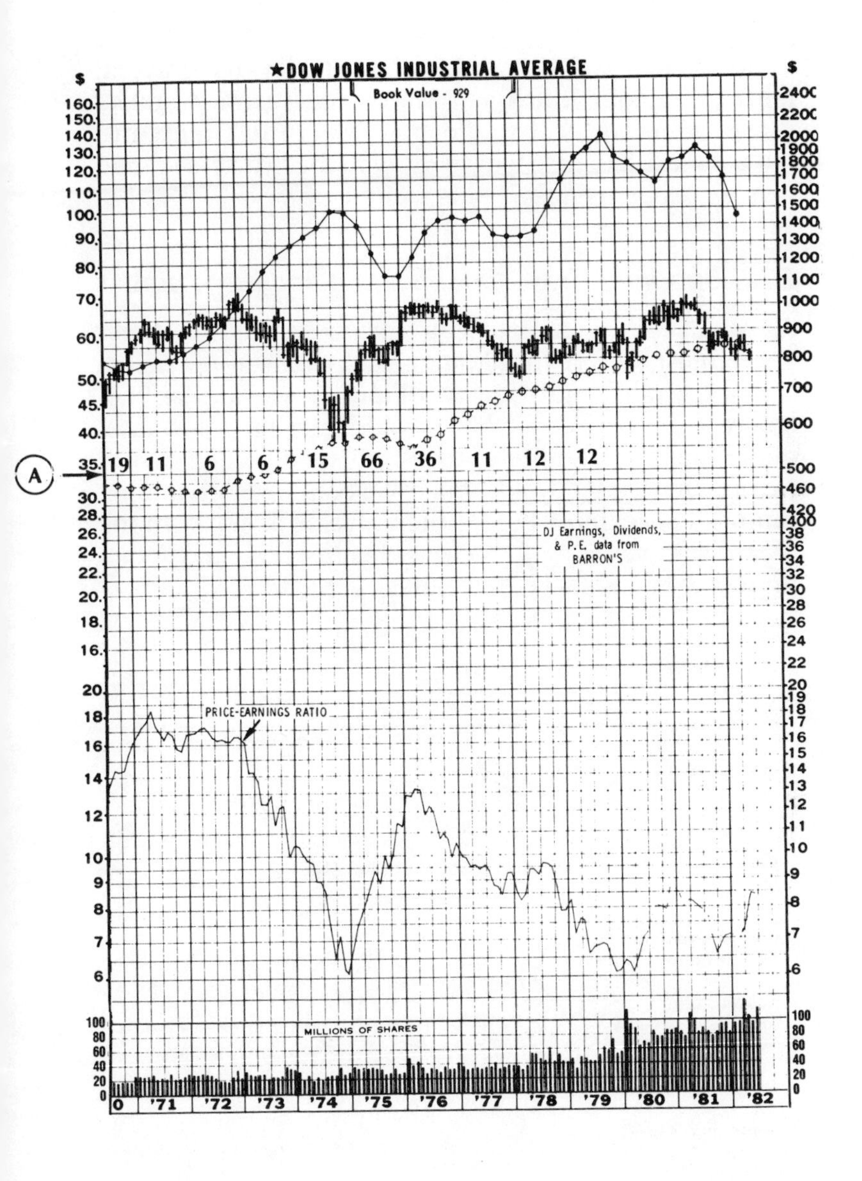

Note: A = Number of buy signals in each year based on 1,100 stocks used in compiling 1970–80 record.

traded stocks as were used in the sample, so the actual figures are four times as great. Even in the worst of years, then, you still would find twenty to twenty-five buyable stocks. In good years, you'd have to separate candidates by using the plus factors.

Distribution of Crash Qualification and Buy-Points

As you can see from the figures *below* on the Dow Jones chart, most Perfect Investment stocks appear just before a market rally and the fewest purchases appear just before a market peak. You should rely on this "automatic" appropriateness of investing vis-a-vis the overall market to reduce your anxiety about overall market timing. These figures cover the universe of stocks in the record sample only. If you include *all* stocks, the actual figures would each be four times as great.

FOOTNOTE TO TABLE—The Perfect Investment Record →

Bottom Pattern Codes:
1. Double bottom.
2. Vee after 90 percent decline (bought on six-month high).
3. Vee plus flag.
4. Vee plus correction.
5. Vee plus gap.
6. Reverse head-and-shoulders bottom.
7. Saucer or congested.
8. Climax.
9. Saucer plus gap.

Note: For purposes of compiling this record, stocks that doubled from their qualifying low before showing earnings (and thus becoming buyable if they had previous deficits) were eliminated. I suggest this modification to all investors—it's a useful risk-reduction technique.

The Perfect Investment Record

Stock	Buy Price . . . Date	First-Year Close—H-L	Second-Year Close—H-L	Third-Year Close—H-L	Five-Year High	Bottom* Pattern
AccuRay	4 . . . 1/79	6.8-6.8-3.5	10.5-13.5-4.3	8-13-7.4	17.5	6
Alberto-Culver	6.5 . . . 1/76	7.3-9.5-8	7.5-7.8-6	10-11-7	17	1
Alco Standard	4.3 . . . 1/75	7.8-8-4.25	10.5-11-7.8	11-12-10	18.5	9
Alexander & Alexander	11 . . . 1/74	13-14-10	17-18.5-12.5	19-19.5-14	36	4
Alleghany Corp.	1.5 . . . 11/75	3-3.3-1	5.5-6.5-2.5	4.5-8-3.8	8	3
Allegheny Beverage	9 . . . 10/70	13-18-19	12-15-10	8-14-8	18	1
Allegheny Ludlum	16 . . . 6/73	16-22-14	16-20-14	26-28-15	28	1
Allied Products	16 . . . 12/70	20-20-15	20-25-16	13-22-12	25	4
Amcord	6.5 . . . 1/76	11-11-6.5	15-15.5-10.5	17-20-14	24	3, 6
American Building Maintenance	7.5 . . . 1/75	11-12.5-7	11-12-9	14-14-10	20	2
American Family	4 . . . 12/70	7.5-14-4	6.5-10-6	5.5-8.5-3.8	14	5
American Greetings	10 . . . 1/76	9.5-11-8	11-13-9	11.5-14.5-10	22	1
American Medical Int.	6 . . . 1/76	12-13-6	17-17-10	28-34-17	34	4, 3
American Standard	12 . . . 6/73	14-16-10.5	14-15-8	26-27-12	52	7
Anheuser-Busch	22 . . . 12/79	28-31-21	41-43-28	68-71-39	76	1, 6
Anthony Industries	5.5 . . . 8/71	15-30-5.5	6-15-5	2.5-5-1.8	30	3
APL	4 . . . 11/74	12.5-12.5-4	14-17-12.5	12.5-15-12.5	17	1
Arcata	7 . . . 3/74	10-10-5.3	14-14-8	16-17-12	26	7
Armstrong Rubber	15 . . . 10/75	20-21-15	28-34-18	26-32-19	40	7
ASA Ltd.	20 . . . 8/77	28-29-19	27-31-22	85-90-25	90	3
Athlone	5 . . . 3/74	9-9-5	14-14-7	16-16-12	22	1
Atlantic Richfield	32 . . . 7/72	42-44-32	42-56-42	52-55-37	70	1
ATO	6 . . . 2/75	9-10-6	10-11-7.5	9-12-9	15	4
Augat	5.5 . . . 5/77	10.5-11.5-5.5	13.5-14-8.5	21-23-12.5	35	1, 7
Avco	8 . . . 1/76	15-16-8	17-17-13	21-34-16	34	4
Avery International	17 . . . 1/79	20-22-16	24-24-16	24-28-19	40	1
AZL Resources	5.5 . . . 3/79	9-15-4.5	17-21-8	21-32-15	32	4
Bairnco	2 . . . 1/75	2.8-3.5-2	5.3-5.8-2.8	6-6-4.5	10.5	1, 5

Stock	Buy Price . . . Date	First-Year Close—H-L	Second-Year Close—H-L	Third-Year Close—H-L	Five-Year High	Bottom* Pattern
Bandag	14 . . . 1/79	19-19-12	23-23-14.5	26-26-20	45	1
Bangor Punta	5 . . . 1/76	13-13-5	21-24-12.5	22-30-18	30	3
Barry Wright	4.5 . . . 12/70	4.3-6.8-3.3	6.5-7-3.5	2.5-6.8-2.5	7	4
Barry Wright	3.3 . . . 6/75	4-5-2.6	6.5-7-3.6	12-14-6	24	3
Belco Petroleum	11 . . . 1/72	10-13-8	10-12-5.8	9.5-10-5.6	23	1
Belco Petroleum	9.5 . . . 1/75	11-14-8.5	18-19-10	22-23-16	40	1
Bergen Brunswig	3.3 . . . 6/78	6.3-6.5-3	8.-8.3-4.3	22-23-8	42	7
Berkey Photo	9 . . . 1/71	18-18-9	17-27-16.5	14-17-9	26	4
Best Products	2 . . . 3/75	12.5-13-2	14-16-9	20-21-12	34	2
Beverly Enterprises	2 . . . 2/76	2.8-3.8-1.5	4.3-4.5-2.4	7-9-3.5	20	4
Block, H. & R.	10.5 . . . 9/74	15-16-9.5	19-20-15	24-24-18	26	1
Blue Bell	9 . . . 1/75	22-22-8	30-31-18	20-30-20	38	1
Boeing	6 . . . 1/71	9-9-4.8	7.8-9-6.8	4-8-4	10.5	4
Boeing	7 . . . 3/75	9-10.5-6.8	15-15-8.5	23-23-14	46	5
Boise Cascade	12 . . . 7/73	13.5-19-12	22-27-10	26-34-21	34	7
Brockway Glass	8.5 . . . 9/74	15-16-7	21-24-14.5	18-24-18	24	4
Caesar's World	.9 . . . 4/75	.9-1.4-.6	1.1-1.1-.6	4-4-.9	36	1
Caldor	5.5 . . . 3/75	11-11-5.5	11.5-12.5-9	15-15.5-11	22	5
Cessna Air	7 . . . 2/75	12.5-13-6.5	13.5-15.5-11	16-18-13	29	1
Charter Company	2.4 . . . 9/70	7-10-2.3	5-8.5-4.3	4.5-6-2.8	10	5
Church's Fried Chicken	3 . . . 2/75	8.5-9.5-3	11-12-7.5	16-17-9.5	30	1
Circle K	6.8 . . . 7/76	12-13-6.5	14-15.5-11.5	16-18.5-13	18.5	1
Coastal Corp.	10 . . . 1/76	15.5-16-8.5	15-25-11	17.5-20-13	52	6
Cole National	11 . . . 12/70	21-21-11	23-25-19	11.5-23-7.5	25	4
Coleman Co.	9 . . . 3/75	16-19-9	16.5-18-12.5	16-17-13.5	22	5
Collins & Aikman	7.5 . . . 5/75	11.5-15-7.5	11-13-9.5	11.5-13-10	15	5
Colt Industries	11 . . . 12/71	14-18-10	13-15-9	19-19-12	38	1
Combustion Equipment	8 . . . 2/71	13-14-6.8	14-20-13	8-14-7	20	4
Computer Sciences	3.3 . . . 2/75	6.8-8-3	7.3-9-5.3	9-10-6.8	24	2
Condec	3 . . . 1/75	7-7.5-3	9.5-11-6.5	8-10.5-7.5	19	2, 9

Cooper Labs	7 . . . 1/76	11.5-12-6.5	25-25-10	21-29-15	38	7, 1
Cross & Trecker	6 . . . 1/76	10-10-6	10.5-11.5-8.5	17.5-20-10.5	38	6
Dart Industries	21 . . . 3/75	34-38-20	38-38-29	42-46-30	55	5
Dataproducts	4 . . . 3/75	9.8-12-3	10.5-14.5-8	15.5-19-9.5	24	2
Dayton Hudson	12 . . . 4/75	33-35-12	32-38-26	42-44-30	52	2
Dekalb Agresearch	22 . . . 12/78	32-34-22	54-60-26	25-54-23	60	7, 1
Dennison Manufacturing	7.5 . . . 9/70	10.5-13.5-6.5	13.5-15.5-9.5	9.5-14.5-7.3	15.5	2
Dennison Manufacturing	7 . . . 9/75	10-11.5-6.5	14-14.5-9.5	15-18-11.5	22	3
Denny's	11 . . . 12/71	17.5-20-10.5	8.5-20-7.5	10-14-6	23	1
Denny's	12 . . . 2/75	24-25-12	20-26-18	29-30-19	34	2
Diebold	8.5 . . . 11/77	12-16-8	19.5-21-12	37-37-19	78	7, 1
Dreyfus Corp.	2.5 . . . 1/76	2.7-3-2.3	3.8-3.8-2.5	4.8-6-3.3	17	3
Eastman Kodak	51 . . . 12/79	77-85-80	75-77-60	86-98-63	98	1, 7
Electronic Data Systems	8.5 . . . 2/78	9.5-12-8	12.5-14-9.5	22-22-9.5	56	7, 1, 8
Esterline	2.5 . . . 5/75	3.5-4.5-2.3	3.3-3.8-3	4.8-6-3.3	21	3
Fairchild Industries	3.3 . . . 1/76	4.3-4.8-3	6.5-6.5-3.6	11.5-14-5.8	34	1, 6
Farah Manufacturing	4 . . . 6/79	3.5-4.5-2.8	13-15-3	6-13-5	20	7, 1
Federal Signal	1.5 . . . 3/75	3.5-4-1.5	4.8-5.5-2.8	6-7-4.5	10.5	5
Filmways	4 . . . 3/75	7-8.5-3.2	9.3-10.5-5	9-9.5-6.5	17	1, 5
Fisher Scientific	11 . . . 9/70	15-19-10.5	14-20.5-11	7-14-6.8	20.5	5, 8
Fleetwood Enterprises	9.8 . . . 10/74	10.5-18-8	16.5-20-10	10-19-9.5	20.5	1
Freeport Minerals	12 . . . 1/71	13-18-10	18-20.5-12.5	17.5-22-13.5	22.5	7
Garan	5.5 . . . 10/70	12-12.5-5	12-16.5-11	10-16-8.5	16.5	2
GDV	5 . . . 1/76	6-6.8-4	7-7.8-4.5	8-14-6.3	14	1
Gelco	6 . . . 2/75	11-11-6	10-11.5-9.5	13.5-16.5-9.8	25	5
General Cinema	6.5 . . . 1/75	11-12-6.5	11.5-13-8.5	14-16-10.5	18	5, 2
General Portland	7.5 . . . 1/77	11-12-6.3	13.5-16-10			3
Gerber Scientific	.6 . . . 7/76	1.3-1.5-.6	4-5.5-1	10.5-10.5-3	26	1
G. K. Technologies	9 . . . 2/75	13.5-14-9	10.8-12.5-9.5	15-15.5-10.5	21	7
Global Marine	14.5 . . . 12/70	16-22-1.5	19.5-27-16	15-24-10	27	4
Gray Drug Stores	6.5 . . . 3/75	12-13-6.5	11-12.5-9.5	14-15.5-11	20	3
Grow Group	4 . . . 10/73	4.5-4.5-3	5-6.5-3	8.5-8.8-4.5	11	7

Stock	Buy Price . . . Date	First-Year Close—H-L	Second-Year Close—H-L	Third-Year Close—H-L	Five-Year High	Bottom* Pattern
Grumman	10 . . . 2/74	11.5-13-7.5	16.5-18-11.5	18-19-15.5	24	1
Gulf & Western	6 . . . 9/70	10-11-5.5	13-16-7.8	9.5-14-8	16	8
Gulf Research & Chemical	9 . . . 6/73	9.5-15-8.5	20-25-6.5	17-21-13.5	25	1
Handleman	5.5 . . . 3/77	12-12-5	14.5-24-12	8-14.5-8.5	24	1
Hercules	15 . . . 7/78	20-22-14.5	21-25-15	21-26-18	35	7, 8
Hilton Hotels	4.5 . . . 2/75	9.5-10-4.5	10.5-11.5-7.5	13.5-13.5-8	36	5, 8
Hospital Corp. of America	3.3 . . . 1/75	6.5-7-3.3	7.5-7.5-5.5	8-9-5.8	21	2
Host International	9 . . . 9/75	9.5-16-9	12-12.5-8.5	21-27-11	27	1
Humana	3.5 . . . 2/75	6-6.5-3.5	7.5-8.5-5.5	10-10.5-6.5	33	5
Ideal Toy	3.5 . . . 3/75	6.8-7.3-3.3	6.5-7.5-5	6-8.5-5	8.5	7, 1
Imperial Oil Ltd.	20 . . . 11/78	38-39-19.5	31-50-27	24-32-20	50	7
Interpublic Group	10 . . . 4/75	17.5-17.5-9	22-22-14.5	28-30-21	37	5
Itek	12 . . . 1/76	16-18.5-12	23-23-11	21-32-14	36	1
James, Fred S.	8 . . . 1/76	12.5-13-8	17-18.5-12	22-28-15	34	1, 6, 7
Jim Walter	19.5 . . . 10/74	40-43-18.5	36-43-28	28-40-26	43	1
Kaiser Cement	6 . . . 1/76	11.5-11.5-6	15-15-9.5	23-29-15	34	3, 7, 5
Kaiser Steel	13 . . . 7/73	19.5-22-12.5	39-43-17.5	41-47-30	47	1
Kane-Miller	7 . . . 9/70	7.5-13-7	5-9-5	8-8-5	13	2
Keene Corp.	4.5 . . . 1/75	5.5-7-4	10.5-11.5-5.5	12-12-9	17	5
Lear Siegler	7 . . . 2/76	14.5-15.5-7	13.5-17-13.5	18.5-24-13	42	3
Levi Strauss	9 . . . 2/75	23.5-25-9	28-30-19	28-32-24	40	1
Lockheed	5 . . . 2/75	7-14-5	10-12.5-6.5	13-19-9	46	9
Loew's	28 . . . 9/70	50-56-28	46-60-35	25-52-23	60	7
Loew's	24 . . . 1/76	36-38-24	32-36-27	47-55-32	93	6
Loral	4 . . . 1/75	10.5-13-4	15-17-10.5	20-22-14	48	9
LTV Corp.	8 . . . 1/79	12-12.5-6.5	21-21-8	16.5-25-12	25	7
McDermott	8.5 . . . 1/71	9-11.5-7.5	19-20-9	23-27-12.5	27	3
McDonnell Douglas	16 . . . 12/70	27-30-16	28-37-26	14.8-30-14	37	3
McGraw-Hill	8 . . . 1/75	14.5-15.5-8	16.8-17-13	17-20-16	34	1
M/A Com.	5 . . . 12/70	10-11-5	10.5-15-9.5	5.5-10.5-5.5	15	3

Maremont	6.5 . . . 9/70	17.5-17.5-9.5	40-40-14.5	33-55-32	60	6, 3
Marine Midland	12 . . . 1/77	14-14.5-11.5	15-18-11	20-20-13	25	9
Marion Labs	13.5 . . . 3/78	15-17.5-12	15-16.5-11.5	22-23-14	60	1
Mark Controls	2 . . . 9/74	7.8-9-1.5	15-18-6.8	16-22-13	22	6
Mary Kay Cosmetics	3.5 . . . 4/79	8.5-8.5-3.5	27-30-8.5	27-37-16	66	7
Medtronic	11 . . . 6/78	22-22-11	34-36-21	35-54-32	56	7
Metromedia	9 . . . 3/75	22-22-9	29-32-22	46-46-25	75	5
Midland-Ross	7 . . . 1/75	10.5-10.5-6.5	15-15-10.5	14.5-17-14.5	30	1, 7
Milton Bradley	10 . . . 11/75	13-17.5-9	13-14.5-10.5	20-24-11	28	3, 6
Mitchell Energy & Development	7 . . . 1/76	23-24-7	19-24-16	17-25-14	45	3
Morse Shoe	2.3 . . . 3/75	8.5-8.5-2.3	7.5-10.5-7.3	13.5-17-7.5	20	5
Narco Scientific	9 . . . 4/75	14.5-15.5-9	12-14.5-10	18-18-10	32	6, 3
Nashua	16 . . . 6/76	23-28-15	27-31-17	21-38-21	38	6, 8
National Can	8.5 . . . 11/74	11.5-13.5-8	14-16.5-10.5	15.5-15.5-12	23	1
National Medical Care	2 . . . 2/75	4.8-5.5-2	6.8-7-3.8	6.5-7-4.5	14.5	5
National Medical Enterprises	3.5 . . . 1/76	6.8-6.8-3.5	9.8-10.5-5.5	15-21-9.8	57	6
NCH	17 . . . 6/79	24-26-16.5	18-29-17	12.5-18.5-12	28	7
New England Nuclear	3 . . . 12/70	7.5-7.5-3	11-12.5-6.5	12-16-6.5	16	3, 8
Northwest Industries	9 . . . 1/71	16-17-9	13-20-13	9.5-13.5-7.5	20	6
Oak Industries	7 . . . 1/72	11.5-14.5-7	6.8-11.5-6	5.3-8.5-3.5	14.5	4, 1
Ogden	11 . . . 12/70	15-20-11	14-18-11.5	12-18.5-12	21	4
Overseas Shipholding	11 . . . 1/76	23-24-10	21-30-20	22-28-20	60	1
Papercraft	7 . . . 2/76	10-10.5-7	12.5-13-10	14-16.5-10.5	18.5	6
Pitney-Bowes	10 . . . 2/74	15-16-8	16-20-13	18-19-13.5	29	8
Pneumo	2.3 . . . 9/74	5.3-5.5-1.9	6.3-7.3-5	7-8.5-5.8	14	6
Pueblo International	3.5 . . . 2/77	5.3-5.3-3	4.3-8.5-3.5	3.3-5.3-3.3	9.5	1
Quaker State Oil	12 . . . 3/79	12.5-19.5-10.5	17-23-11.5	10-20-10	23	1
Ramada Inns	4.5 . . . 3/78	11.5-17-4.3	7.5-14-7	10-11.5-5.8	17	1, 7
Ranco	7.3 . . . 6/76	14.5-16-7	13.5-15-10	15-24-13	24	3, 4
Raymond International	7 . . . 1/72	6.5-8.5-5.3	8-10.5-5	6.3-8.5-4	20	1

Stock	Buy Price . . . Date	First-Year Close—H-L	Second-Year Close—H-L	Third-Year Close—H-L	Five-Year High	Bottom* Pattern
Reynolds Metals	17 . . . 8/73	18-26-15	21-24-13	40-42-18	43.5	1
Rohm & Haas	36 . . . 1/79	42-48-33	54-55-33	57-70-54	90	1
Rohr	7 . . . 11/77	16-20-6.3	14.5-19-11.5	14-20-10	20	7
Saga	6.5 . . . 10/75	10.5-15-6	11.5-14-9.5	10.5-17-10.5	17	6
Sargent-Welch Scientific	7 . . . 1/75	11.5-14-7	14-14-11	13.5-16-13	19	7
Savin	2.5 . . . 10/75	6.5-8-2.5	14-25-6	12-25-11.5	25	4
SCA Services	2.8 . . . 1/77	4.5-5.5-2.5	7.8-9.5-4	9-9.5-7.5	20	1, 7
Schering-Plough	31 . . . 1/79	36-38-37	41-46-30	31-41-26	47	1
SCOA	1.5 . . . 3/75	3.5-3.8-1.5	3.3-3.5-2.5	5-5-3	11	1
Searle, G. D.	13 . . . 4/78	16-16-11	21-24-13	27-30-20	50	7
Seligman & Latz	4.5 . . . 11/71	6.8-7-4	9-10.5-6.5	6.8-10.5-5.5	10.5	1, 5
Simmonds Precision	4 . . . 1/75	6.3-9.5-4	6.5-9-5	9.5-10-5.5	21	5
Singer	15 . . . 2/76	21-26-15	18.5-26-18.5	24-24-13.5	26	1, 2
Skyline	17 . . . 8/74	18-26-15	18-22-13	13-20-12	26	1
Syntex	10.5 . . . 1/78	18-19-10	21-22-15	29-38-15	61	7
Taft Broadcasting	10.5 . . . 10/75	14.5-16-9.5	14-17-12	18-26-14	35	6
Talley Industries	6.5 . . . 1/75	8.5-8.5-6.5	11-12-8	11.5-15-10.5	15	1
Tektronix	14 . . . 2/75	27-30-13	29-37-24	35-40-29	65	5
Telex	3 . . . 12/77	5.5-9.5-2.8	4-7-3.3	5-6.5-2.5	27	1
Texasgulf	17 . . . 11/72	27-33-17	26-36-20	30-36-24	36	1
Tokheim	2.5 . . . 3/75	5-5.5-2.5	7.5-9-4.3	9-9-6.5	17	1, 5
Tyco Labs	10 . . . 12/71	14.5-23-10	10-14-6	9.5-12-4.8	23	1
Tyler	3 . . . 10/70	6-6.8-2.5	6.3-8.5-5	4.8-7.5-3	8	5
United Inns	4.5 . . . 11/75	4.3-7.5-4.3	9.3-9.3-4.3	11-19-9	24	5
United Technologies	14 . . . 10/74	26-31-13.5	35-37-22	38-52-32	52	1
Unitrode	6 . . . 12/70	11-14.5-5.5	13-18-10	9-13-6	18	4
Upjohn	36 . . . 3/78	44-55-36	52-52-40	62-70-50	70	1
U. S. Home	4 . . . 1/75	5.3-6.5-3	6-8.5-5	5.3-6.8-5.3	14	2
Varo	3 . . . 6/75	12-13-3	11-13-7	11-15-9	15.5	2, 3, 5
Viacom International	2.5 . . . 2/70	5-6-2.3	7.3-7.8-3.8	9.5-11-6.3	22	9

Wackenhut	5.5 . . . 2/75	7.3-9-4.8	6-7.5-4.8	8.3-8.3-5.5	8.3	1
Wallace-Murray	8.5 . . . 10/75	15-16.5-7.5	19-23-14	18.5-26-18	30	6
Wang Labs	1.8 . . . 1/76	1.8-2.5-1.3	3.3-3.8-1.8	8.5-9-3	46	1
Warnaco	7 . . . 9/77	12-13-6.5	11-13-7.5	15-18-9.4	35	1
Warner Communications	3.3 . . . 1/75	6-6.5-3	8-8.5-5	8.5-9.5-7	50	4
Waste Management	2.8 . . . 6/76	5.8-5.8-2.3	7.5-8.5-4.8	10.5-11-7.5	40	4, 1
Western Pacific	10 . . . 2/76	17-18-9.5	25-26-16.5	40-42-24	67	9
Whittaker	4 . . . 1/76	6-7-3.8	7-8-4.5	13.5-19-7	50	4
Wometco	6 . . . 2/75	12-13-6	11.5-13.5-10	13.5-16-10.5	21	5, 8
Wynn's International	4 . . . 1/76	7.5-8-5.5	9.5-10.5-6.5	15.5-18-9.5	22	6
Xerox	50 . . . 5/78	60-65-50	57-69-48	60-72-54	72	1
XTRA	5.5 . . . 7/76	13-16-5	21-21-11	19-25-14	29	1, 7
Yates	12 . . . 7/72	16.5-17-11	8.5-25-8	9.5-12-4.5	25	3

Stocks That Qualified on Crash Criteria and Whose Earnings Rose in 1973–74

Stock	1974 Low	1980 High
Adobe Oil & Gas	4.25	60
Airborne Freight	2.75	26
Alco Standard	6.5	38
Allied Maintenance	8.5	17
Allis-Chalmers	6	36
American District Telegraph	15	30
American Express	18	40
American Family	2.25	11
American Standard	4	37
American Stores	5.25	30
APL	2.25	11
ATO	3.25	22
Automatic Data	10.5	52
Avnet	4.25	60
Bard, C. R.	9.5	24
Barry, R. G.	2.12	10.5
Brown-Forman Dist.	7	57
Caldor	2.25	31
Centronics Data	5.25	42
Coastal Corp.	3.75	51
Cole National	4.5	23
Colonial Penn	13	22
Combined Int.	5.25	21
Combustion Engineering	7.5	55
Compugraphic	4.25	42
Cox Broadcasting	4.25	61
Curtiss-Wright	5	42
Data General	9	88
Dataproducts	2	38
Dennison Manufacturing	3.75	20.5
Dexter	5.25	35
Dillingham	4.25	19.5
Disney	16	54
Eckerd, Jack	10	37
E G & G	3.5	47
Fischbach	14	36
Foster Wheeler	1.5	30
Gelco	3.25	37
Golden West Fin.	1.75	15
Gordon Jewelry	5.5	29
Hall, Frank B.	8	31
Harte-Hanks Comm.	3	35

Stock	1974 Low	1980 High
Hospital Corp. of America	2.25	55
Host International	5	24
House of Fabrics	3.5	7.5
Humana	1.25	74
Imperial Oil	4.5	35
Kidde	8	47
King's D.S.	4	12
Lear Siegler	3.5	42
Lifemark	1.25	42
Lockheed	2.75	37
Loral	1	49
McGraw-Hill	5.5	46
M A Com.	.75	33
Meredith	7	55
National Medical Care	.5	23
National Medical Ent.	.88	38
New England Nuclear	4.25	49
Revco D.S.	6	36
Rollins	6.5	40
Ryan Homes	5.5	30
Sargeant-Welch Sci.	5	22
SCM	8.5	32
Simmonds Prec.	2.25	19
Storage Technology	1.25	26
Tampax	22	36
Tandy	1.25	50
Texas Oil and Gas	1.5	42
TRW	10	60
V.F.	9	32
Viacom	2.5	59
Warner Communications	1.88	42
Totals	391.89	2,698
Average gain, 1974 low to 1980 high		588%
Average monthly gain (divided by eighty months)		7.35% per month
Average annual gain, 1974 low to 1980 high		88.2%

Note: Most stocks hit low in 1974 in about September–October, though some were later and some were earlier. Highs in 1980 were reached at various times during the year; there would be a statistically insignificant variance on the above figures if each stock were calculated for percent gain over exact time from low to high.

A Glance at 1974

The crash that began in 1973 and ended in 1974 was a dazzling moment for the Perfect Investment system. For investors who could keep their heads when all about them was in chaos, it was the opportunity of a lifetime. Though 1974 crash stocks were excluded from the record to make it more realistic, you might be interested to see the performance of crashed stocks whose earnings *increased* in 1973 and 1974—in other words, stock sold out of sheer anxiety, and not for any of the investors' standard catalog of rationalizations. The stocks haven't gone straight up but have wiggled and wobbled over the years, so many would have been sold prior to their 1980 highs. But you can see how very well an investor who *buys right* and holds on can do from the table below.

If there's one lesson to be learned from 1974 (and the entire Perfect Investment method) it is this: *Buy* bargain stocks; don't run from them for the emotional security of the middle of the pack.

16

Conclusion: Ten Points to Remember

Perfect Investment stocks that have met the crash criteria and passed through the fivefold screen *have no place to go but up.*

1. *Remember, there is a company behind the stock.*

Often stocks seem abstract, or like stars in the sky, some shining, some falling. But a stock is not just a price that goes up and down with no connection to any reality on earth. We are dealing with significant businesses that have been around for years and are large enough to be publicly traded. In today's world a company that's survived even ten years (most existed far longer as private enterprises before selling stock) has seen itself through at least one major recession, through the oil price shock, through competition of all kinds, through high interest rates and low, through technological changes.

The company must have some intrinsic ability to make money, too, for investors only recently paid *many times* the current price for its stock. No management is infallible, and there are more ways to stumble in business than anyone can count. There are just as many ways, though, to recover or start on a new path—if you've got the capital, personnel, and asset base from which to work. Often a company falters through mere bad luck. Remember that few mistakes are fatal, and ill fortune can just as easily be followed by the smiles of Fate.

2. *Your profits come from buying right.*

"Buy low and sell high" is an old saw with a very sharp cutting edge. Now, it is true that any stock on which you make a profit has been bought lower and sold higher. But this is known only in retrospect, when it becomes clear that the buy price was lower than the sell price. What you also know, then, is that you bought at the "right" price. At the moment you bought, in effect, you created your future profit.

We never know how high a stock may go, so it's impossible to tell what "high" will be in advance. But we *do* know what low is. We know, for example, that a stock can't go below zero, that it must sell higher than that. We know that there is certain minimum value for a going concern, for its assets and earning power. We may not know how much an investor will pay for this company, but we know the level at which genuine, sensible investors will find the value irresistible.

Perfect Investment stocks are always bought "right" because they are always low in an absolute sense. Selling high follows naturally, because the profit was built in at the time of buying.

3. *Don't rush to buy.*

Since buying right is the key to investment success, the buy should be made cautiously, deliberately, and with a calm mind. There is often a sense among investors that the train is leaving the station *right now* and one must run down the platform to catch it. For the long-term investor, the kind of agility implicit in this idea is rarely productive.

The single pitfall in actually operating the Perfect Investment system is buying a stock during a short-term rally when the overall trend is still declining. There are always going to be some rallies within a downtrend as bargain hunters undertake tentative accumulation and/or short sellers decide to cover (buy back) stock they had earlier borrowed and sold short. It's of utmost importance that you wait for the bottom and turn patterns to be fulfilled—this is one case in which the early bird doesn't always catch the worm. Since many sellers have long felt that Perfect Investment stocks are better sold than bought, it will be a rare case in which you are unable to make your purchase after a moderate short-term decline, at a "right" price that ensures future profits. Don't permit yourself to chase a stock or feel that it's running away from you. There are plenty of other fish in the sea, and the fish you've got your eye on will most likely accommodate you by pulling back into a better buying range.

4. *Sell with as much rigor as you buy.*

Selling usually is more of a problem for investors than buying. If the stock has not done so well, we tend to keep hoping against hope that tomorrow, or next month, or next quarter the issue we bought so carefully and felt so strongly about will finally fire. Or, if the stock has made spectacular gains, we get the taste of victory, the magic of unearned profits on our tongues. We want more, more, more.

In the former case, with a mediocre performer, you've got to think of the stock as your employee. If it doesn't do the job, it gets a pink slip. Sometimes it seems that your sale was just the boost your stock needed to take off—leaving you watching in dismay from the sidelines—but that's part of the emotional stresses that can go along with investing. You need to detach yourself, become cold and objective, never feel a thing as you stick to your strategy. You are probably *more* likely to score with a reinvestment in a new stock than by holding on to one that hasn't followed the Perfect Investment script. On the other hand, you'll never succeed if you nervously flit from issue to issue, refusing to give one a chance to grow and develop.

When your stock has soared, continue to apply your trend lines with discipline. It's tempting to want to cheat yourself and change the trend line to effect an extended holding period. If this stock has been so great, you think, it will be great forever. But nowhere is the cycling of things more apparent than in the market, and just as stocks can't go below zero, neither can they rise to infinity. Holding on too long—after the properly drawn trend line has been broken—can lead only to disappointment and recriminations. These are the sorts of emotional states that cloud your analysis and interfere with your entire investment behavior.

Do not marry. Do not even fall in love. When the trend line is broken, buyers no longer have the positive charge and avarice they once displayed. It's your signal that the party's over.

5. *The rules are more important than the principles.* Some readers will glean from this book only the idea that you should buy a stock after it has been sold down and then looks as if it's going to come up again. Although that's true in the most general sense, it forgets the most important reason for developing a set of rules in the first place. Principles provide us with a rough guide to the realms in which we're likely to find good investments. But they provide a rough guide at best and leave ample room for emotional distortions and guesses. The rules that are generated from ideas have been tested against reality through extensive research. Slowly the sorts of stocks that seem as if they would be good investments but truly aren't get screened out of the system. By the time the rules have been fine-tuned to exclude definable classes of losers and include stocks that are virtually certain to be winners, we have something far more valuable than a concept about investing. *We have the probabilities behind us*. To know, at the moment you invest, that this particular kind of stock, with this particular set of characteristics, has gone up within twelve months practically since there have been markets at all is the great secret to avoiding the emotional mistakes that devour most investors. To follow only the principles and not the rules that have emerged from them is like having a nice car and being completely lost on the highway. Investing really is like a trip: You've got to know why you're going to a particular place, how you're going there, when you expect to arrive, and when you expect to leave.

If you follow only the principles and not the rules, anything can sway you. A company's ads on TV exert an influence. Or a broker's chatter. Or an article in *Barron's*. Whether you're familiar with their products. A brand name you believe is "solid." An appearance on the list of most actively traded stocks, or best gainers. The rules prevent you from risking your hard-earned capital on these kinds of irrelevant ephemerals.

6. *Check out the facts.*

Your effectiveness in operating any system depends on your belief that the system will work as proposed. You need faith, but it should not be blind faith. Don't simply take my word for it. Get a set of charts—and back issues of the information services—and see what happens to Perfect Investment stocks. The more truth you have in front of you, the less anxiety you'll have about taking a position. It's not always easy to buy and hold these stocks that no one's talking about or hyping. Everything you can do to immunize yourself from negativity, fear, and contraction is a further step toward greater profits.

7. *Don't let a bear market scare you.*

One of the hardest times to invest is when the economy (and the world!) seems to be going to hell in a handbasket and the overall market has been declining for months with no bottom in sight. Everything's being dragged down, down, down. Faith in the American corporate economy has disappeared. Bearish investment advisers are calling for another 50 percent drop. Volume has dried up. There's not a buyer for miles.

It's hard to look at stocks when the promise of riches is not oozing out of their pores, but that is precisely the time to create your shopping list. You need not jump in prematurely, but you must be getting ready to buy when things look horrible. *The biggest market gains, and the best Perfect Investment stock gains, are made after prolonged bear markets that have affected most stocks.* Obviously, you don't have to wait just for bear markets before you invest, but those infrequent times are the moments when you should pull out all the stops, hock the family jewels, breathe deeply, and go for it.

8. *Watch interest rates.*

When I was a novice investor I used to think rates were, well . . . a different world. I wasn't interested in bonds or bills, so why should I pay attention to interest rates? I was a stock investor; rates were for other people doing other things. But I've learned, sometimes the hard way, that no investor can afford to ignore the trend of interest rates. When rates are high, the large investors (pension and mutual funds) who control the market prefer to reap their gains in the less risky bond and bill market, pulling money out of stocks for the more certain returns. It is not until rates begin to fall that stocks become attractive to them relative to the alternatives. Not only do interest rates exert a powerful influence on the course of business in general, but also the returns on interest rate instruments are *competitors* of stocks in attracting institutional investment dollars.

You don't have to be an expert, and you don't have to be able to predict what rates will be a some distant point in the future. Fortunately, rates are the "trendiest" of all investment factors; that is, when rates go up, the probabilities are very strong that they'll continue going up. When they go down, they're likely to go down some more. The market *follows* rates. You're unlikely to see a major rally up from a bear market until rates begin to fall. Investors ordinarily don't try to anticipate the fall, they wait for it to happen; the most recent example is the August 1982 upside explosion. Rates fell *first*. Likewise, when rates begin to rise, a bull market's days are numbered. The most significant times for investors are when rates are near historic highs and begin to fall (bullish) or are near the low end of their range in recent years and begin to rise (bearish). Keep one eye on rates. They help clarify the world and its future.

9. *Think of your stock as property.*

Most of us understand investing in real estate much better than we understand stock investing, probably because real estate is more tangible, you can see the building, you can see the neighborhood, you know what the costs are, you're close to what's happening. The separation we feel from our dollars and the thing they're invested in in the stock arena causes us to lose sight of what we know on the most basic levels about investing. If you buy a house, you want to do everything you can to get it at a good price. You don't expect to sell it in three months. You know you're going to have to wait a while for your profits to develop and that if you bought at a good price compared to the relative value, develop they will. You don't torture yourself by reading the real-estate section every day to find out how much the value of your property has changed; you check it out now and then. You know that the market is kind of slow-moving, but it moves in one direction for a while, up or down. You know a good time to buy is when there aren't many buyers around, and a good time to sell is when there are far more buyers than houses and everyone is mad to take on huge mortgages and creative financing. You also know that the most profit in real property exists when it is possible to *improve* the property (or when the neighborhood is improving) and make it worth as much as its neighbors. Think of the management of your company as house improvers. Buy that "fixer-upper" and hold it until the renovation work is done. Smile smugly as buyers enter the fixed-up property, eyes bulging at the beautiful new and gleaming surfaces. Take a good offer when the time is right and move on to the next property.

10. *Time is on your side.*

Perfect Investments are automatically bought low and sold high. Long-term investing of this sort works because time is on your side. Time heals. Time heals old wounded companies and old wounded share prices. Time heals the feelings of investors who "always knew" the stock was really worth its old high price, and time slowly allows them the will to return it there. Time lets markets return. Time lowers high interest rates. Time retires aged company founders and stuck-in-the-mud managers who can't adjust to new realities. Time makes tangible assets worth more. Time pays down debts. Time

Slowly the quality of their loan portfolio will build up again. Their earnings will resume the steady march upward. Both the Illinois and the federal governments will be happy to see this, for they would *never* let an institution like CIL go under: Too much of the commerce of Illinois and the rest of the Midwest depends on Continental, its resources, and its expertise. Too, if CIL went down there would be a nationwide crisis of confidence, not to mention perfect havoc in the banking system. In fact, CIL can take its losses; it's strong enough.

If there's one thing I would bet my investment capital on, it's that Continental Illinois will survive and prosper once again. My bet is this: They won't make the same mistake twice.

The stock, on the other hand, will hang low for quite a while. There'll be plenty of time to buy it. Investors who want banks will look elsewhere. It'll be a long time before they believe anything CIL has to say, a long time before they believe CIL can actually make money on a credible, sustainable basis. I'll be watching the stock. When I see the bottoming and turning patterns coming clear, I'll buy without a moment's hesitation, for I'll know then that pension funds, mutual funds, and brokerage houses have finally come to the same conclusion that's apparent to me right now: Seen from a long-term perspective, *this stock is like money in the bank.*

Good luck with your investments, then, though you really shouldn't need it.

If you would like free copies of any further refinements that may be discovered for Perfect Investment stocks in the coming years, or if you are interested in Perfect Investment-based advisory services, please write:

Lowell Miller
Box 549
Woodstock, New York 12498

Appendix

Charts and Information Sources

Below you will find the chart-reading instructions for the Securities Research, Inc., long-term monthly basis charts that have been used in this book. Available charts in the marketplace include monthly, weekly, and daily basis versions—the "basis" is the unit of time each bar on the graph covers. A daily basis chart, for example, shows each *day* of price changes for the period covered.

Generally, you will need to look at a long-term chart to locate the crash and bottom pattern, and a shorter term (daily or weekly) chart to locate the turning pattern. Sometimes you can get by with just one chart. *Daily Graphs* and *Trendline*, for example, show you the five-year high and low prices, in addition to the daily price action for the past year. If the bottom and turn happen to appear in the particular chart you're looking at, you'll need go no farther.

THE DESIGN AND FEATURES OF CYCLI-GRAPHS

The charts in this quarterly publication provide the investor with easy-to-read factual portrayals of both the market record and the underlying investment record of a large number of listed stocks which are actively traded on the New York and American Stock Exchanges. They represent a broadly diversified list of industrial, railroad, and utility enterprises. Each chart depicts the latest 12 years of monthly PRICE RANGES (with their relation to the general market) and TRADING VOLUMES plotted against the running background of per share EARNINGS and DIVIDEND trends. All data have been fully adjusted for all stock dividends and splits and are drawn on uniform semi-logarithmic (ratio) scale grids. The charted trends reflect relative, or percentage, changes. Thus, in this scale, the vertical linear distance for a 100% move is the same any place on the chart — irrespective of whether the rise is from $5 to $10, $20 to $40, etc.

These long-range charts complement the graphs found in the weekly-plotted and monthly-issued SECURITY CHARTS book which furnish the latest short term trends of the stocks charted herein.

All Capitalization figures are based on company's *latest annual* report.

Bonds include other long term debt.

★Stocks included in the Dow-Jones Averages are designated by a star placed *before the heading*.

Unless prefaced by a "•" for American Stock Exchange or a "#" for Over-the-Counter, all stocks charted are traded on the New York Stock Exchange.

Earnings and Dividends are read from the left-hand scale of each chart.

Earnings Lines — on a per share 12 months ended basis — are represented by the solid black line. Dots show whether company issues quarterly, semi-annual or only annual earnings reports.

Dividend Lines — representing the annual rate of interim dividend payments — are shown by the dashed lines. The small circles show the month in which dividend payments are made. Extra or irregular payments of each year are shown in typed figures.

Note: For closer measurement of percentage changes, price-earnings ratios and dividend yields, see the instructions and use the various rulers on the transparent sheet accompanying each edition of this publication.

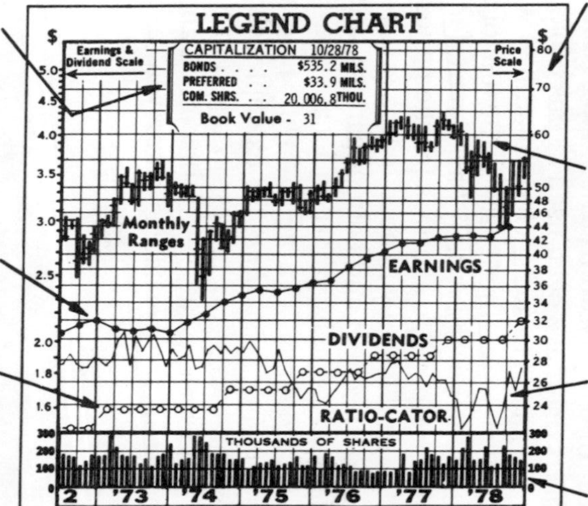

Price Scale — The price ranges are always read from the scale at the right-hand side of each chart. This scale is equal to 15 times the Earnings and Dividend scale at the left, so when the Price Range bars and the Earnings line coincide, it shows the price is at 15 times earnings. When the price is above the earnings line, the ratio of price to earnings is greater than 15 times earnings; when below, it is less.

Monthly Price Ranges represented by the solid vertical bars show the highest and lowest point of each month's transactions. Crossbars indicate the month's closing price. Use the transparent Comparators sheet for comparing the price-earnings-dividend pattern of any stock with the major averages, as well as for measuring percentage price changes, price-earnings ratios, dividend yields, and growth.

Monthly Ratio-Cator: The plottings for this line are obtained by dividing the closing price of the stock by the closing price of the Dow-Jones Industrial Average on the same day. The resulting percentage is multiplied by a factor of 4.5 to bring the line closer to the price bars and is read from the right hand scale. The plotting indicates whether the stock has kept pace, outperformed, or lagged behind the general market as represented by the DJIA.

Volume: The number of shares traded each month is shown by vertical bars at the bottom of each chart on an arithmetic scale.

Following are samples of various useful charts and where you can get them. Most have low-cost trial subscriptions. *Don't forget: Most brokers and libraries have subscriptions to at least one chart service, where you can look for your Perfect Investments at no charge, and only when you're ready to invest.*

Securities Research *Blue Book*—monthly basis
Securities Research, Inc.
208 Newbury Street
Boston, Mass. 02116

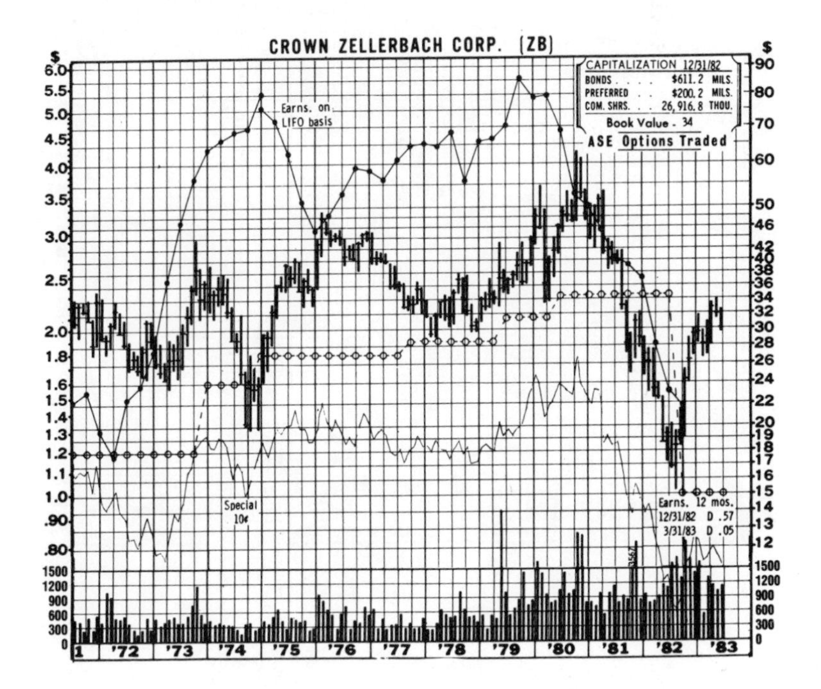

Securities Research *Red Book*—weekly basis
Securities Research, Inc.
208 Newbury Street
Boston, Mass. 02116

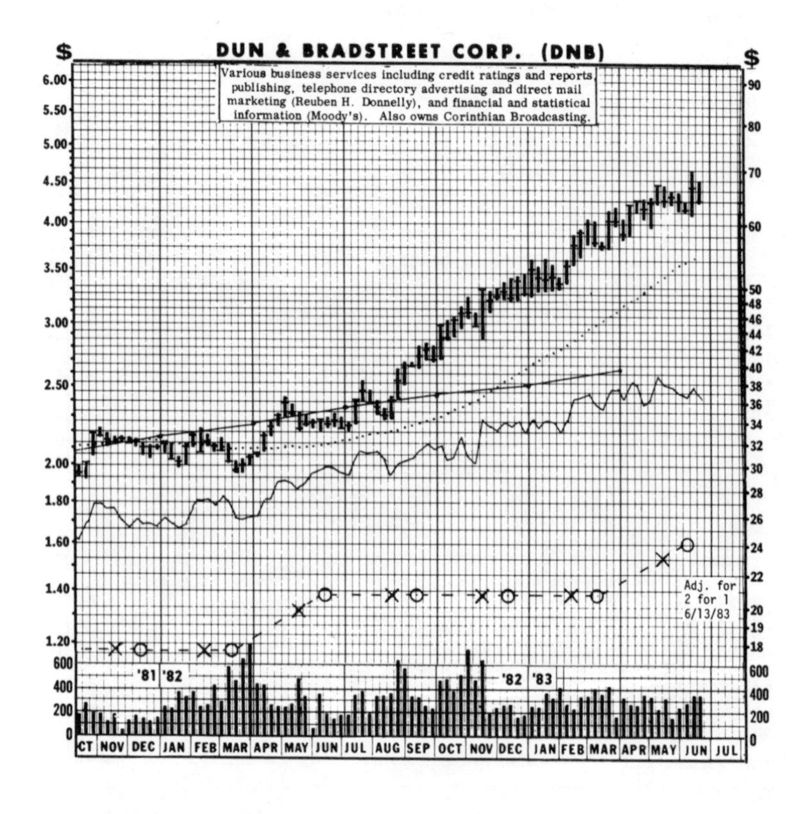

Long-Term Values—monthly basis
William J. O'Neill & Co.

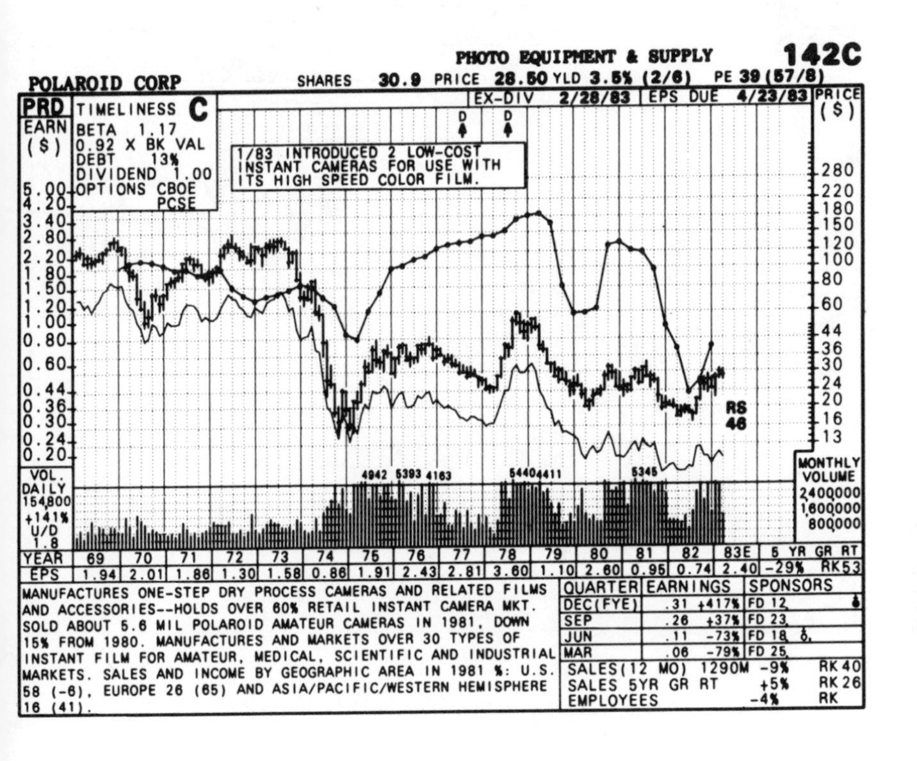

YEAR	69	70	71	72	73	74	75	76	77	78	79	80	81	82	83E	5 YR GR RT
EPS	1.94	2.01	1.86	1.30	1.58	0.86	1.91	2.43	2.81	3.60	1.10	2.60	0.95	0.74	2.40	-29% RK53

MANUFACTURES ONE-STEP DRY PROCESS CAMERAS AND RELATED FILMS AND ACCESSORIES--HOLDS OVER 60% RETAIL INSTANT CAMERA MKT. SOLD ABOUT 5.6 MIL POLAROID AMATEUR CAMERAS IN 1981, DOWN 15% FROM 1980. MANUFACTURES AND MARKETS OVER 30 TYPES OF INSTANT FILM FOR AMATEUR, MEDICAL, SCIENTIFIC AND INDUSTRIAL MARKETS. SALES AND INCOME BY GEOGRAPHIC AREA IN 1981 %: U.S. 58 (-6), EUROPE 26 (65) AND ASIA/PACIFIC/WESTERN HEMISPHERE 16 (41).

QUARTER	EARNINGS		SPONSORS
DEC(FYE)	.31	+417%	FD 12
SEP	.26	+37%	FD 23
JUN	.11	-73%	FD 18
MAR	.06	-79%	FD 25

SALES(12 MO)	1290M	-9%	RK40
SALES 5YR GR RT		+5%	RK26
EMPLOYEES		-4%	RK

Daily Graphs—daily basis
William J. O'Neill & Co.

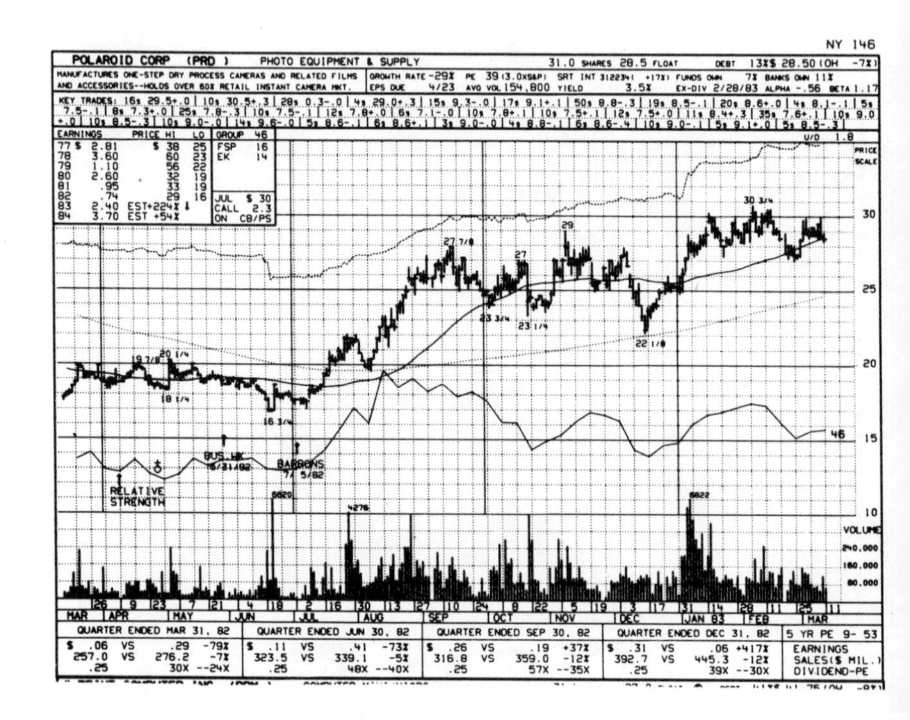

Trendline—daily basis
Standard & Poor's, Inc.

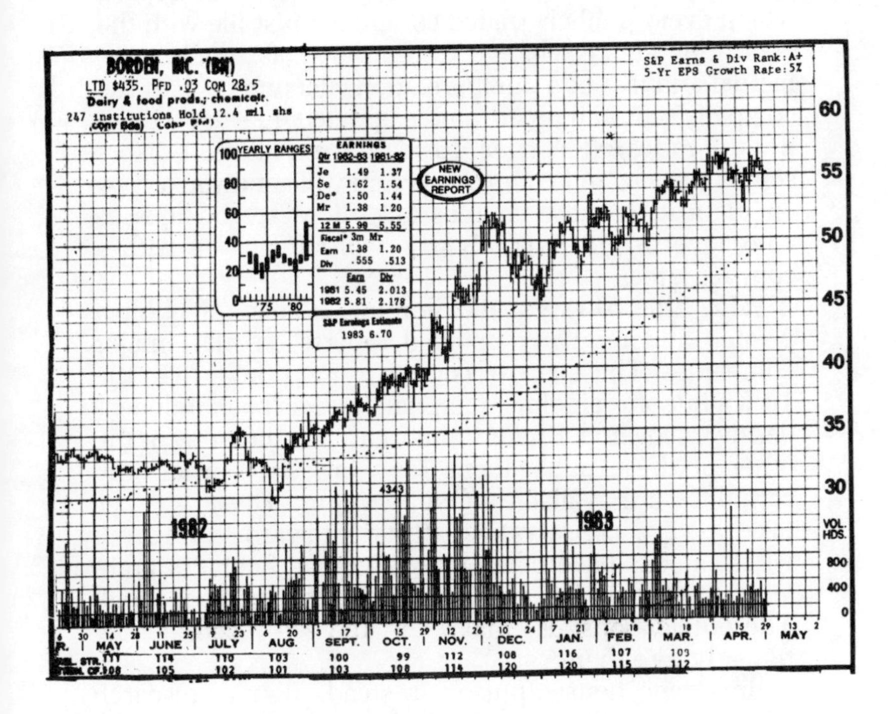

Information Sources

The most direct way of finding out what's happening to a company right now is in its 10-K report. This report, which every publicly traded company must file with the Securities and Exchange Commission, is much more factual and less of a public-relations document than the company's annual report and is updated quarterly. Business libraries often have 10-K's on microfilm, brokers sometimes do, and companies often will send you a copy on request. If those sources fail, there are businesses who advertise in *Barron's* who will supply you with a copy for a fee.

Value Line, Moody's, and Standard & Poor's all publish printed and regularly updated reports on most major companies. These are, of course, much briefer than the 10-K's but often include material that has been independently uncovered. Brokers almost always have one or the other of these publications (and low-priced trial subscriptions are available). One warning: These services take a very conservative attitude toward companies whose stocks have fallen or who've had business problems. Cast their *interpretive* comments from your mind. The publications also make buy and sell recommendations: Ignore them!

Brokerage houses put out a steady flow of research reports. They tend to avoid spending much time on Perfect Investment-type stocks because it's too hard to sell their clients on a stock that's declined. What's most useful about brokerage reports is the familiarity their analysts have with the entire industry in which the company you may be interested in operates. Sometimes you can get a good overview of the competition and industrywide factors that might be affecting your company. Again, as with the information services, resist the temptation to buy anything the brokerages say to buy, or sell anything they think should be sold. Their record is poor.

One quick way to get information is through the electronic data services of Dow Jones News Retrieval. At the push of a button you can locate all the recent articles and information about a particular company. If you have a personal computer you can have the News Retrieval service coming in regularly. If you don't, you'll find that most good libraries can now direct an inquiry to the service for you at a very low charge. And nearly all brokers have access to DJNR as well.

BANDAG INC. NYSE-BDG

RECENT PRICE 38 | P/E RATIO 12.8 (Trailing: 13.8; Median: 14.0) | EARN'S YLD 7.8% | DIV'D YIELD 2.6% | 130

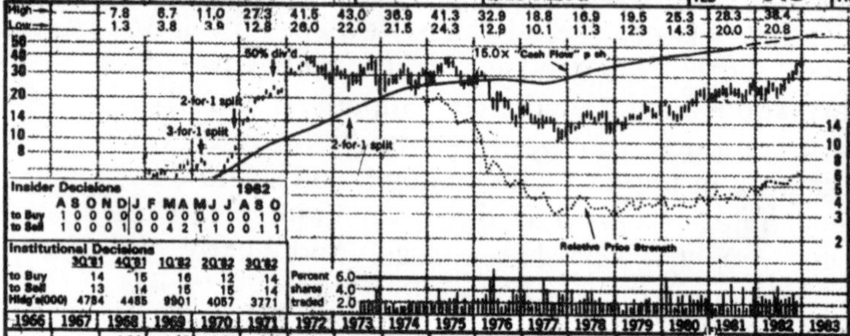

	1968	1969	1970	1971	1972	1973	1974	1975	1976	1977	1978	1979	1980	1981	1982
High	7.8	6.7	11.0	27.3	41.5	43.0	36.9	41.3	32.9	18.8	16.9	19.5	25.3	28.3	38.4
Low	1.3	3.8	3.9	12.8	26.0	22.0	21.5	24.3	12.9	10.1	11.3	12.3	14.3	20.0	20.8

50% div'd
2-for-1 split
3-for-1 split
2-for-1 split
15.0 x "Cash Flow" p sh
Relative Price Strength
Target Price Range
Percent shares traded 6.0 4.0 2.0

Insider Decisions 1982

	A	S	O	N	D	J	F	M	A	M	J	J	A	S	O
to Buy	1	0	0	0	0	0	0	0	0	0	0	0	0	1	0
to Sell	1	0	0	0	1	0	0	4	2	1	1	0	0	1	1

Institutional Decisions

	3Q'81	4Q'81	1Q'82	2Q'82	3Q'82
to Buy	14	15	16	12	14
to Sell	13	14	15	15	14
Hldg's(000)	4784	4485	9901	4057	3771

1984	1985	1986	1987

Dec. 31, 1982 Value Line

TIMELINESS 2 Above Average
(Relative Price Performance Next 12 Mos.)
SAFETY 3 Average
(Scale: 1 Highest to 5 Lowest)
BETA 1.00 (1.00 = Market)

1985-87 PROJECTIONS

	Price	Gain	Ann'l Total Return
High	105	(+175%)	31%
Low	70	(+ 85%)	19%

1966	1967	1968	1969	1970	1971	1972	1973	1974	1975	1976	1977	1978	1979	1980	1981	1982	1983	© Arnold Bernhard & Co., Inc.	85-87E
--	--	1.26	1.85	2.52	3.58	4.86	7.56	10.44	13.26	14.30	15.70	19.49	23.63	27.66	25.77	28.50	31.45	Sales per sh	46.65
--	--	.15	.25	.38	.60	.82	1.17	1.59	1.77	1.88	1.83	2.19	2.56	2.89	3.30	3.85	4.25	"Cash Flow" per sh	6.40
--	--	.12	.20	.31	.47	.64	.96	1.35	1.49	1.55	1.44	1.70	1.99	2.27	2.60	2.80	3.40	Earnings per sh (A)	5.25
--	--	--	--	--	--	--	--	--	--	.20	.35	.50	.60	.70	.80	.90	1.00	Div'ds Decl'd per sh (B)	1.70
--	--	.19	.12	.25	.49	.31	.34	.65	.27	1.04	.35	.45	.68	1.17	.71	.80	.80	Cap'l Spending per sh	1.50
--	--	.38	.63	1.09	1.58	2.30	3.91	5.26	6.83	8.19	9.28	10.47	11.79	13.04	14.80	14.65	17.25	Book Value per sh (C)	25.70
--	--	10.87	10.80	11.27	11.30	11.43	12.59	12.59	12.74	12.74	12.74	12.70	12.55	11.96	12.13	10.50	10.50	Common Shs Outst'g (D)	10.50
--	--	25.4	28.0	21.3	42.8	53.0	32.5	21.7	21.3	13.9	9.8	8.4	7.8	8.3	9.1	9.8		Avg Ann'l P/E Ratio	17.0
--	--	3.9%	3.6%	4.7%	2.3%	1.9%	3.1%	4.6%	4.7%	7.2%	10.3%	11.8%	12.9%	12.0%	11.0%	10.2%		Avg Ann'l Earn's Yield	5.9%
--	--	--	--	--	--	--	--	--	--	.9%	2.5%	3.5%	3.9%	3.7%	3.4%	3.3%		Avg Ann'l Div'd Yield	1.8%

CAPITAL STRUCTURE as of 9/30/82
Total Debt $16.8 mill. **Due in 5 Yrs.** $6.5 mill.
LT Debt $12.8 mill. **LT Interest** $1.7 mill.
Incl. $3.6 mill. capitalized leases.
(8% of Cap'l)
Leases, Uncapitalized Annual rentals $2.8 mill.
Pension Liability None in '81 vs. None in '80
Pfd Stock None
Common Stock 10,460,138 shs. (92% of Cap'l)

1972	1973	1974	1975	1976	1977	1978	1979	1980	1981	1982	1983		85-87E
53.3	95.1	131.5	168.9	182.1	200.1	247.5	296.5	330.9	312.5	310	330	Sales ($mill)	490
29.7%	27.0%	26.1%	24.0%	23.1%	19.9%	19.0%	17.5%	17.2%	20.8%	22.5%	22.5%	Operating Margin	23.5%
1.9	2.7	3.0	3.6	4.1	4.9	6.2	6.9	7.3	8.5	8.5	8.5	Depreciation ($mill) (E)	12.0
7.5	12.1	17.0	19.0	19.8	18.4	21.6	25.3	27.4	31.5	32.0	36.0	Net Profit ($mill)	55.0
45.8%	48.3%	48.4%	49.0%	49.2%	49.3%	49.9%	48.7%	49.2%	48.5%	48.5%	48.0%	Income Tax Rate	48.5%
14.0%	12.7%	12.9%	11.3%	10.9%	9.2%	8.7%	8.5%	8.3%	10.1%	10.3%	10.9%	Net Profit Margin	11.2%
17.5	34.4	47.2	68.2	83.1	97.0	105.7	118.8	120.4	146.0	120	145	Working Cap'l ($mill)	235
3.2	3.5	3.1	3.5	10.4	10.6	14.2	13.7	14.7	12.4	13.0	13.0	Long-Term Debt ($mill)	18.0
26.3	49.3	66.3	87.0	104.3	118.2	133.0	147.9	156.0	179.5	155	180	Net Worth ($mill)	270
25.6%	23.1%	24.6%	21.1%	17.5%	14.6%	15.1%	16.0%	16.4%	16.8%	18.5%	18.5%	% Earned Total Cap'l	20.0%
28.5%	24.5%	25.6%	21.8%	19.0%	15.6%	16.3%	17.1%	17.5%	17.5%	20.5%	18.5%	% Earned Net Worth	20.5%
28.5%	24.5%	25.6%	21.8%	16.6%	11.8%	11.5%	11.9%	12.2%	12.1%	14.5%	13.5%	% Retained to Comm Eq	13.5%
--	--	--	--	13%	24%	29%	30%	31%	31%	30%	30%	% All Div'ds to Net Prof	32%

CURRENT POSITION ($mill.)	1980	1981	9/30/82
Cash Assets	42.8	54.9	41.8
Receivables	81.4	91.1	79.1
Inventory (LIFO)	46.7	36.9	25.7
Other	2.5	8.8	4.6
Current Assets	173.4	191.7	151.2
Accts Payable	22.0	12.2	9.3
Debt Due	5.0	4.3	4.0
Other	26.0	29.2	25.1
Current Liab.	53.0	45.7	38.4

ANNUAL RATES of change (per sh)	Past 10 Yrs	Past 5 Yrs	Est '79-'81 to '85-'87
Sales	25.5%	15.0%	10.5%
"Cash Flow"	21.5%	11.0%	14.0%
Earnings	21.5%	9.5%	15.0%
Dividends	--	28.5%	16.0%
Book Value	28.0%	14.5%	11.5%

Calendar	QUARTERLY SALES ($ mill.) Mar. 31	June 30	Sept. 30	Dec. 31	Full Year
1979	64.8	71.5	74.6	85.6	296.5
1980	78.3	76.2	83.6	92.8	330.9
1981	68.7	74.5	81.7	87.6 (F)	312.5
1982	68.3	74.5	78.3	88.9	310
1983	70.0	78.0	85.0	97.0	330

Calendar	EARNINGS PER SHARE (A) Mar. 31	June 30	Sept. 30	Dec. 31	Full Year
1979	.39	.48	.49	.63	1.99
1980	.47	.48	.58	.74	2.27
1981	.53	.63	.71	.73	2.60
1982	.51	.67	.82	.80	2.80
1983	.80	.75	.90	1.15	3.40

Calendar	QUARTERLY DIVIDENDS PAID (B) Mar. 31	June 30	Sept. 30	Dec. 31	Full Year
1979	.125	.15	.15	.15	.58
1980	.15	.175	.175	.175	.68
1981	.175	.20	.20	.20	.78
1982	.20	.225	.225	.225	.88
1983					

BUSINESS: Bandag, Inc. is the world's largest manufacturer of precured tread rubber, equipment and supplies for the tire retreading industry (81% of sales). Also custom compounds rubber and manufacturers industrial hose (19% of sales). Heavy Duty Parts Group, a rebuilder and distributor of vehicle replacement parts, sold in 1981. Has 8 plants. Serves about 1,000 dealers in U.S. and 100 foreign countries. Employees costs: 15% of sales. '81 deprec. rate; 10.9%. Est'd plant age: 4 yrs. Has 1,999 employees, 2,798 shareholders. Carver family owns 45% of stk. Chrmn. & C.E.O.: M. G. Carver. Pres.: C.E. Edwards. Inc.: Iowa. Address: Bandag Center, Muscatine, Iowa 52761.

Bandag keeps rolling along. We estimate that the company's retread material sales showed worldwide unit growth of 1% in the December 1982 quarter. (This performance was similar to the prior quarter.) Operating profits, aided by easing raw material costs and tight expense controls, probably rose significantly more. Lower LIFO charges, and a reduced number of shares outstanding (Bandag acquired 1.6 million shares in the open market) also helped. The sale of two subsidiaries trimmed share earnings by 20¢ to 25¢. These shares remain ranked 2 (Above Average) for year-ahead performance.

Bandag's retreading business has benefited from the recession. We believe retreading's cost advantage (it's only 1/3 to 1/2 the price of a new tire) appeals even more to Bandag's truck and bus customers in today's sluggish times. Bandag also benefits from the greater number of radial heavy-truck tires on the road. Radials have better quality casings, which are more suitable for retreading than most conventional tires and may be retreaded more than once.

Bandag is poised for a good gain in 1983. We think worldwide business activity will climb during 1983, especially in the second half. That's a plus for the dominant retread business, and also for the company's three nonretread subsidiaries, which traditionally move in step with the economy, and were weak performers in 1982. The absence of loss-ridden off-the-road retreading units will also help. Furthermore, Bandag's per share earnings during the first three quarters will be boosted slightly by the share repurchase.

Bandag shares are also a solid holding through 1985-87. This opinion stems from our belief that the company's share of the total U.S. bus and truck tire retreading market will expand significantly because of its cost advantage. Overseas markets, where Bandag's penetration is considerably less than at home, also hold significant promise. And Bandag's financial strength permits the company to consider expansion into retreads for light duty trucks and passenger cars.

New strategies might be required toward this decade's end. If the passenger business doesn't open up, Bandag's retread operations might approach maturity. The company would then have three options: 1) run the business as a cash cow; 2) sell it to someone else to milk; or 3) find a faster growing company to invest in.

J.H.K./M.S.

(A) Based on avg. shs. outst'g. Next earn'gs rep't due late Jan. Est'd constant-dollar egs./sh.: '81, $2.10. (B) Next div'd meet'g about Feb. 22. Goes ex about Mar. 21. Div'd paym't dates: Jan. 20, Apr. 23, Jul. 23, Oct. 20. (C) Incl. intangibles. In '81, $7.0 mill., 56¢/sh. (D) In mill., adj. for stock splits & div'ds. (E) Deprec. on accel. basis. (F) Continuing operations only.

Company's Financial Strength	A
Stock's Price Stability	65
Price Growth Persistence	35
Earnings Predictability	95

Reprinted courtesy Value Line

AVERY INTERNATIONAL

LISTED	SYM.	LTPS•	STPS•	IND. DIV.	REC. PRICE	RANGE (52-WKS.)	YLD.
NYSE	AVY	123.7	98.7	$0.90	40	42 - 24	2.3%

MEDIUM GRADE. THE COMPANY HAS A DOMINANT POSITION THE MANUFACTURE OF SELF ADHESIVE-LABELS AND LABELING SYSTEMS.

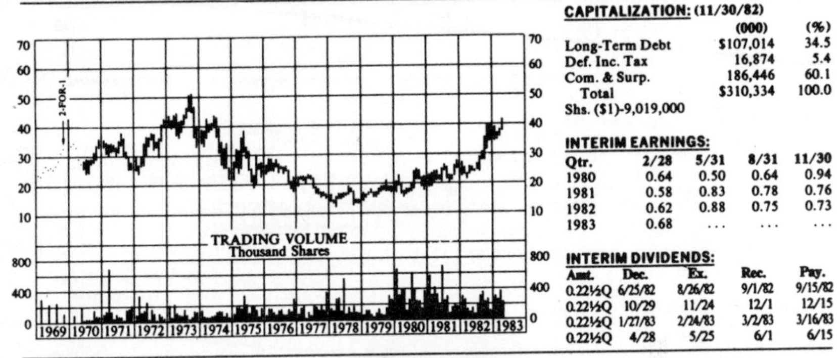

CAPITALIZATION: (11/30/82)

	(000)	(%)
Long-Term Debt	$107,014	34.5
Def. Inc. Tax	16,874	5.4
Com. & Surp.	186,446	60.1
Total	$310,334	100.0

Shs. ($1)-9,019,000

INTERIM EARNINGS:

Qtr.	2/28	5/31	8/31	11/30
1980	0.64	0.50	0.64	0.94
1981	0.58	0.83	0.78	0.76
1982	0.62	0.88	0.75	0.73
1983	0.68	...	...	...

INTERIM DIVIDENDS:

Amt.	Dec.	Ex.	Rec.	Pay.
0.22½Q	6/25/82	8/26/82	9/1/82	9/15/82
0.22½Q	10/29	11/24	12/1	12/15
0.22½Q	1/27/83	2/24/83	3/2/83	3/16/83
0.22½Q	4/28	5/25	6/1	6/15

BACKGROUND:

Avery International operates in two principal industry segments. Materials Units, which contributed to 63% in fiscal 1982 sales (54% in operating income), produces self-adhesive base materials, which are sold to customers who convert or adapt these products for a wide variety of industrial applications. Converting Units segment, 39% (46%), produces and sells converted products such as self-adhesive labels as well as tags, indexing and tabbing guides, and other products lines. Integrated sales contributed -2% sales (00% profits). AVY also designs and produces specialized application equipment for use with its converted products. Foreign operations, conducted primarily in Western Europe, contributed 38% of total sales and 28% of profits.

RECENT DEVELOPMENTS:

For the quarter ended 2/28/83, net income rose 10% to $6.2 million, on sales of $180.2 million, up 6% over the similar period last year. Positive results reflected strong performances by the Materials Group in the U.S. and the Fasson Industrial Division in Europe. Improvements also were recorded by the Avery Label operations in Europe and the Thermark Division in the U.S. These results more than offset weakness at the Permacel and Soabar units.

PROSPECTS:

Near-term profits should resume its upward trend. Current order trends are encouraging and there are indications of economic improvements in the U.S. Effective cost controls and improved productivity will help. However, international business will probably continue to suffer from the higher U.S. dollar. Longer-term prospects have been enhanced by the acquisition of Aigner and Permacel. Aigner will augment the office product line, while Permacel's technological and marketing capabilities compliment those of industrial tape products.

STATISTICS:

YEAR	GROSS REVS. ($mill.)	OPER. PROFIT MARGIN %	RET. ON EQUITY %	NET INCOME ($mill.)	WORK CAP. ($mill.)	SENIOR CAPITAL ($mill.)	SHARES (000)	EARN. PER SH.$	DIV. PER SH.$	DIV. PAY. %	PRICE RANGE	P/E RATIO	AVG. YIELD %
11/30													
a73	242.7	12.3	—	12.8	63.5	21.7	9,517	1.39	0.25	18	51½ - 33	30.4	0.6
74	296.3	13.2	14.9	16.9	81.6	44.7	9,528	1.76	0.30	17	44 - 22	18.8	0.9
75	282.6	6.1	4.3	h4.3	79.9	55.5	9,534	h0.44	0.30	59	38¾ - 19	56.6	1.0
76	361.9	9.0	10.3	12.8	89.8	59.5	9,692	1.32	0.33	25	29⅛ - 17½	17.7	1.4
77	423.5	9.2	11.5	15.3	105.0	69.6	9,539	1.60	0.40	25	23½ - 15⅛	12.1	2.1
78	484.4	9.4	12.1	18.0	113.4	76.7	9,002	1.94	0.48	25	19½ - 12¼	8.2	3.0
b79	562.1	8.3	13.7	21.1	121.6	74.3	9,011	2.35	0.56	24	21½ - 14¼	7.6	3.1
80	618.7	8.6	14.2	24.5	119.6	62.0	9,011	2.72	0.72	26	25¼ - 15½	7.5	3.5
81	638.0	8.6	14.7	h26.5	101.4	79.9	9,011	h2.95	0.80	27	28 - 18⅞	7.9	3.4
82	**712.2**	**8.5**	**14.3**	**26.8**	**112.5**	**107.0**	**9,019**	**2.98**	**0.90**	**30**	**40⅛ - 21½**	**10.4**	**2.9**

•Long-Term Price Score — Short-Term Price Score; see page 4a. a-Incl. acquisitions. b-Reflects change to LIFO. h-Restated to reflect change in accounting for foreign currency translations.

INCORPORATED:
Sept. 21, 1946 – Del.

PRINCIPAL OFFICE:
150 N. Orange Grove Blvd.
Pasadena, CA 91103
Tel.: (213) 304-2000

ANNUAL MEETING:
Last Wed. in March

NUMBER OF STOCKHOLDERS:
2,198

TRANSFER AGENT(S):
Security Pacific National Bank,
Los Angeles, Cal.

REGISTRAR(S):
Security Pacific National Bank,
Los Angeles, Cal.

INSTITUTIONAL HOLDINGS:
No. of Institutions: 73
Shares Held: 5,032,780

OFFICERS:
Chairman
H.R. Smith
Pres. & Ch. Exec. Off.
C.D. Miller
Sr. V.P.-Fin. & Ch. Fin. Off.
P.M. Neal
Vice Pres. & Treas.
W.H. Smith
Vice Pres., Gen. Coun. & Sec.
R.G. Van Schoonenberg

Reprinted courtesy Moody's

Searle (G.D.)

2001K

NYSE Symbol SRL Options on ASE (Feb-May-Aug-Nov)

Price	Range	P-E Ratio	Dividend	Yield	S&P Ranking
Feb. 14'83	1983				
43⅞	50-39	16	0.52	1.2%	A-

Summary

This leading ethical drug producer is also one of the largest domestic optical products retailers, and manufactures specialty chemicals and gases. Earnings have trended upward in recent years, following the 1977 streamlining of operations which included the discontinuance of about 20 businesses. Greater contributions from new products, especially aspartame low-calorie sweetener products and several new cardiovascular drugs, enhance future earnings prospects.

Current Outlook

Earnings for 1983 are projected at about $3.60 a share, up from 1982's $2.77.

Dividends should remain at $0.13 quarterly.

Sales for 1983 are expected to show further progess, reflecting continued strength in major markets and contributions from new products. Greater contributions are also expected from the company's aspartame low-calorie sweeteners. Despite heavy R & D and start-up costs and a likely rise in the tax rate, profitability should benefit from the better volume, some easing in foreign exchange pressures and greater overall operating efficiency.

Net Sales (Million $)

Quarter:	1982	1981	1980	1979
Mar.	235	217	249	214
Jun.	257	235	263	211
Sep.	257	233	284	226
Dec.	288	258	286	248
	1,037	942	1,082	898

Sales for 1982 (preliminary) rose 10% from those of the year before, aided by contributions from SRL's aspartame tabletop sweetener product. Profitability, however, was hurt by lower sales and earnings of ethical drugs in the U.S., heavy drug marketing costs, higher research and development costs, start-up expenses, and adverse foreign exchange. Pretax income edged up 0.2%. After taxes at 24.0%, against 29.0%, net income was up 7.3%. Earnings were equal to $2.77 a share, versus $2.52, which was before losses of $0.50 from discontinued operations and a special charge of $0.12 from an accounting change.

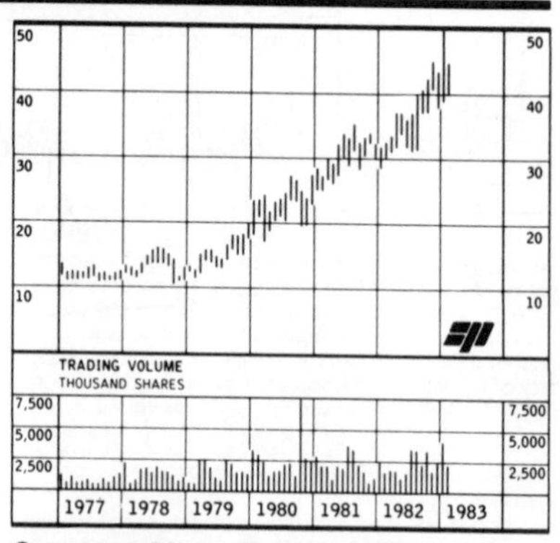

Common Share Earnings ($)

Quarter:	1982	1981	1980	1979
Mar.	0.56	0.51	0.43	0.38
Jun.	0.64	0.56	0.46	0.37
Sep.	0.70	0.67	0.32	0.47
Dec.	0.87	0.78	0.57	0.46
	2.77	2.52	1.78	1.68

Important Developments

Jan. '83—The company announced commitments to invest $55 million in manufacturing capacity to produce NutraSweet, its new low-calorie food sweetener product. SRL was awaiting approval from the FDA to market NutraSweet for carbonated beverages.

Next earnings report due in mid-April.

Per Share Data ($)

Yr. End Dec. 31	1982	1981	[2]1980	[2]1979	1978	1977	1976	1975	[1]1974	[2]1973
Book Value	**NA**	10.53	9.75	8.67	7.89	7.06	7.90	7.26	6.17	5.34
Earnings[3]	**2.77**	2.52	1.78	1.68	1.37	0.68	1.18	1.56	1.41	1.24
Dividends	**0.52**	0.52	0.52	0.52	0.52	0.52	0.52	0.50½	0.46	0.44¾
Payout Ratio	**19%**	20%	29%	31%	38%	77%	44%	32%	33%	36%
Prices—High	**45¼**	35½	27⅝	20	16⅜	13¾	18	25¾	28¼	40⅝
Low	**28⅝**	25⅛	17¼	11½	10⅝	10⅞	10¾	13½	11⅜	22¾
P/E Ratio—	**16-10**	14-10	16-10	12-7	12-8	20-16	15-9	17-9	20-8	33-18

Data as orig. reptd. Adj. for stk. div(s). of 200% Jun. 1973. **1.** Reflects merger or acquisition and accounting change. **2.** Reflects merger or acquisition. **3.** Bef. results of disc. opers. of -0.50 in 1981, -0.17 in 1980 & -0.02 in 1979, -1.21 in 1977, and spec. item(s) of -0.12 in 1981, +0.24 in 1980. NA-Not Available.

February 22, 1983

Standard & Poor's Corp.
25 Broadway, NY, NY 10004

2001K

G.D. Searle & Co.

Income Data (Million $)

Year Ended Dec. 31	Revs.	Oper. Inc.	% Oper. Inc. of Revs.	Cap. Exp.	Depr.	Int. Exp.	Net Bef. Taxes	Eff. Tax Rate	[6]Net Inc.	% Net Inc. of Revs.
[2]**1981**	**942**	**228**	**24.2%**	**87.6**	**37.3**	**36.1**	[5]**197**	**27.1%**	[7]**131**	**13.9%**
[1]1980	1,082	202	18.7%	67.0	30.9	37.2	[5]154	29.6%	94	8.7%
[1]1979	898	180	20.0%	49.3	26.4	28.8	146	31.9%	89	9.9%
1978	848	138	16.2%	40.4	22.2	30.9	117	29.2%	72	8.5%
[2]1977	750	119	15.9%	51.2	21.5	32.2	89	51.4%	35	4.7%
1976	761	99	13.0%	37.1	19.3	29.9	84	19.4%	62	8.1%
1975	712	115	16.1%	43.5	17.0	26.1	100	12.8%	[7] 81	11.3%
[3]1974	621	106	17.0%	37.6	14.2	19.2	[5] 97	19.1%	72	11.7%
[4]1973	472	87	18.5%	24.9	11.2	11.1	[5] 80	24.9%	60	12.7%
1972	272	63	23.1%	17.0	7.0	5.6	[5] 53	21.5%	42	15.4%

Balance Sheet Data (Million $)

Dec. 31	Cash	Current Assets	Current Liab.	Ratio	Total Assets	Ret. on Assets	Long Term Debt	Common Equity	Total Cap.	% LT Debt of Cap.	Ret. on Equity
1981	**222**	**591**	**246**	**2.4**	**1,094**	**11.9%**	**192**	**578**	**811**	**23.7%**	**23.6%**
1980	192	656	436	1.5	1,130	8.4%	90	549	658	13.7%	18.3%
1979	203	655	327	2.0	1,132	8.4%	246	489	769	32.0%	19.4%
1978	92	505	154	3.3	977	7.5%	342	427	784	43.7%	17.9%
1977	79	471	198	2.4	960	3.6%	344	381	734	46.9%	8.6%
1976	146	526	210	2.5	1,014	6.4%	344	436	785	43.8%	14.6%
1975	111	451	134	3.4	898	9.8%	347	399	747	46.4%	21.7%
1974	81	390	165	2.4	734	10.8%	206	341	552	37.3%	23.1%
1973	139	361	74	4.9	577	12.6%	199	269	488	40.8%	28.0%
1972	90	219	71	3.1	314	14.7%	49	130	235	20.8%	35.1%

Data as orig. reptd. **1.** Excludes discontinued operations and reflects merger or acquisition. **2.** Excludes discontinued operations. **3.** Reflects merger or acquisition and accounting change. **4.** Reflects merger or acquisition. **5.** Incl. equity in earns. of nonconsol. subs. **6.** Bef. results of disc. opers. in 1981, 1980, 1979, 1977, and spec. item(s) in 1981, 1980. **7.** Reflects accounting change.

Business Summary

G.D. Searle is a research-based pharmaceutical company with other interests in prescription eyewear and specialty gases and chemicals. The medical products business was discontinued in 1981. Contributions by industry segment in 1981:

	Sales	Profits
Pharmaceutical/consumer	68%	83%
Optical group	24%	12%
Other	8%	5%

International operations contributed 39% of sales and 30% of operating profits in 1981.

Important products in the Pharmaceutical/Consumer group are Aldactone, Aldactazide, and Soldactone antihypertensives, Metamucil for constipation, Flagyl for vaginitis, and Norpace antiarhythmic. Other items are Enovid, Ovulen, and Demulen oral contraceptives, Dramamine anti-nauseant, Lomotil antidiarrheal, and the Cu-7 intrauterine contraceptive.

Searle markets aspartame, a low-calorie sweetener, under the brandnames NutraSweet, Equal, Egal and Canderel. Approval for one or more uses has been received in 22 countries.

Searle is a leading U.S. retailer of optical products and has 989 owned and franchised optical stores operating in 41 states and five countries.

Dividend Data

Dividends have been paid since 1935. A dividend reinvestment plan is available.

Amt. of Divd. $	Date Decl.	Ex-divd. Date	Stock of Record	Payment Date
0.13	Apr. 26	May 4	May 10	Jun. 4'82
0.13	Jul. 28	Aug. 4	Aug. 10	Sep. 3'82
0.13	Oct. 26	Nov. 4	Nov. 10	Dec. 3'82
0.13	Feb. 3	Feb. 8	Feb. 14	Mar. 9'83

Next dividend meeting: late Apr. '83.

Capitalization

Long Term Debt: $195,900,000.

Common Stock: 49,992,384 shs. ($0.33⅓ par). Institutions hold about 37%; the Searle family controls about 34%.
Shareholders: 26,600.

Office—4711 Golf Rd. (P.O. Box 1045), Skokie, Ill. 60076. **Tel**—(312) 982-7000. **Pres & CEO**—D. H. Rumsfeld. **Secy**—B. M. Windon. **Treas**—D. L. Seeley. **Investor Contact**—W. H. Clarkin. **Dirs**—D. C. Searle (Chrmn), W. G. Anlyan, C. M. Bliss, W. M. Dixon, Jr., D. F. Grisham, K. J. Isselbacher, D. P. Kelly, D. S. Perkins, R. F. Richards, D. H. Rumsfeld, W. L. Searle, A. M. de Staercke, A. M. Wood. **Transfer Agent & Registrar**—Harris Trust and Savings Bank, Chicago. **Incorporated** in Illinois in 1908; reincorporated in Delaware in 1955.

H.B. Saftlas

Index

Note: Page numbers in italics refer to charts and tables.

ABOUT THE AUTHOR

Lowell Miller is a private investor and investment adviser. His earlier work on stock trading, *The Momentum-Gap Method,* received wide praise and was named Stock Market Book of the Year in 1978. In addition to his experience with securities, Mr. Miller has founded enterprises in publishing and manufacturing, providing him with hands-on knowledge of the business realities any stock ultimately represents. He currently provides investment guidance and management in a variety of formats. A newsletter based on Perfect Investment stocks will be available in early 1984.